Growing Fruit in the Upper Midwest

Growing Fruit
in the Upper Midwest

Don Gordon

University of Minnesota Press
Minneapolis   Oxford

Published by the University of Minnesota Press
2037 University Avenue Southeast, Minneapolis, MN 55414
Printed in the United States of America on acid-free paper

Library of Congress Cataloging-in-Publication Data

Gordon, Donald. 1939-
    Growing fruit in the upper Midwest / Don Gordon.
      p. cm.
    Includes index.
    ISBN 0-8166-1869-0 (hc)
    1. Fruit-culture–Lake States. 2. Fruit-culture–Middle West.
  I. Title.
  SB355.G63 1991
  634'.0977–dc20   90-39498
                                                               CIP

A CIP catalog record for this book is available from the British Library

The University of Minnesota is an
equal-opportunity educator and employer.

Contents

Preface

This book is an outgrowth of several horticultural classes taught at Mankato State University and from my newspaper column on horticulture and the environment, published weekly since 1976 in the *Mankato Free Press*. It also reflects the experience gained from growing fruit as a hobby and from owning and operating a commercial pick-your-own raspberry business for several years.

Several excellent books have been published on fruit production in the United States, but this is the first to deal exclusively with the Upper Midwest. Despite the harsh climate that prevails in this area, it is possible to successfully grow hundreds of excellent fruit cultivars.

The goal in writing this book was not only to provide a practical "how-to" guide to growing fruit for home gardeners and small commercial growers, but also to present the interesting and often forgotten historical and economic aspects of fruit production in the Upper Midwest. This information will be of interest to large commercial growers, undergraduate and technical-school students, extension personnel, and teachers.

This book is nontechnical in nature and for that reason is not extensively referenced, but readers who desire more information will find an expanded list of references at the end of each chapter.

Acknowledgments

This book would not have been possible without the assistance of several people who offered advice on cultivar selection, provided reference material, or aided in other ways in the preparation of the text. Specifically, the author wishes to thank the following individuals:

Illinois	Professor Allen Otterbacher
Iowa	Professors Ervin Denisen, Paul Domoto, and Gail Nonnecke
Minnesota	Professors Leonard Hertz, Emily Hoover, Jim Luby, and Henry Quade, as well as Dave Bedford, Research Scientist at the Minnesota Horticultural Research Center, John Marshall, grape grower, and Paul Otten of North Star Gardens
North Dakota	Professors Arthur Boe, Neil Holland, and Earl Scholz
Oregon	Professors F. J. Lawrence and Melvin Westwood
South Dakota	Professor Ronald Peterson
Wisconsin	Professors Malcolm Dana, George Klingbeil, and Robert Tomesh, and grape grower Elmer Swenson

I would also like to thank Laverne Dunsmore for the line drawings, John Rongstad for preparation of the maps, Jean Spellacy for typing the manuscript, and the staff of the Anderson Horticultural Library at the Minnesota Landscape Arboretum for assistance in securing reference material.

Last, but not least, a special thanks to my wife, Kathy, who typed several preliminary drafts of the book, assisted in editing, and offered continued encouragement.

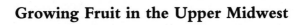

Growing Fruit in the Upper Midwest

Chapter

1

Introduction

Plant Classification

Plant classification is one of the few things in the world on which all nations agree. The scientific name of the peach, *Prunus persica*, has the same meaning in Japan as it does here and in all other nations of the world. The correct name of a plant is the key to tracing its history and, in the case of fruit, to unlocking the diaries of past growers. Their successes and failures form the foundation of modern fruit culture.

There are many categories of plant classification, but those most likely to directly benefit the home gardener include the following:

Family. This is a group of related genera or, in some cases, a single genus. Names of botanical families are easy to recognize because most end in *aceae* as in Rosaceae or Vitaceae. Plants in the same family have structural and often cultural similarities. The most important plant family for fruit in the Upper Midwest and throughout much of the world is the Rosaceae. Familiar fruits in this family include apples, pears, peaches, cherries, plums, apricots, strawberries, blackberries, raspberries, and other brambles.

Genus. The genus (genera is the plural) is a subdivision of the family and includes one or more closely related species. Usually, species in the same genus have much in common morphologically. *Malus* (apples) and *Pyrus* (pears) are examples of closely related genera in the family Rosaceae.

Species. This term is both singular and plural—it is possible to have one species or several species. Botanists do not agree on a precise definition of species, but it is commonly used for a group of plants in a genus which closely resemble one another. In other words, morphologically they are more similar to each other than to other species in the genus. In the animal world it is often customary to classify members of the same species together if they can interbreed but are reproductively isolated from other species. This sometimes works for plants, but plenty of named plant species cross or hybridize. Hybrid species names are easy to recognize when an "x" is used between the genus and species. For example, *Malus* x *domestica* denotes a hybrid origin for the cultivated apple.

Variety. A variety is a subdivision of the species and should not be confused with the cultivar, which will be discussed next. The botanical variety is commonly used for members of the same species which share common morphological characters and usually occupy a particular geographical area. In these cases, a third name is added to create a trinomial. For example, *Prunus armeniaca* variety *sibirica* is one of three varieties of the apricot.

Cultivar. Considerable confusion exists over the difference between the botanical variety and the term *cultivar*. Botanical varieties are not genetically uniform, and they usually reproduce themselves in nature by seed. Cultivars, in contrast, are genetically uniform, named plants that are propagated. To maintain genetic uniformity, cultivars are usually propagated vegetatively, though through carefully controlled crosses or hybridization, some cultivars can be maintained by plants grown from seed. Cultivars that are vegetatively propagated are also known as clones. In nature, a single plant possessing desirable characteristics may appear among the millions of seedlings, or sometimes a mutation or sport may occur. By cloning these discoveries, an unlimited number of genetically identical plants can be produced. For example, all 'Delicious' apples grown throughout the world are clones from a single tree. Two methods are commonly used to distinguish cultivar names. The name may be preceded by "cv." or enclosed by single quotes. For example, Montmorency cherry would be either *Prunus cerasus* cv. Montmorency or *Prunus cerasus* 'Montmorency'.

Dwindling Diversity

The development of a new fruit cultivar that may possess cold-hardy characteristics, disease resistance, or increased productivity is usually welcomed by all growers and breeders, but there is a dark side to the release of new cultivars. Unfortunately, all too often not only are the older inferior cultivars replaced, but they are lost forever. This loss of germplasm translates into a smaller gene pool for future fruit breeding. In 1905, there were about 8,000 apple cultivars and all but about 1,200 have been lost or are extinct (*Ag. Research*, May 1986). Similar horror stories exist for grapes and for many other important horticultural crops.

When a disease or pest threatens a plant, breeders respond by trying to find germplasm that may provide resistance or immunity. If that germplasm is not found in existing cultivars, breeders must turn to this last line of defense, which exists only in wild plants. Unfortunately, with a rapidly expanding population, no one is certain how long the genetic landscape of these plants can be maintained.

On a positive note, a conscious effort is being made to preserve genetic diversity through the establishment of national clonal repositories at various locations throughout the United States. For example, Corvallis, Oregon, is the repository for pears and small fruit. Grapes, kiwifruit, and stonefruit germplasm is being preserved at Davis, California, and the New York State Agricultural Experiment Station at Geneva serves as the home for apple and American grape germplasm.

Plant Parts, Growth, and Development

Roots

Roots absorb water and nutrients from the soil and transport these to the base of the stem. They also anchor the plant and store food produced through photosynthesis in the leaves.

When a seed germinates, the first part to emerge is the radicle, which gives rise to the root. As a young root grows downward through the soil, it may form extensive lateral branches resulting in a fibrous root system, but when only minimal branching occurs a taproot system is formed.

The type of root system that develops is to a certain extent genetically controlled, but this can be altered. For example, transplanting and/or root pruning are techniques used by nurseries to increase lateral branching of roots. The root system may also be altered by soil conditions, a high water table, or root competition. Some fruit trees that normally produce roots that grow vertically will develop a more shallow horizontal root system if the plants are spaced too closely together in the orchard. Planting over a compacted plow furrow or a hardpan layer produces essentially the same results. Planting on soils that are waterlogged for extensive periods also results in a poor root system.

For many kinds of fruit, the grower has a choice of not only which cultivar to select, but also which rootstock goes along with it. The rootstock that is grafted or combined by budding to the cultivar is also important. The following chapters give specific recommendations for rootstock selection.

Bud, Shoot, and Spur Development

Buds located at the tips of branches are called terminal and these contain meristematic (dividing) cells, which result in shoot elongation. Active lateral buds located on the sides of stems also have meristematic capabilities, and these produce short lateral branches or spur shoots. Stems may also contain dormant or inactive buds. These latent buds may become overgrown with bark tissue and remain dormant until they are forced to develop by shoot wounding or severe pruning.

Buds may be strictly vegetative, giving rise to shoots and leaves; others may produce only flowers or inflorescences as in cherry, peach, and plum. Mixed buds produce both vegetative structures and flower primordia as in apples, grapes, and kiwifruit.

Buds, in preparation for the outset of winter, enter a dormancy or resting period to ensure that growth does not resume when weather conditions are unfavorable. To satisfy the resting requirement, buds must be exposed to a minimum number of hours of cool temperatures before normal bud growth can resume in the spring. This chilling requirement varies from species to species and even within a given species. Table 1, adapted from Ryugo (1988), provides some examples.

Table 1. Time period below 45° F. needed to satisfy the resting requirement of selected fruits

Species	Hours	Days
Apricot	700–1,000	29–41
Apple	1,200–1,500	50–62
Cherries, sour	1,200	50
Peach	1,000–1,200	42–50
Pear, European	1,200–1,500	50–62
Plums, European	700–1,100	29–46

Source: Modified, with permission, from Ryugo, 1988.

The Flower

In the geological timeframe, the flower is a recent addition to the botanical world, appearing in the fossil record long after the algae, fungi, mosses, ferns, and gymnosperms. Plants possessing flowers (angiosperms) have been enormously successful, and today they are the dominant plant group throughout the world.

The angiosperm flower develops from a bud and is typically composed of

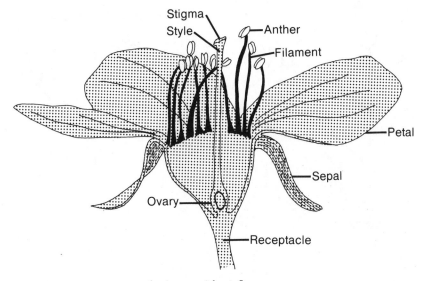

Angiosperm (plum) flower.

modified leaves called sepals, petals, stamens, and carpels, which are attached to a swollen stem tip or receptacle.

Sepals. Collectively known as the calyx, these are usually green and are the outermost floral organs.

Petals. Collectively called the corolla, these organs are located above the sepals and frequently serve to attract pollinators.

Stamens. These are the male pollen-producing organs, which are located above the petals. The stalk of an individual stamen is the filament and the pollen-producing sac is the anther.

Carpels. These are the female floral organs located in the center of the flower. One or more carpels make up the pistil, which is composed of stigma, style, and ovary.

Flower Variation

Complete Flowers. Possess sepals, petals, stamens, and carpels.

Incomplete Flowers. Lack one or more of the floral organs in complete flowers.

Perfect Flowers. These are bisexual flowers possessing both stamens and pistils.

Imperfect Flowers. Unisexual flowers. Those with only stamens are called staminate and those with only pistils, pistillate. *Monoecious* means having staminate and pistillate flowers on the same plant. *Dioecious* is a condition where staminate and pistillate flowers are borne on separate plants.

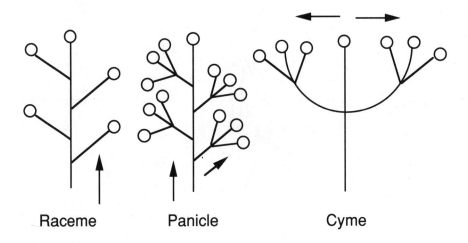

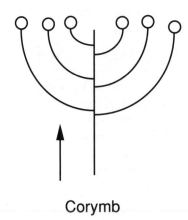

Inflorescence types. Arrows indicate flowering order.

Inflorescences

An inflorescence is a cluster of two or more flowers. Examples of inflorescences found among the species discussed in this book include the following:

Raceme. Individual flowers supported by a short stalk are borne on an axis that elongates for an indefinite period. The lowest flower on the axis blooms first and finally the terminal bud forms the last flower. Example: red currant.

Panicle. This is a compound inflorescence with several main branches, each of which bears flowers supported by short stalks or pedicels. The oldest flowers are at the bottom of the inflorescence. Example: grape.

Corymb. This inflorescence is like a raceme except that the pedicels of individual flowers elongate, forming a more or less flat-topped inflorescence with the oldest flowers on the outside. Example: pear.

Cyme. This term illustrates another branched inflorescence like the panicle, except that it is more or less flat-topped and the central flowers open first. Example: raspberries.

Pollination

Pollination is the transfer of pollen from the anther to the stigma. Once on the stigma, the pollen grain germinates and produces a pollen tube, which grows down through the style to the ovary, where fertilization occurs. After fertilization, the seeds begin to form and the ovary enlarges.

In the absence of pollination, the flower soon begins to wither and the ovary fails to develop into a fruit. This may occur when insect pollinators are absent or when adverse weather conditions limit their activity. Honeybees, for example, which are the major pollinators for most fruits discussed here, rarely fly during cold, rainy, or windy days. They are most active on sunny days when the temperature is above 65° F. During favorable conditions, Naeve (1985) reported that honeybees may visit 5,000 blossoms in a day. Honeybees and other insect pollinators are susceptible to pesticides, and these should never be used during the blooming period.

Some fruit cultivars are described as being self-fruitful. This simply means that when pollen is transferred from the anther to the stigma on the same flower or to the stigma of another flower of the same cultivar, and fertilization will occur.

In contrast, some plants have an incompatibility problem with their own pollen, and cross-pollination with another cultivar must occur for fruit production. In these self-unfruitful plants, pollen from the anther of one cultivar must be transferred to the stigma of a different cultivar.

Fruit

The botanical definition of a fruit is a mature ovary and other flower parts associated with it. Ovules inside the mature ovary are the seeds. With this liberal interpretation, a ripe tomato or the pods of beans and peas would be fruits, though they are commonly classified as vegetables.

In this book, the term *fruit* is restricted to the more common usage and

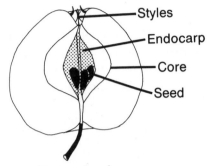

Pome-Apple

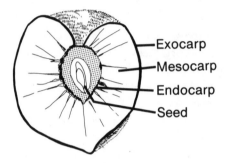

Drupe-Peach

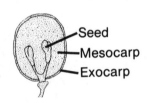

Berry-Grape

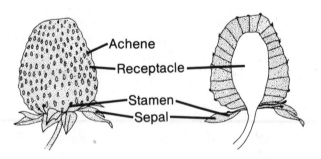

Aggregate-Strawberry

Fruit types.

Table 2. Mineral particle sizes

Particle	Range in diameter of particles (mm)	Range in diameter of particles (in.)	Approximate number of particles required to form a line 1 in. long
Sand	0.05–2	0.002–0.08	12–500
Silt	0.002–0.05	0.0008–0.002	500–12,500
Clay	<0.002	<0.0008	>12,500

Source: University of Minnesota Extension Bulletin 383.

covers ripened ovaries and associated flower parts that are fleshy and usually sweet and pulpy. Fruits in this category are classified as follows:

Pome. The ripened ovary is often referred to as the core and is usually not consumed. The edible portion is the fleshy, expanded receptacle that grows around the ovary. Examples: apple, pear, saskatoon.

Drupe. The fruit is divided into three distinct layers. The outer portion (skin) is the exocarp; the middle edible portion, the mesocarp; and a hard inner pit, the endocarp. These are also known as stone fruits. Examples: cherry, plum, apricot, peach.

Berry. Except for the exocarp, the entire ovary remains fleshy at maturity. Examples: grape, gooseberry, currant.

Aggregate. The fruit here is formed from the fusion of several different ovaries produced in a single flower. Individual ovaries in the flowers may become drupes as in blackberries and raspberries, or small, dry, one-seeded achenes as in strawberries. The edible fleshy portion of the strawberry is expanded receptacle tissue.

Soil

Before planting any type of fruit, it is beneficial to have some knowledge of the soil in which the plant will grow. Some types of fruit have exacting soil requirements, while others will grow in a variety of soils. The challenge for the fruit grower is to improve or modify soil conditions to fit the needs of the types of fruit being grown.

Soil Composition

Soil is composed of mineral particles, air, water, soluble chemical compounds, organic matter, and a variety of living organisms. These organisms play no small role in this dynamic mixture — their diversity and numbers are enormous. For example, Waksman (1952) reported that ¼ teaspoon of fertile

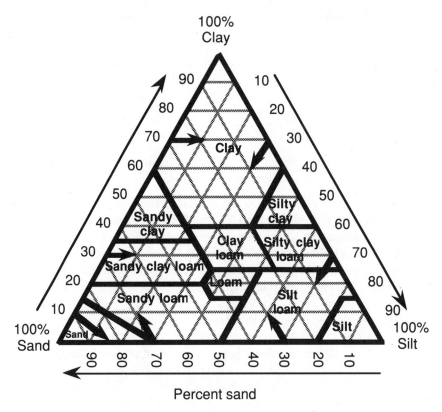

Soil texture chart.

soil may contain 50 nematodes, 62,000 algae, 72,000 fungi, 2,920,000 actinomycetes, and 25,280,000 bacteria.

One acre of soil may contain more than a million earthworms, and the bacteria alone may weigh one ton or more. Most soil organisms have beneficial effects since they aid in decomposition of organic matter, help release nutrients for plant uptake, and play an important role in soil aeration.

Soil Texture

Other than organic soils, which predominantly contain decaying organic matter (65 percent or more), most soils in the Upper Midwest are classified texturally by the content of the mineral particles, clay, sand, and silt. The relative size of these particles is listed in Table 2.

The chart above provides a convenient way to determine a soil's textural class. To use this chart, follow the respective percentage lines for sand, silt, and clay until they intersect. For example, a soil with 20 percent clay, 40 percent silt, and 40 percent sand would be classified as loam.

Soil texture can be used as a guide for cultural practices, and it is a major determinant of the soil's available nutrient and water capacity. For example, sandy soils, because of particle size and space (pores) between particles, have poor water-holding capacity. When it rains, most of the water will drain through quickly, and plant nutrients may be lost; thus, supplemental water and frequent fertilization may be necessary. On the plus side, sandy soils can be cultivated earlier than other soils in the spring and also soon after a rain because there is little danger of compaction.

In contrast to sandy soils, clay soils have the ability to hold a large amount of water, and they attract and hold nutrients better. On the negative side, they exhibit slow movement of air and poor drainage. In addition, clay soils have a great deal of plasticity. This simply means that the soil may be easily molded when it is wet. Cultivating clay soil before it has sufficiently dried results in large clods and often compaction, especially if large equipment is used. The test for when to cultivate is to take a handful of soil and attempt to compress it into a ball. If the soil resists molding, crumbles, and falls apart, it is ready for cultivation.

Between the extremes of clay and sand are the loam soils. These soils are considered ideal for growing many kinds of fruit. Loam soils do not exhibit the plasticity of clay soils and thus can be worked much sooner after a rain. They also hold water and nutrients much better than sandy soils.

Organic Matter

Most soils can be improved by periodic addition of organic matter. Organic matter added to sandy soils increases water- and nutrient-holding capacity. On clay soils, it improves soil structure, thus allowing for better drainage and air movement.

The choice for what type of organic matter to add to the soil should be dictated largely by price and availability. Animal manures, compost, and various types of green manure crops are all excellent sources of organic matter.

Soil pH

A soil's pH is a measure of acidity or alkalinity. It is measured on a logarithmic scale that ranges from 0 to 14. A pH of 7 is neutral, neither acidic nor alkaline. Above 7 is alkaline or basic and below 7 is acidic.

The optimum pH range of soil for each fruit is discussed in the following chapters. In general, most of the cultivars perform best if the pH is slightly acidic.

Soil pH may be adjusted by the addition of various materials to the soil, but this should be done preferably before, not after, planting. A pH test in

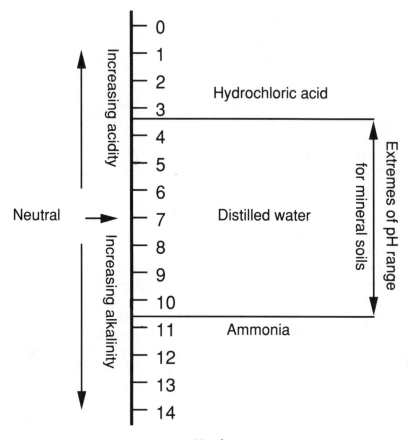

pH scale.

the fall before spring planting is ideal since it usually takes several months for completion of the complex chemical reactions required to change soil pH.

To make the soil more alkaline, some type of lime may be added to the soil. The least expensive is ground limestone ($CaCO_3$) or calcitric limestone. Dolomitic limestone ($CaMgCO_3$) is also used and has the added feature of supplying magnesium, a nutrient that may be in short supply in some soils.

Specific recommendations for making the soil more acidic are given in the chapter on blueberries and in the section on cranberry culture.

Soil Testing

Inexpensive, home soil-testing kits are frequently advertised in gardening magazines and nursery catalogs, but many are notoriously unreliable and often provide only ballpark estimates of soil conditions. For precise determination of soil pH and soil mineral content, use either state university or private, professional soil-testing laboratories. Information on how to contact these labs, sampling methods, and cost is available at all county extension offices.

Nutrient Requirements

At least 16 nutrients are essential for the proper growth of the plants discussed here. In the photosynthetic process,

$$\text{Light}$$
$$6CO_2 + 6H_2O \longrightarrow C_6H_{12}O_6 + 6O_2$$
$$\text{Chlorophyll}$$

Carbon (C) and oxygen (O_2) in the form of carbon dioxide (CO_2) enter the leaf through tiny pores called stomates. Water (H_2O) and other required elements enter the plant in the soil through the roots. The sugar glucose ($C_6H_{12}O_6$) manufactured in photosynthesis is used as an energy source and for the construction of the plant parts. Oxygen exits the plant as a by-product through the stomates.

The three elements most likely to be in short supply in soils are nitrogen (N), phosphorus (P), and potassium (K).

Nitrogen (N) is required in large quantities and is essential for formation of chlorophyll and plant protein. Nitrogen is leached easily from soil, and on sandy soils with poor water-holding capacity, it may be required at more frequent intervals than on other soil types. Table 7 (in the chapter on apples) serves as a guide for judging the nitrogen status of fruit trees.

When nitrogen is deficient, the leaves turn pale green to yellow and the older leaves are affected first. In severe cases, all the leaves turn yellow and growth may be stunted. Too much nitrogen produces excessive vegetative growth and poor fruit growth.

Phosphorus (P) plays a role in flowering, fruiting, and root development. It is a major component of nucleic acids and is present in some plant proteins. Phosphorus in the form of rock phosphate is relatively immobile and is unavailable for plant uptake except when released by soil acids. Addition of organic matter to soils helps improve phosphorus uptake. Inorganic fertilizers that contain phosphorus in the acid form (HPO_4) can be used to correct a deficiency. When phosphorus is deficient, the oldest leaves are affected first, and they may appear reddish purple. Too much phosphorus may induce a zinc or iron deficiency.

Potassium (K) is an important enzyme activator and is essential for sugar movement. It also plays a role in the formation of chlorophyll, as well as flower and fruit coloring. In addition, it is essential for strong root development. Potassium is quite soluble and may be leached from the soil. When deficient, the oldest leaves are affected first and may develop gray or tan areas near the margins. Excess K application can cause salt burn and induce a magnesium deficiency.

Three additional elements are needed by plants in fairly large quantities, but these are usually present in adequate amounts in most soils.

Calcium (Ca) is an essential element in plant cell walls, and it plays a role in the permeability of cell membranes. When deficient, young leaves are affected, and the growing points of the plant may be stunted or die. A calcium deficiency may occur on acid and/or dry soils.

Magnesium (Mg) is a part of the chlorophyll molecule and it plays a role in protein synthesis. When lacking, the oldest leaves turn yellow between the veins, and when severe, all leaves may be affected. Deficiencies have been reported in acid soils, sandy soils, and where potassium levels are high.

Sulfur (S) plays a role in photosynthesis and is found in many plant proteins. Deficiency symptoms are similar to those for nitrogen except the youngest leaves are affected first. This element may be in short supply in sandy soils low in organic matter.

Other elements are required by plants in small amounts (micronutrients).

A boron (B) deficiency may affect root and shoot elongation. It is also thought to play a role in flowering and in the breakdown of carbohydrates. When deficient, growing points may die, and younger plant tissue is affected first. In time, leaves may appear distorted. This deficiency is most likely to occur on sandy soils low in organic matter. Excess boron often causes margin scorching on older leaves.

Chlorine (Cl) deficiencies are practically unknown. Excess amounts may cause marginal scorching of older leaves. Chlorine plays a role in photosynthesis.

Copper (Cu) deficiencies occur most often on organic soils (muck, peat). The youngest leaves are affected first, and they may exhibit yellowing or dieback. Excess copper may induce iron chlorosis and stunt root growth. This element plays a role in certain enzymatic reactions and is involved in photosynthesis.

Iron (Fe) chlorosis (yellowing between the veins of the youngest leaves) occurs when iron is not readily available. This may occur on alkaline soils (pH greater than 7.2) and is usually more severe in cold, wet soils. Susceptibility of plant species varies. In blueberries, for example, a pH as low as 5.5 to 6.0 may cause chlorosis. Excesses are rare, but high levels of iron may cause a manganese deficiency. Iron also plays a role in photosynthesis and respiration.

Manganese (Mn) is involved in enzymatic reactions, and it plays an essential role in photosynthesis. A manganese deficiency produces yellowing between the veins of younger leaves, thus mimicking an iron deficiency. Often, only the main veins remain green. In some species, older leaves develop gray streaks or dots. This deficiency may occur on soils with a pH greater than 7.2 or on organic soils with a pH greater than 6.0. Excess manganese can occur on soils with a pH less than 4.5. Symptoms of excess are chlorosis and brown spots on the leaves.

Molybdenum (Mo) deficiencies are rare and usually occur only on acid soils with a pH less than 5.0. When lacking, the leaves may be pale and distorted. This element plays a role in enzyme systems and is involved in some reactions involving nitrogen.

Zinc (Zn) plays a role in several enzymatic reactions. When deficient, younger leaves are usually affected first and may exhibit yellowing between the veins. Internodes may be short, producing a rosette effect in some trees. A zinc deficiency is most likely to occur under conditions similar to those which cause an iron deficiency. Zinc in excess may also induce an iron deficiency.

Pests and Diseases

It is very disheartening to fight drought, weeds, blisters, and sore muscles only to find an insect so small it can barely be seen suddenly devouring the fruits of one's labor. The initial reaction may be to quickly visit the local garden store for a spray or dust to immediately eliminate this new intruder. Another option would be to become more knowledgeable about the life cycle of the pest and to initiate steps that will lessen the problem in the future.

Many insect and disease problems can be minimized or eliminated by a combination of good cultural practices. These include pruning regularly, providing water and chemical nutrients in needed amounts, controlling weeds, and employing preventive measures to avoid winter physiological and dessication injury. Since several disease organisms can overwinter on fallen fruit, leaves, and twigs, growers with just a few plants can solve many problems by raking and removing debris from the orchard.

Choosing cultivars that offer some natural resistance to specific diseases is also an important point to consider, and the disease susceptibility of cultivars should be carefully evaluated before a selection is made.

A growing trend nationwide among commercial fruit growers is to use a technique called IPM or integrated pest management. This technique does not completely eliminate the need for pesticides, but it certainly has the laudable goal of cutting down on their use.

Many commercial orchardists may spray a particular fruit such as apples with chemicals 13 or more times during the growing season, but for the homeowner or small grower, this is not necessary nor advised. Without some method of pest or disease control, damage is inevitable, but a less-than-perfect fruit can be acceptable and usable. In most cases, growers with just

The diversity of available chemicals is enormous, but home gardeners can eliminate the need for many of these products by selecting disease-resistant cultivars and by using good cultural techniques.

a few plants will find they can raise more fruit than they can possibly use with a minimum of spraying and some proven IPM techniques. Tips for reducing pesticide use are scattered throughout the book.

For those who choose to use the commercial pesticides, the list seems endless since there are several thousand types currently available in the United States. A major problem with pesticides is that it is nearly impossible for the average person, let alone the professional, to sort through the maze of claims and counterclaims of competing manufacturers. Unfortunately, even many of the people who sell pesticides do not know the ingredients of the products, nor do they have the necessary training to properly evaluate their effects.

My advice on choosing pesticides is to pick the ones that will do the job with a minimum of damage to the environment. Avoid pesticides that are persistent, that is, those that do not degrade in a matter of days.

Choose a pesticide with a low toxicity to humans and pets. This can be determined by observing the signal word on the label: *Caution* = low toxicity or comparatively free of danger; *Warning* = moderately toxic; *Danger* = highly toxic. Also, some pesticides used in orchards are classified for "restricted use." In order to purchase and use them, one must become certified.

Check with your local county extension service for certification requirements.

Here are some safety "don'ts" when handling pesticides:

Don't use around children, pets, foods, utensils, or eating areas.

Don't leave a partial or empty container in an open garbage can.

Don't smoke while handling pesticides.

Don't take pesticides out of the original container to store in another container.

Don't mix pesticides unless you are sure they are compatible.

Don't use around birdbaths, wells, or cisterns.

Don't unnecessarily expose body parts to pesticides. Wear long-sleeved shirts, pants, gloves, and preferably a mask.

Don't use pesticides when pregnant women are present.

Above all, do follow manufacturers' directions on dosage and safety precautions. This is especially important when harvesting fruit since the elapsed time between applications and the safety period for human consumption varies considerably with the different pesticides. Fruit sprayed with pesticides should be thoroughly washed before it is eaten.

Choice of a pesticide and timing of application are very important for protecting pollinators. For example, insecticides applied during the blooming period will kill honeybees, which are the major pollinators of most types of fruit. Misapplication of certain pesticides will also result in scorching of foliage, heavy russeting of fruit, excessive fruit thinning, or in extreme cases, total fruit drop.

Information on the relative safety of chemicals changes rapidly, so for the sake of safety, specific chemicals are not recommended here, except those of a general nature. Growers requiring information on chemicals to treat specific pests should contact their county extension service for detailed, up-to-date information.

Hardiness Zones

Success with fruit production begins with choosing cultivars that are adapted to local growing conditions. To assist the reader, zone maps with a guide to cultivar selection have been prepared for each state. These maps reflect the fruit-hardiness zones currently used by extension personnel in each state. It is important to note that each state has a different zone map, and that the zones do not overlap. For example, Zone 1 in Wisconsin should not be confused with Zone 1 in Minnesota.

Most hardiness maps have severe limitations, and this one is no exception.

Hardiness zones for each state.

The zones presented here do not take into account variation in soil types and rainfall. They are, therefore, only approximate guides for cultivar selection.

Locating Cultivars

One of the best sources for locating cultivars discussed in this book is the 1989 *Fruit, Berry and Nut Inventory*, edited by Kent Whealy. This publication (available from Seed Savers Publications, R.R. 3, Box 239, Decorah, IA 52103) is an inventory of almost all the fruit, berry, and nut cultivars grown in the United States. It contains a listing of nearly 250 nurseries and over 4,140 cultivars.

Another excellent source for locating fruit cultivars and horticultural plants of all kinds is the 1989 AHL source list of plants and seeds (available from the Anderson Horticultural Library, Minnesota Landscape Arboretum, 3675 Arboretum Drive, Box 39, Chanhassen, MN 55317). This publication contains a listing for over 40,000 plants commercially available in North America.

Readers will find that a few cultivars listed in this book are no longer commercially available. These are included largely for historical purposes and to alert growers to their rarity.

SELECTED REFERENCES

Acuff, G. 1989. "Second Stage" IPM Cuts Pesticide Use. *American Fruit Grower* 109(5): 36–38.

Fuller, H. J., and O. Tippo. 1958. *College Botany*. New York: Holt.

Janick, J. 1986. *Horticultural Science*. 4th ed. New York: Freeman.

Lawrence, G. H. M. 1951. *Taxonomy of Vascular Plants*. New York: Macmillan.

Lockeretz, W., ed. 1983. *Environmentally Sound Agriculture*. New York: Praeger.

Naeve, L. 1985. *Tree Fruit Pollination*. Iowa State University Coop. Ext. Ser. Pub. F-5-85.

Radford, A. E., W. C. Dickinson, J. R. Massey, and C. R. Bell. 1974. *Vascular Plant Systematics*. New York: Harper and Row.

Rosen, C. J. 1989. Diagnosing Nutrient Deficiency and Toxicity Symptoms in Fruit and Vegetable Crops. *Minnesota Fruit and Vegetable Growers Assoc.* 3(3): 12.

Ryugo, K. 1988. *Fruit Culture—Its Science and Art*. New York: Wiley.

Sill, W. H., Jr. 1982. *Plant Protection—An Integrated Interdisciplinary Approach*. Ames: Iowa State University Press.

Waksman, S. A. 1952. *Soil Microbiology*. New York: Wiley.

Apples

Brown (1975) has described the apple as the most ubiquitous of all fruits because of its widespread use and cultivation. It is the most valuable tree fruit and can be found almost everywhere except in the very hottest and coldest regions of the world.

The exact origin of the apple is unknown, but according to Teskey and Shoemaker (1978), it probably originated in the region south of the Caucasus Mountains in Asia Minor. Many wild *Malus* species are indigenous there, and it seems likely that the apple arose as a result of interspecific hybridization. To reflect the hybrid origin, this member of the rose family is now known scientifically as *Malus* x *domestica* Borkh.

How long humans have been using the apple is unknown, but its history can be traced back 2,900 years to the time of Homer. Korban and Skirvin (1984) point out that the apple was well known to the ancient Greeks, and it was mentioned by the Father of Botany, Theophrastus, in the third century B.C. The Romans probably were responsible for the spread of the apple throughout Europe and into Asia.

In this country, the first apples were grown from seed brought by the early European colonists. The seed continued to be the vehicle for the transport of the apple from the Atlantic states to the West. It was carried by the Indians, the early settlers, and of course, by the legendary Johnny Appleseed (John Chapman, 1774–1845). Chapman, a pioneer planter, distributed both seeds and sprouts throughout the Ohio Valley. By the late 1860s, the apple was grown coast to coast (Teskey and Shoemaker, 1978).

In the Upper Midwest, the early settlers found growing apples and many other types of fruit a challenging and often exasperating experience. Horace

Greeley in 1860 once told Wilford L. Wilson, "I would not live in Minnesota." "Why?", asked Wilson. "Because," replied Greeley, "you cannot grow apples there."

The History of the Minnesota Horticultural Society, published in 1873, gives us a glimpse of the problems faced by early fruit growers from the society's first meeting in Rochester in 1866 to its last at St. Paul in 1873. Some excerpts follow.

Early Letters from Fruit Growers

From David Berry, Afton, Washington County, February 20, 1866: "Sir, In answer to your inquiries regarding apple trees, I beg to say that on the 9th day of May, 1854, I set out 25 three-year old trees. Came, I understood, from Iowa. None have escaped injury."

From Joseph Bell, Marshall, Dakota County, February 13, 1866: "Most people have no faith in raising orchards in Minnesota, but I have no doubt of success, although the quince, pears and cherries I planted have all died."

From S. Hunt, Hudson, St. Croix County, Wisconsin (no date): "In the spring of 1852, a small quantity of apple seeds, selected from the most hardy varieties of fruit raised in Canada and the State of Maine, was planted on the farm of Otis Hoyt in St. Croix County. The result was several hundred fine young trees which grew vigorously for two years, then they began to gradually die out from the effects of our climate, until at the end of five years, two only remained."

Similar tales of grower frustration were commonplace in all of the Upper Midwestern states. In Iowa, for example, toward the end of the nineteenth century, apple cultivars were imported from Russia supposedly to solve the cold-hardiness problem. Literally thousands of these "Russians," as they were called, were distributed to growers at a nominal price, but, unfortunately, their fame was short-lived because the trees proved quite susceptible to fireblight (Bolluyt, 1982).

The early settlers were aware of the technique of grafting, since this art had been practiced for centuries in Europe. Smock and Neubert (1950) reported that by 1647, apples were being grafted on seedling rootstock in Virginia. Despite this knowledge, progress in developing hardy, disease-resistant cultivars for the North was slow. Attempts to develop new apple cultivars through controlled hybridization did not begin in this country until the late 1700s (Korban, 1986). The late N. E. Hansen of South Dakota was a pioneer in securing hardy germplasm for apple production. He was instrumental in introducing the imported 'Dolgo' crab from Russia, which could be used as a hardy rootstock for desirable cultivars. In addition, his breeding work yielded close to 100 named cultivars.

It is surprising that some of our best and most enduring apple cultivars arose not through conscious breeding efforts, but rather appeared as chance seedlings in home or commercial orchards. The 'McIntosh' apple, Wisconsin's leading cultivar, is a case in point. In about 1811 in Dundas County, Ontario, Canada, John McIntosh discovered 20 apple seedlings on his farm. He gambled and moved the plants to an area near his cabin. Years passed and his wife, Hana Doran, took a fancy to one of the trees that produced unusually bright red, top-quality fruit. Their son Alan was also fascinated by the tree, and after learning budding and grafting techniques, he established a nursery so he could distribute the plants to friends and relatives. As a circuit-riding lay preacher, Alan became Canada's Johnny Appleseed. From this original chance discovery, the famous 'McIntosh' apple has spread worldwide.

The 'Delicious' apple, and its improved strains, is number one in production in the United States. The original 'Delicious' appeared as a chance seedling in 1870 on the farm of Jesse Hiatt near Peru, Madison County, Iowa. The apple was acquired by Stark Nursery in 1894, and by 1922 the 'Delicious' crop was valued at $22 million (Frecon, 1979). From this original tree, literally millions of apple trees have been propagated, and several hundred named sports or mutant strains have been identified.

In 1916, Stark Bros. Nursery paid $5,000 for the propagation rights to a golden yellow apple that appeared as a chance seedling on the farm of A. H. Mullins in West Virginia. That apple, named 'Golden Delicious', is the most widely planted apple in the world.

Production

During the last two decades, apple production has increased significantly in the United States. From 1970–72 to 1984–86, production went up 30 percent, and the value of the 1989 crop was $1.04 billion. The four top apple-producing states listed in order of importance are Washington, California, Michigan, and New York.

In the Upper Midwest, Wisconsin, Minnesota, and Iowa are the major apple producers. The value of the 1989 crop was $11,098,000 in Wisconsin, $7,645,000 in Minnesota, and $2,247,000 in Iowa (*Noncitrus Fruits and Nuts*, January 1990).

Apple Propagation

Standard Trees

Today, virtually all apple trees sold commercially are grafted or budded to form a unique combination of two or more distinct genetic types. Standard-

Two-year-old apple tree with a well-branched root system. The swollen graft-union area is clearly visible on the trunk.

size trees are produced in the following manner: First, the seed of a hardy cultivar, like 'Dolgo' crab, is planted and allowed to develop for one to two years. Next a bud from a desired cultivar such as 'Haralson' or 'McIntosh' is selected, and this (called the scion) is inserted onto the hardy seedling rootstock in July or August. The following spring, the rootstock is cut back to the bud.

If the sprouts from the hardy rootstock are allowed to develop, it is possible to end up with two types of apples being produced on the same tree. Sprouts that develop from the base of the plant should be removed.

5-1 Apples

Many nurseries advertise 5-in-1 apple trees. These are produced just like the normal standard variety except that buds or scions from five cultivars are used. These trees are novelty items, and in terms of productivity, their higher cost is rarely justified. Another disadvantage is that often some of the cultivars are not hardy for a particular region. When that happens, the grafts may freeze out, and one may end up with fewer cultivars. In addition, the sur-

5-1 apple trees are considered novelty items and are rarely worth the extra price, but growers who wish to experiment with grafting often find it a rewarding experience. Here Minnesota grower G. A. Stroebel has successfully budded scions from eight cultivars onto this apple tree. Photo by J. Cross.

viving cultivars may grow unequally and make tree pruning and shaping more difficult.

Dwarfed Trees

Dwarfed trees may be produced by using dwarfing rootstocks or dwarfing interstocks. Rootstocks used in the dwarfing process are obtained from small (dwarf) apples. The rootstock is propagated vegetatively by rooting shoots of these dwarf apple types. After the shoot has properly rooted, a bud or scion of the desired cultivar is grafted onto the rootstock and the top portion is cut off. In this case the dwarfing effect of the rootstock limits the size of the tree.

Most dwarfing rootstocks used in the Upper Midwest were classified in England at the East Malling Research Station and carry the designations M.1, M.9, and so on, or were classified jointly by the East Malling Station and the John Innes Horticultural Station located at Merton, England. These later rootstocks carry the designations MM.106, MM.111, and so on. Some of these original rootstocks were infected with viruses, but today nurseries carry virus-free stock, which is often labeled or designated as EMLA (East Malling Long Ashton — research stations) rootstock.

Since there are many kinds of dwarfing rootstocks, each with different characteristics, *it is important not to buy a tree labeled simply as "dwarf."* Reliable nurseries tag each tree with the name of the cultivar and the dwarfing rootstock used. For example: McIntosh/MM.106.

Dwarf Interstems

By means of a double graft, a dwarfing interstem (stem section) such as M.8 may be inserted between a seedling rootstock and a scion of the desired cultivar. The major disadvantage of this dwarfing method is the weak points of the two grafts. This often results in brittle wood and wind breakage near the interstem.

At the present time, the use of dwarfing interstems should be approached with extreme caution. Many growers throughout the Upper Midwest have experienced considerable tree death and early decline with interstem trees.

Selecting Apple Rootstocks

Standard seedling rootstocks continue to be the best choice for growers who live in the *colder* portions of the Upper Midwest. These rootstocks can withstand + 14° F. *root zone temperature.* In contrast, the dwarfing rootstocks now being used are injured when root temperatures drop to + 18° F. to + 22° F. (Hertz and Hoover, 1987). Dwarfing rootstocks have performed very poorly throughout North Dakota, and they are not recommended there or in northern Minnesota and Wisconsin. Researchers in Minnesota have found that the dwarfing rootstocks are reasonably hardy when grown under sod in the southern portion of the state. Even there, rootstocks can be injured during winters with little snowcover or when the plants are grown under clean cultivation without a mulch.

In favorable apple-growing regions, the dwarfing rootstocks have become increasingly popular with commercial growers during the last few years. In Minnesota, for example, by 1988, 211,342 or over 62 percent of the apple trees were being grown on dwarfing rootstocks (Minnesota Ag. Stat. Service, November 1988). In Wisconsin by 1986, 72 percent of the apples in commercial orchards were dwarf or semidwarf varieties (Wisconsin Ag. Stat. Service, December 1987).

Before purchasing trees with dwarfing rootstocks, consider both the advantages and the disadvantages. The dwarf trees are more manageable, and the fruit is easier to pick. The trees do start bearing at an earlier age than stan-

Young dwarf 'Red Haralson' trees in flower (top) *and with fruit* (bottom).

dard trees, and they take up much less space; thus, homeowners with small lots will find them very desirable.

In contrast, the dwarfs are more expensive to purchase than standard trees, and they are less productive. In addition, because of their weaker, less hardy root system, the trees will have to be mulched, and they often require staking or support.

When choosing a rootstock, Forshey et al. (1986) suggest the following characteristics to keep in mind:

> It should be winter hardy.
> It should provide good anchorage for the tree in the soil.
> It should be resistant to disease.
> It should sucker very little or not at all.
> It should be tolerant of unfavorable soil conditions.
> It should promote early bearing and continued heavy production.
> It should be easily propagated.
> It should provide some degree of size and vigor control over the scion without adverse effects on productivity.

Unfortunately, none of the rootstocks currently available provide all of these characteristics. Growers are advised to read carefully the following descriptions of common dwarfing rootstocks and to pick those that best fit local growing conditions.

Malling Rootstocks

M.7. This rootstock produces a dwarfing effect equal to about 55 to 65 percent the size of standard trees. It seems to be the least hardy of all dwarfing rootstocks used in the Upper Midwest; thus, adequate snow-cover and/or mulching may be essential in some areas. This type is well adapted to most soils except heavy clay, and it is widely used in commercial orchards. Trees on this rootstock are precocious (early bearing) and quite productive. The major disadvantage to M.7 is that it has a tendency to sucker, especially if it is planted too shallow. For best results, plant the graft union two inches above the soil line. Disease-free clones of this rootstock are often labeled M.7a.

M.9. A tree equal to about 25 to 40 percent the size of standard trees is produced with this rootstock. M.9 is slightly hardier than M.7, and it performs best on deep, well-drained soils. This rootstock is susceptible to burrknot, fireblight, and suckering. It should be planted at the same depth as M.7. The tree must be staked or supported because its roots and wood are very brittle and break easily. M.9 is rarely used by commercial growers, but because of its size-producing effect, early blooming, and heavy productivity, it has been popular with amateur fruit growers and is widely used as an interstem and in European orchards.

M.26. The dwarfing effect of this selection is 40 to 50 percent of standard trees. This is the most hardy of all the commonly used rootstocks, but M.26 is very susceptible to burrknot, fireblight, and suckering. This selection should also be planted on deep, well-drained soils. It is not tolerant of prolonged wet-soil conditions. With most cultivars, M.26 is precocious and heavy bearing.

M.27. This is the most dwarfing rootstock now available. Trees produced on this selection are only about 25 percent the size of standard. Because of poor anchorage, these trees require support. M.27 is slightly less hardy than M.9 and should be planted deep and mulched. It performs best on deep, well-drained soils. It is very precocious and heavy bearing.

Malling Merton Rootstocks

MM.106. This is a semidwarf rootstock producing trees 60 to 75 percent the size of standards. These trees perform best in loam and sandy loam. Collar rot can be a problem with MM.106, especially if the trees are deep planted or are grown on poorly drained soils. Cultivars on this selection usually fruit early and are very productive. A major disadvantage is that trees budded on this selection often grow late in the fall and exhibit delayed dormancy.

MM.111. This is a semistandard rootstock that results in trees about 90 percent the size of those grown on seedlings. MM.111 is very tolerant of most soils, and it is probably the best choice for droughty soil conditions. It is not early fruiting, but productivity may exceed cultivars grown on seedling rootstocks.

For more information on rootstocks, see Hertz and Hoover (1987), Ferree and Carlson (1987), and Domoto and Nonnecke (1988).

Spur-Type Trees

For some cultivars, special strains exist that yield trees that are more compact because of restricted branching. Besides the reduction in size of trees (75 to 90 percent of normal), the fruit develops from more closely spaced spurs that are borne on the principal limbs. The spur-type trees produce fruit that is easy to pick, and pruning is somewhat more simplified. These trees are excellent in combination with size-controlling rootstocks.

A small sample of the apple cultivars grown in the Upper Midwest.

Pollination and Fruit Set

Most apple cultivars are self-unfruitful or self-sterile. This means they will not set fruit with their own pollen. For this reason, plant at least two cultivars of apples near one another and make sure that the pollenizers bloom at the same time and are cross-compatible.

Strains of named cultivars cannot be relied on for effective pollination of other strains of the same cultivar. For example, 'Macspur' pollen cannot be used for standard 'McIntosh' and vice versa.

Even when two different cultivars are present, there still may be a problem with pollination. This is particularly true when the cultivars share a common genetic heritage. For example, 'Connell Red' and 'Fireside' are so similar that their pollen is incompatible. In addition, some apple cultivars such as 'Stayman', 'Winesap', and 'Mutsu' produce inviable pollen. Thus, when a cultivar produces poor or inviable pollen, a third cultivar must be present to provide cross-pollination.

During the last few years some commercial growers have experimented with ornamental flowering crabs as a pollen source. Some of these crabs have been shown to be effective pollenizers for apples, but more testing is needed before an extensive list of cultivars can be recommended for the Upper Midwest.

How close cross-compatible trees need to be to each other depends on the foraging activities of bees, which are largely responsible for the transport of the pollen from one cultivar to another. In commercial orchards, the pollenizing cultivar is often interplanted every fourth row or every 100 feet. One strong colony of bees is recommended for each three acres of apples.

In urban areas or where one lives within 100 feet of a neighbor with apples or flowering crabs, it may be necessary to plant only one cultivar. Another alternative where only one cultivar is present would be to bring in flower bouquets from another pollenizing cultivar and place them in water under the tree.

What to Plant

Consider cultivar preference. When choosing cultivars, give important consideration to the preference of each family member. It is a good idea to visit large orchards and to sample a number of cultivars. On numerous occasions, I have had my classes sample as many as 30 cultivars of apples and to rate each one. As might be expected, there was a wide difference of opinion on which ones tasted best. In the Upper Midwest, there is an old saying, "One man's apple is another man's hog feed."

Consider maturity times. Apple cultivars vary considerably in their maturity

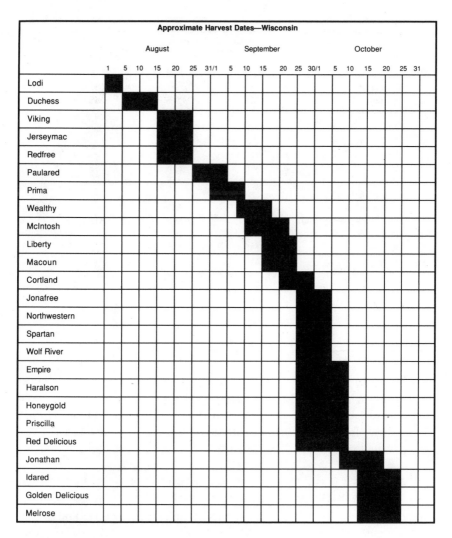

Approximate Harvest Dates—Wisconsin																			
August							September							October					
1	5	10	15	20	25	31/1	5	10	15	20	25	30/1	5	10	15	20	25	31
Lodi																		
Duchess																		
Viking																		
Jerseymac																		
Redfree																		
Paulared																		
Prima																		
Wealthy																		
McIntosh																		
Liberty																		
Macoun																		
Cortland																		
Jonafree																		
Northwestern																		
Spartan																		
Wolf River																		
Empire																		
Haralson																		
Honeygold																		
Priscilla																		
Red Delicious																		
Jonathan																		
Idared																		
Golden Delicious																		
Melrose																		

Source: Stang, 1984.

times. By selecting the right cultivar, the apple harvest can be extended from August through mid-October, as the harvest chart indicates.

Consider storage qualities. In general, early maturing apples do not store well. They must be used fresh or prepared for canning or freezing. The best keeping apples are usually those that mature late in the season. Examples follow Table 3.

Table 3. Disease resistance

	Fireblight	Cedar-apple rust	Apple scab
Beacon	S	S	–
Red Baron	MR	MR	–
Lakeland	S	S	MS
Minjon	MS	MS	MS
McIntosh	MR	R	S
Cortland	MR	MR	S
N.W. Greening	R	R	–
Honeygold	S	–	–
Haralson	MR	MR	MS
Prairie Spy	S	MS	S
Red Delicious	R	R	–
Golden Delicious	MR	MS	–
Fireside (Connell Red)	MS	MR	MS
Redwell	MS	MS	–
Regent	MS	MS	MS
Keepsake	MR	MR	–
Wealthy	S	S	–
Redfree	MR	R	R
Prima	R	R	R
Liberty	R	R	R
Jonafree	R	R	R
Priscilla	MR	MR	R

R = resistant, MR = moderate resistance, S = susceptible, MS = moderately susceptible.

Storage 1 to 3 weeks. Mantet, Oriole, Duchess, Beacon.

Storage 1 to 3 months. Wealthy, Red Baron, Lakeland, Minjon, Cortland, Jonathan, Northwestern Greening, Redwell, State Fair, Paulared, Hazen, Sweet Sixteen, McIntosh, Honeygold, Mandan, Dakota.

Storage more than 3 months. Haralson, Regent, Fireside, Connell Red, Red Delicious, Golden Delicious, Keepsake.

Consider space available. A standard apple tree requires about 600 to 800 square feet per tree; semidwarfs (M.7, MM.106), 250 to 400 square feet; dwarfs (M.9, M.26), 40 to 100 square feet.

Consider bearing age. Standard trees may not bear fruit for 5 to 10 years or more; semidwarfs bear in 3 to 4 years. Dwarf trees may bear in 1 to 3 years.

Consider yield. Standard trees, on the average, yield 8 to 12 bushels of fruit per plant; semidwarf, 4 to 6; and dwarf, 1 to 2.

Consider disease resistance. The three major diseases affecting apples in the Upper Midwest are fireblight, cedar-apple rust, and apple scab. Apple cultivars vary widely in their resistance to these diseases as Table 3 indicates.

Barerooted apple trees mulched to protect the roots from drying out.

Selection of Nursery Stock

Nursery trees are graded on the basis of diameter (caliper), height, and root development. Commercial growers usually plant one-year-old trees that range in size from ½ inch to ¾ inch (caliper) or are 4 to 7 feet tall.

Trees sold to homeowners through retail outlets and nursery catalogs are usually two-year-old branched trees that range in size from 3 feet up. Trees smaller than 3 feet or less than 7/16-inch caliper are not advised. Likewise, the purchase of three- or four-year-old ("jumbo") trees is rarely worth the extra money since these plants do not produce earlier, and they are often more difficult to transplant.

More and more nurseries now offer apple and other fruit cultivars as "certified virus indexed." This simply means that the plants are free of known harmful viruses. When available, they are the preferred choice.

Bareroot Stock

Most apple trees are sold in the spring as bareroot. Nearly all bareroot stock is dug the previous fall and stored through the winter in temperature- and humidity-controlled warehouses. Although the plants when offered for sale

During the last few years, potted fruit trees have become very popular,
but they offer no advantage over barerooted trees unless planting
must be delayed until late spring.

are still in a dormant condition, the roots can easily be damaged if they are allowed to dry out by exposure to the air and sun. When buying plants locally, check to see if the plants are stored out of the sun in a cool area. Also notice if the roots are covered and kept damp with sawdust, peat, marsh hay, or other material.

Use caution in purchasing bareroot trees in package form. These types of trees are especially popular in shopping centers and in stores that sell plants only in the spring. Often these plastic packages, when exposed to the sun, can become like an oven in a few short hours. In some cases, they remain exposed for up to two months before sold to some unsuspecting buyer.

Container-Grown Stock

During the last few years, apples planted in asphalt, peat, plastic, or metal containers have become increasingly popular. This container stock is usually more expensive to purchase and offers no advantage over bareroot stock — unless it becomes necessary to delay planting until late in the growing season.

For example, apples planted after early June or during the summer months must be container grown.

When to Plant

Apple trees perform best if planted early in the spring, as soon as the soil can be worked. The longer planting is delayed, the more difficult it will be to get the tree established and to recover from the transplant shock. Fall planting of apple trees is not advised in the Upper Midwest.

Cultivar Characteristics

Beacon. ('Early Delicious', 'Miller Red' and 'Fenton', but not the 'Fenton' described in 1873). This old-time (1936) Minnesota cultivar arose as a chance seedling of 'Malinda', open pollinated. It has very poor storage qualities (rarely beyond September), and is susceptible to both fireblight and cedar-apple rust. This multiple-use cultivar has red skin, and the flesh is mildly acid.

Centennial. Introduced in 1957 at Excelsior, Minnesota, from 'Dolgo' x 'Wealthy', this crab apple is about 1½ to 2 inches long and ¼ inch less wide. The skin is striped red over orange-yellow, and the flesh is yellow, crisp, and juicy. It is used primarily for fresh eating, jelly, and sauce. The tree has a tendency toward biennial fruiting and is moderately resistant to fireblight.

Chestnut. This is another open-pollinated seedling of 'Malinda' introduced at Excelsior, Minnesota, in 1946. The fruit is a crab type averaging about 2 inches in diameter. The skin is light red over yellow and is russeted. The flavor is subacid, and the apple is used for fresh eating, pickles, and sauce. It is moderately susceptible to apple scab and fireblight.

Chieftain. This cultivar was introduced at Ames, Iowa, in 1966 from 'Jonathan' x 'Delicious'. It ripens toward the end of September in Iowa and has good storage qualities. The skin is bright red, and the flesh is juicy and subacid. It is used fresh and for cooking. Resembling 'Jonathan', the tree has intermediate resistance to fireblight, cedar-apple rust and scab.

Connell Red. ('Connell Fireside'). Introduced in 1957 by William F. Connell in Dunn County, Wisconsin, this is a bud mutation of 'Fireside', which it resembles in nearly all characteristics except for the more intense red color of the fruit. See 'Fireside'.

Cortland. This 'Ben Davis' x 'McIntosh' hybrid was introduced in 1915 at Geneva, New York. This is a medium-size red apple with white flesh that holds its color well after being cut. It is a multiple-use fruit that stores from September to January. The tree is moderately resistant to cedar-apple rust and fireblight but susceptible to scab.

Dakota. Introduced in 1965 at Mandan, North Dakota, from a cross of 'Wealthy' x 'Whitney', this medium red apple is used for fresh eating and cooking. In North Dakota, it matures about September 1 and will keep in storage for about two months. The tree is moderately resistant to fireblight.

Delcon. This cultivar was introduced in 1948 by Paul H. Shepard in Mountain Grove, Missouri, from a cross of 'Conrad' x 'Delicious'. The apple, which has light to dark red skin over yellow, is used fresh and for cooking. In Iowa, it matures about September 18 and keeps well in storage.

Dolgo. This extremely hardy crab apple was imported from Russia by N. E. Hanson and introduced in 1917. Seeds of this crab have been used to produce hardy rootstocks for a number of northern-grown cultivars. In North Dakota, this cultivar is frequently topworked (grafted) for tender cultivars. The bright red, small (1½ inch) fruits are used mainly for jelly.

Duchess (of Oldenburg). This Russian apple was imported to America from England about 1835. It ripens very early in August or September and does not store well. The skin is pale yellow, striped with red. The flesh is tart and crisp, suitable for pie and sauce. It is intermediate in resistance to cedar-apple rust. 'Red Duchess' is a color strain with similar characteristics.

Empire. This McIntosh-type red apple is popular in Wisconsin. The flesh is cream colored, crisp, juicy, and subacid. This apple is suitable for fresh eating and cooking and stores well for three to five months. It was introduced in 1966 at Geneva, New York, from a cross of 'McIntosh' x 'Delicious'. It is intermediate in resistance to cedar-apple rust.

Fireside. Of unknown parentage, this apple was introduced from Excelsior, Minnesota, in 1943. The medium red skin is lightly striped with dark red on a yellow ground. This is an excellent storing, multiple-purpose apple with a mild taste approaching sweetness. The tree is large, late maturing, and is moderately susceptible to scab and fireblight. It is slightly subject to cedar-apple rust. 'Connell Red' is a bud mutation of 'Fireside'.

Gala. This apple originated in Greytown, Wairarapa, New Zealand, and was introduced by J. H. Kidd in 1960 from a cross of 'Kidd's Orange' x 'Golden Delicious'. The skin is a pale yellow to golden yellow, heavily striped with red. It is grown in central and southern Iowa and ripens in late August or early September. The flesh is yellow, very sweet, and used primarily for cooking. It is susceptible to fireblight.

Garrison. This is a hybrid selected from 'Duchess of Oldenburg' x 'Starking Delicious' and introduced in 1957 from Mandan, North Dakota. The fruit is red with carmine stripes and is similar in taste to 'Delicious'. It matures early and is best used for fresh eating and cooking, since it does not store well. This hybrid may be difficult to locate.

Golden Delicious (Yellow Delicious). This apple originated as a chance seedling in the orchard of A. H. Mullins from West Virginia and was introduced by Stark Bros. Nursery in 1916. The skin on the fruit is golden yellow with numerous small dots. The flesh is firm, crisp, juicy, and mildly subacid and is multipurpose. This is a late-maturing apple with excellent storage qualities. The tree lacks hardiness in more northerly areas and is slightly susceptible to cedar-apple rust. It is moderately resistant to fireblight.

Golden Grimes. The parentage of this apple is unknown. It originated in West Virginia as a chance seedling and has been cultivated for over 150 years. The skin is tough, deep yellow with scattered dots. The yellow flesh is crisp, subacid, and suitable for fresh eating and cooking. In Iowa, where it is principally grown, the fruit matures about September 18. The tree is intermediate in resistance to fireblight and cedar-apple rust.

Haralson. This open-pollinated seedling of 'Malinda' was introduced in 1923 at Excelsior, Minnesota. Because of its excellent taste and hardiness, this is the most popular apple grown in Minnesota. The fruit is red with moderately conspicuous dots, and the white, firm, crisp flesh is suitable for multiple use. In Minnesota, the average harvest is September 30–October 8. This apple will keep in storage until March. The tree has a tendency toward the biennial bearing habit. It is slightly susceptible to fireblight and cedar-apple rust but only moderately susceptible to scab. 'Haralred' is a red selection of 'Haralson' with similar characteristics, except it ripens earlier and is sweeter.

Hazen. Neal S. Holland, North Dakota State University, Fargo, introduced this 'Duchess' x 'Starking Delicious' in 1980. The fruit is dark red with a mild, slightly subacid flavor. In North Dakota, the fruit matures about August 25 and will keep in storage about a month. The tree is semidwarf and may bear early after three to four years. It is moderately resistant to fireblight.

Honeygold. This 'Golden Delicious' x 'Haralson' cross was introduced in 1969 at Excelsior, Minnesota. The skin is yellow with a bronze blush, and the flavor of the flesh is similar to 'Golden Delicious'. This selection is recommended as a substitute in colder areas where 'Golden Delicious' is marginal. The fruit is multipurpose and will keep in storage from October to February. The tree is susceptible to fireblight.

Idared. Introduced in 1949 in Moscow, Idaho, this apple was selected from a cross of 'Wagener' x 'Jonathan'. The skin is red, inconspicuously streaked with carmine. The flesh is white, mildly subacid to sweet, and is suitable for fresh eating and cooking. In Iowa, the fruit ripens midseason and has a tendency to drop early. The tree is susceptible to fire-blight and scab. It is intermediate in resistance to cedar–apple rust.

Jerseymac. This is a complex hybrid with 'Melba', 'Wealthy', 'Starr', 'Red Rome', and 'Julyred' involved in the breeding. It was introduced in New Brunswick, New Jersey, in 1971. The skin is light green, blushed with red. The white flesh, with excellent flavor, resembles 'McIntosh'. This apple matures in mid to late August in Wisconsin and will keep in storage for only two to three weeks. The tree in growth habit resembles 'McIntosh' and is susceptible to fireblight.

Jonadel. This apple was introduced in Ames, Iowa, in 1958 from a cross of 'Jonathan' x 'Delicious'. The red fruit is milder and larger than 'Jonathan', but it ripens at about the same time, which is early September in Iowa. This is a multipurpose apple with good storage qualities. The tree has a tendency to drop fruit early and is resistant to fireblight and scab.

Jonafree. Purdue University, Rutgers University, and the University of Illinois cooperated to produce this 1979 introduction from complex parentage. This cultivar is rated as immune to apple scab and is resistant to fireblight and powdery mildew. The fruit ripens with 'Jonathan' and is very similar to that cultivar.

Jonagold. Geneva, New York, is the home of this 'Golden Delicious' x 'Jonathan' selection introduced in 1968. The large fruit has a yellow skin with red striping. The flesh is similar to 'Jonathan' in flavor. In Iowa, fruit is harvested about October 1 and will keep in storage for several months. This is a triploid cultivar, and it cannot be used as a pollenizer. The tree resembles 'Golden Delicious' and is intermediate in resistance to cedar–apple rust, fireblight, and scab.

Jonalicious. Anna Morris Daniels selected this chance seedling from Abilene, Texas, and it was introduced by Stark Bros. Nursery in 1960. The large fruit's yellow skin is blushed dark red. In Iowa, the fruit is harvested in mid–September and will keep in storage for three to four months. This cultivar resembles 'Jonathan' in many ways. The tree is resistant to fireblight and scab.

Jonamac. Roger D. Way introduced this 'McIntosh' x 'Jonathan' selection from Geneva, New York, in 1972. The fruit is medium size, and the skin is dark red with some striping. This multiple-use apple ripens in early September and has only fair storage qualities. The tree is considered superior to 'McIntosh' in many ways, and the fruits are less likely to drop prematurely. It is susceptible to fireblight and intermediate in resistance to cedar–apple rust and scab.

Jonathan. This cultivar originated as a chance seedling on a farm in Ulster County, New York, about 1800. The name honors Jonathan Has-brouck, who first called attention to the apple. The fruit is small, and the skin is solid bright red. The flesh is white tinged with yellow and is firm and crisp. This is a multiple-use apple that will keep from October to December. The tree lacks hardiness in more northerly areas and is susceptible to fireblight and cedar-apple rust. It is intermediate in resistance to scab.

Keepsake. The parentage of this apple is open-pollinated 'Malinda' x 'Northern Spy'. It was introduced in 1978–79 from crosses made by W. H. Alderman at the University of Minnesota. The tree is fully hardy in central Minnesota, but it may not be suitable for more northerly areas because 155–170 days are required from bloom to harvest. The skin is red with scattered red dots, and the flesh is light yellow, firm, and crisp. This apple stores well with high humidity from October to May. The tree is moderately resistant to fireblight and cedar-apple rust.

Killand. This 'McIntosh' x 'Dolgo' selection was introduced in 1957 at Mandan, North Dakota. This small to medium apple has bright red skin with darker red stripes. The flesh is firm, juicy, and subacid and has been rated very good in cooking tests. In North Dakota, the fruit matures after mid-September and keeps well in storage. This apple may be difficult to locate.

Lakeland. This open-pollinated seedling of 'Malinda' was introduced at Excelsior, Minnesota, in 1950. The fruit is medium size with a solid red skin. The flesh is creamy yellow, sometimes tinged red, and it is mildly acid, changing to subacid in storage. This multipurpose apple, which matures September 17–25 in Minnesota, will keep in storage until November. The tree is susceptible to cedar-apple rust and fireblight and is moderately susceptible to scab.

Liberty. The pedigree of this apple is complex and involves such widely known cultivars as 'Rome Beauty', 'Jersey Black', 'McIntosh', 'Wealthy', and 'Macoun'. It was introduced from Geneva, New York, in 1978. In that state it was grown for 23 years without any fungicidal sprays. It is scab-free and resistant to cedar-apple rust and fireblight. The skin is bright red striped over a greenish yellow ground color. The flesh is crisp, juicy, and slightly coarse in texture. This is primarily a dessert apple that keeps well in storage until January.

Lodi. ('Early Golden', 'Golden Lodi', 'Improved Transparent', 'Large Transparent'). Introduced in 1924 at Geneva, New York, this is a selection from 'Montgomery' x 'Yellow Transparent'. The skin is light green or yellow, and the flesh is firm, crisp, and tart. This apple matures very early and does not store well. It is best suited for pies and sauce. The tree is very susceptible to fireblight.

Macoun. Geneva, New York, is the home of this 1923 'McIntosh' x 'Jersey Black' introduction. This apple is similar to 'McIntosh' but is smaller and develops a black red color at maturity. It ripens in Wisconsin a few days before 'McIntosh' but does not store as well. In that state the trees may be relatively short-lived. It is susceptible to scab and is intermediate in resistance to cedar-apple rust and fireblight.

Mandan. Developed at Mandan, North Dakota, this 'Duchess' x 'Starking' Delicious cross was introduced in 1965. The red fruit is medium size, and the flesh is crisp, juicy, and mildly subacid. This multipurpose apple matures about September 1 in North Dakota. It will keep approximately two months in storage and is moderately resistant to fireblight.

Mantet. This open-pollinated seedling of 'Tetofski' was introduced in 1929 from Morden, Manitoba, Canada. The skin is yellow, striped, and blushed with red. The flesh is fine-grained, juicy, and sweet. This apple matures in North Dakota about August 20 and will keep only one week in storage. The tree is susceptible to fireblight.

McIntosh. This is the most popular apple grown in Wisconsin. It originated as a chance seedling from unknown parentage in Dundas County, Ontario, Canada, about 1870. This is a medium-size apple with nearly solid bright red skin. It has excellent fresh-eating qualities but tends to be soft when cooked. The tree often drops fruit prematurely and it is very susceptible to apple scab. Spur-type strains such as 'Macspur' or 'Spur McIntosh' are available, as are improved color strains such as 'Rogers', 'Geneva', and 'Boller'.

Melrose. A 'Jonathan' x 'Delicious' cross introduced in 1944 from Wooster, Ohio, this fruit is similar to 'Jonathan' in color and shape, but is less tart. The apple matures in mid-October in southern Wisconsin and is good for long-term storage. It is rated excellent for all uses.

Milton. This apple was introduced in 1923 at Geneva, New York, from a cross of 'Yellow Transparent' x 'McIntosh'. The skin is pinkish red, and the flesh is similar in taste and texture to 'McIntosh'. Many of the tree's characteristics are very similar to 'McIntosh'. 'Milton' ripens over a long season, which makes it a good home garden cultivar.

Minjon. The suspected parentage of this apple introduced in 1942 from Excelsior, Minnesota, is 'Wealthy' x 'Jonathan'. The small fruit resembles 'Jonathan' in many ways. The skin is dark red, and the flesh is yellow, often stained pink or red. This somewhat tart apple is considered multipurpose. In Minnesota it ripens September 9–17 and stores until November. The tree is moderately susceptible to scab, fireblight, and cedar-apple rust.

Mollie's Delicious. New Brunswick, New Jersey, is the home of this ('Golden Delicious' x 'Edgewood') x ('Red Gravenstein' x 'Close') selection introduced in 1966. The very large fruit has a light yellow skin blushed red. This multiple-use apple ripens in Iowa in early September.

Mutsu. This apple was introduced into the United States in 1948 from Japan.

It originated from a cross of 'Delicious' x 'Indo'. In southern Iowa, it matures in mid to late October and will keep in storage for five to six months. It is a multipurpose apple with some resistance to spray injury. The skin is golden yellow, blushed with orange. The flesh is yellowish white, crisp, and mildly subacid. It cannot be used as a pollenizer. The tree is susceptible to fireblight and scab and intermediate in resistance to cedar-apple rust, and is very cold tender.

Northwestern (Greening). This apple of unknown parentage originated in Waupaca County, Wisconsin, and was first described in 1895. The very large, green or yellow cooking apple matures in Wisconsin and Minnesota in late September or early October. It will keep in storage until January, but the fruit tends to scald at temperatures below 36° F. The tree is resistant to fireblight and cedar-apple rust.

Nova Easygro. 'Spartan' x 'PRI 565' is the parentage of this 1971 introduction from the Kentville, Nova Scotia, Research Station. This large apple has greenish yellow skin with red stripes. The flesh is firm, crisp, and somewhat juicy. Blooming time is with 'McIntosh'. The tree is resistant to cedar-apple rust and intermediate in resistance to fireblight.

Oriole. Parentage of this apple, introduced from Excelsior, Minnesota, in 1949, is unknown. This is a large apple with orange yellow skin striped red. The flesh is white, fine grained, juicy, and subacid. In Minnesota, the fruit matures August 7–14 and it must be used fresh or for cooking since it does not store well. 'Oriole' is susceptible to scab, cedar-apple rust, and fireblight.

Paulared. This cultivar of unknown parentage was introduced in 1967 from Sparta, Michigan. The skin is light yellow covered with bright red. The flesh is white, crisp, juicy, and subacid. In Wisconsin, the fruit ripens in late August and has short-term storage qualities. It is best used for fresh eating. The tree is highly susceptible to fireblight and is resistant to apple scab. It is intermediate in resistance to cedar-apple rust.

Peace Garden. Bred at Mandan, North Dakota, this 'Malinda' x 'Duchess of Oldenburg' cross was introduced in 1957. The fruit is medium size, bright glossy red with carmine stripes. In North Dakota, it matures in late September and the eating qualities improve with winter storage.

Prairie Spy. The parentage of this apple introduced in 1940 from Excelsior, Minnesota, is unknown. In Minnesota, the fruit matures September 27–October 5. It is a long-term storage apple, but it has a tendency to scald at temperatures below 36° F. The large red fruit is mild flavored and is considered multipurpose. The tree is susceptible to fireblight and scab and moderately susceptible to cedar-apple rust.

Prima. This disease-resistant cultivar was introduced in 1970 at Urbana, Illinois, from a cross using code numbered breeding stock. The fruit is medium size with a yellow skin blushed with red. The flesh is crisp, rich flavored, and subacid. In Wisconsin, the fruit matures one week before 'McIntosh', and it will store for one to two months. The tree is resistant to cedar-apple rust, fireblight, and scab.

Priscilla. Introduced in 1972 from Lafayette, Indiana, the pedigree of this apple is complex and involves well-known cultivars such as 'Starking Delicious', 'Rome Beauty', 'Golden Delicious', 'McIntosh', and other *Malus* breeding stock. This medium to large apple has a yellow skin almost completely covered with red. The flesh is crisp, medium grained with a pleasant flavor. It ripens in late September to early October in Wisconsin and will store two to three months at 34° F. The tree is scab free and apparently tolerant of fireblight and cedar-apple rust.

Puritan. 'McIntosh' x 'Red Astrachan' is the parentage of this 1953 Massachusetts introduction by F. C. Sears. This red apple resembles 'McIntosh' but matures about three weeks earlier. The tree has a tendency to bear biennially.

Red Baron. This 'Golden Delicious' x 'Daniels Red Duchess' cross was introduced in 1970 from Excelsior, Minnesota. The red fruit is medium size, and the flesh is crisp, juicy, and subacid; it tends to discolor when cut. In Minnesota, the fruit matures September 12–20 and will store until November. It is used primarily for fresh eating. The tree has a moderate resistance to fireblight and cedar-apple rust.

Red Delicious (Delicious). This apple of unknown parentage was discovered by Jesse Hiatt, Peru, Iowa, and introduced in 1895 by Stark Bros. Nursery. The large red fruit has five distinctive knobs, and the flesh is light yellow, crisp, and sweet. This apple is not recommended for cooking. It is best when eaten fresh and will store until March. In more northerly areas, the tree lacks hardiness. It is resistant to cedar-apple rust and fireblight.

Redfree. Purdue, Rutgers, and the University of Illinois introduced this 'Raritan' x 'PRI 1018–101' cross in 1981 at Lafayette, Indiana. In Wisconsin, the red apple matures August 15–25 and will store for up to two months. The tree is resistant to apple scab and cedar-apple rust. It is moderately resistant to fireblight.

Red River. This crab-type apple was introduced about 1937 from a cross of 'Dolgo' x 'Delicious' at Fargo, North Dakota. The red crab develops its best color during winter storage, and it matures late in the season.

Redwell. Introduced in 1946 at Excelsior, Minnesota, this is an open-pollinated seedling of 'Scotts Winter'. This large red apple matures September 29–October 7 in Minnesota and will keep in storage until January. The fruit is suitable for fresh eating, sauce, and baking. The tree is moderately susceptible to cedar-apple rust and fireblight.

Regent. Because of its excellent taste, this has become one of the most popular apples grown in Minnesota. It was introduced in 1963 at Excelsior from a cross of 'Daniel's Red Duchess' x 'Delicious'. The medium fruit has a skin with bright red stripes over light yellow. The flesh is creamy white, juicy, and very crisp. The flavor is somewhat suggestive of 'Delicious'. In Minnesota, the harvest is October 9–17, and the multipurpose fruit will store until April. The tree lacks extreme winter hardiness and is moderately susceptible to cedar-apple rust, fireblight, and scab.

Rescue (Scott 1). Bred in Scott, Saskatchewan, Canada, this open-pollinated seedling of 'Blushed Calville' was introduced in 1933. The fruit is a small crab with greenish yellow skin washed with striped red. The flesh is yellowish white, sweet to subacid. This selection may be difficult to locate.

Rome Beauty ('Belle de Rome', 'Faust's Beauty', 'Gillet's Seedling', 'Press Ewing', 'Phoenix', 'Royal Red', 'Starbuck'). This cultivar was discovered on the Joel Gillet farm in Rome Township, Lawrence County, Ohio, and was named by George Walton in about 1832. The fruit is large and the thick, tough skin is yellowish green with a medium red partial overcolor. The flesh is yellowish white, juicy, and mildly subacid. Fruits mature in Iowa in late October and will store four to five months or longer. The tree is susceptible to cedar-apple rust, fireblight, and scab.

Sharon. This apple was introduced in 1922 at Ames, Iowa, from a cross of 'McIntosh' x 'Longfield'. In Iowa this multipurpose, red-striped apple matures in early September and will store until January. It resembles 'McIntosh' in many respects, and like that cultivar, has a tendency to drop fruit early.

Snow Famen ('Snow Fameuse'). This is an extremely old cultivar of unknown parentage that probably originated in Canada. Hedrick (1922) estimated that it had a history of at least 200 years. The multi-use red apple matures in Iowa in mid-September and has a relatively short storage life. The cultivar has waned in popularity because of its susceptibility to disease.

Spartan. Summerland, British Columbia, Canada, is the home of this 'McIntosh' x 'Newtown' cross introduced in 1936. The red fruit resembles 'McIntosh' in many respects but has better color and shape and stores somewhat longer. If harvesting is delayed, the fruits may have a tendency to develop watercore. The tree is intermediate in resistance to cedar-apple rust and scab and is resistant to fireblight. The tree is very similar to 'McIntosh' but is not as hardy.

Spigold. Geneva, New York, is the home of this 'Red Spy' x 'Golden Delicious' selection introduced in 1962. The large fruit has a yellow skin with red stripes. The fruit has multiple uses and has been rated outstanding for dessert quality. In Iowa, the harvest season begins about October 1. This is a triploid cultivar that cannot be used as a pollenizer.

State Fair. This 'Mantet' x 'Oriole' cross was introduced in 1978–79 at Excelsior, Minnesota. The small to medium fruit has red skin with scattered white dots. The flesh is light yellow, crisp, and juicy. In Minnesota, this multi-use apple matures October 11–19 and will keep in storage until May. The tree is susceptible to scab and intermediate in resistance to fireblight.

Stayman ('Stayman Winesap'). This is a reported seedling of 'Winesap' selected by Mr. J. Stayman at Leavenworth, Kansas, in 1866. Cultivars such as 'Blaxstayman', 'Neipling', 'Cardinal Stayman', and 'Staymared' are sports or bud mutations of this cultivar. This red multi-use apple matures in mid to late September in Iowa. The tree is resistant to fireblight and intermediate in resistance to cedar-apple rust.

Summer Treat ('Stark Summer Treat'). This 1980 introduction from Stark Bros. Nursery originated in Cream Ridge, New Jersey, from a numbered seedling x 'Mollie's Delicious'. In Iowa, the harvest season is in early September.

Sweet Sixteen. Introduced in 1978–79, this apple was selected at Excelsior, Minnesota, from a cross of open-pollinated 'Malinda' x 'Northern Spy'. This multi-use, red-striped fruit matures with 'McIntosh' and will keep in storage until January. The tree is resistant to fireblight and moderately resistant to scab and cedar-apple rust.

Thorberg. Developed at Mandan, North Dakota, this 'Duchess of Oldenburg' x 'Starking Delicious' cross was introduced in 1957. The skin is red with carmine stripes and distinct tan dots. The flesh is firm and somewhat tart. In North Dakota, the fruit matures during the last two weeks of September, and it will keep in storage until early winter. This cultivar may be difficult to locate.

Wealthy. This apple of unknown parentage was introduced from Excelsior, Minnesota, about 1860 by Peter Gideon. The medium, red-striped apple is multi-use but is considered prime for cooking. In Minnesota, it is harvested September 8–16 and will keep in storage until November. The tree is susceptible to cedar-apple rust and fireblight.

Whitney. This large crab apple was grown from seed by A. E. Whitney and was introduced from Franklin Grove, Illinois, in 1869. The skin is yellow with red stripes and the flesh is medium fine, pleasant, and approaching sweet. This crab apple has multiple uses for fresh eating and cooking. The tree is moderately resistant to fireblight and is considered intermediate in resistance to cedar-apple rust.

Winesap. The origin of this apple is unknown, but according to Hedrick (1922), it dates back to the colonial period. The bright red fruit is indistinctly striped, and the yellow flesh is crisp, juicy, and somewhat subacid. In Iowa, the fruit is ripe in late October and is considered

Table 4. Commercial apple trees by cultivar, Wisconsin, 1986

Cultivar	Number of Trees
McIntosh	170,293
Red Delicious	125,034
Cortland	84,413
Golden Delicious	31,738
Spartan	20,183
Empire	19,739
Paulared	19,538
Jonathan	17,512
Idared	16,488
N. W. Greening	15,296
Haralson	11,979
Viking	10,385
Connell Red	6,835
Wealthy	6,071
Jerseymac	4,736
Beacon	4,368
Others	93,657
Total	658,265

Source: *Apple and Cherry Trees in Wisconsin.* 1987. Wisconsin Ag. Reporting Service.

Table 5. Commercial apple trees by cultivar, Minnesota, 1988

Cultivar	Number of trees
Haralson	100,073
McIntosh	33,964
Red Delicious	25,388
Regent	25,028
Connell Red	23,138
Fireside	22,393
Cortland	15,313
Honeygold	14,830
Paulared	9,701
Beacon	9,546
Prairie Spy	6,020
Red Baron	5,970
Wealthy	5,563
Jonathan	5,174
Spartan	4,351
State Fair	3,592
N. W. Greening	2,967
Golden Delicious	2,494
Others*	20,730
Total	336,235

Source: *1988 Apple Tree Survey.* Minnesota Ag. Statistical Service.
*Includes all miscellaneous cultivars. The following cultivars had more than 500 trees in at least three separate orchards: Sweet Sixteen, Keepsake, Chestnut Crab, Redwell, Viking, Lakeland, and Minjon.

multipurpose. The tree is resistant to fireblight and intermediate in resistance to cedar-apple rust.

Wisconsin Viking ('Viking', but not 'Gurney Viking'). This apple was introduced in 1969 from code-numbered crosses made at Sturgeon Bay, Wisconsin. The fruit is medium to large with 75–95 percent of the skin colored red. The flesh is white, juicy, fine grained, and rated of very good quality. In Wisconsin, the harvest season is August 15–25. Overripe fruits have a tendency to develop watercore in storage. The tree tends to be biennial bearing, and it has a moderate tolerance to scab and fireblight.

Wolf River. This cultivar of unknown parentage was discovered in Winnebago County, Wisconsin, about 1881. It is the largest apple grown in Wisconsin. The skin is pale yellow, mottled, and blushed with pink to red overcolor. It is best known as a cooking apple and is considered prime for dried apple slices and apple butter. In Wisconsin, the fruit is harvested September 25-October 5.

Yellow Transparent. This apple of unknown parentage was imported from Russia about 1870. The skin is clear yellow and the flesh is white, juicy,

Fruit zones—
apples and crab apples

Cultivar	Iowa			Minn.				S. Dak.				N. Dak.			Wis.			
	4b	5a	5b	1	2	3	4	1	2	3	4	A	B	C	1	2	3	4
Beacon	X	X		X	X	X	X	X	X	X	T	T	T	T	X	X	T	T
Centennial*				X	X	X	X	X	X	X	X	X	X	X	X	X	X	T
Chestnut*	X	X	T	X	X	X	X	X	X	T		X	X	X	X	X	X	X
Chieftain	X	X	X															
Connell Red	X	X		X	X	X		X	T			G	G	G	X	X	X	
Cortland	X	X	X	X	X	X		X	T						X	X	X	
Dakota												X	X	X				
Delcon		X	X															
Dolgo*	X	X	X	X	X	X	X	X	X	X	X	X	X	X	X	X	X	X
Duchess	X	X	X	X	X	X				X	X	X	X	X	X	X	X	X
Empire	X	X	X	T											X	X	X	X
Fireside	X	X		X	X	X		X	T			G	G	G	T	T	T	
Gala	X	X																
Garrison												T	T	T				
Golden Delicious		X	X	X											X			
Golden Grimes		T	X															
Haralson	X	X		X	X	X	X	X	X	X	T	X	X	X	X	X	X	X
Hazen									X	X	X	X	X	X				
Honeygold	X	T		X	X			X	T			T	T	T	X	X	X	X
Idared		T	T												X	X	X	
Jerseymac	T	X	X												X	X	X	
Jonadel	X	X	X															
Jonafree		X	X												T	T	T	T
Jonagold			X															
Jonalicious		X	X															
Jonamac	X	X	X															
Jonathan		X	X	X											X	X		
Keepsake	X	X	T	X	X	X		X	T						X	T	T	
Killand												T	T	T				

X = recommended for planting; T = recommended for trial; G = recommended for planting but graft on branches of hardy tree such as Dolgo; * = crab apple.
See zone map on page 20.

Fruit zones—
apples and crab apples, continued

Cultivar	Iowa			Minn.				S. Dak.				N. Dak.			Wis.			
	4b	5a	5b	1	2	3	4	1	2	3	4	A	B	C	1	2	3	4
Lakeland				X	X	X	X					T	T	T	X	X	T	
Liberty	X	X	X												X	X	X	X
Lodi	X	X	X												X	X	X	X
Macoun															X	X	X	X
Mandan												X	X	X				
Mantet				X	X	X	X	X	X	T	T	X	X	X	X	X	X	X
McIntosh	X	X	X	X	X			X	T			T	T	T	X	X	X	X
Melrose		T	X												X	X		
Milton															X	X	X	X
Minjon	X	T			X	X						G	G	G				
Mollie's Delicious		X	X															
Mutsu			X												X	X	X	
N.W. Greening	X	X	X	X	X	X		X	T			X	X	X	X	X	X	X
Nova Easygro															X	X	T	
Oriole				X	X	X	X	X	X	T	T	X	T	T	X	X	X	X
Paulared	X	X	X	X	X										X	X	X	
Peace Garden												T	T	T				
Prairie Spy	X	X		X	X	X		X	X	T		G	G	G	X	X	X	X
Prima		X	X												X	X	X	X
Priscilla		X	X												X	X	X	X
Puritan															X	X	X	X
Red Baron				X	X	X	X	X	X	T	T	X	T	T	X	X	T	T
Red Delicious	T	X	X	X											X	X		
Redfree	X	X	X														T	T
Red River*												X	X	X				
Redwell	X			X	X	X	X	X	X	T		X	T	T	X	X	T	T
Regent	X	X		X				T	T						X	X		
Rescue*						X	X		X	X		X	X	X				
Rome Beauty			X															

X = recommended for planting; T = recommended for trial; G = recommended for planting but graft on branches of hardy tree such as Dolgo; * = crab apple.
See zone map on page 20.

**Fruit zones—
apples and crab apples, continued**

Cultivar	Iowa			Minn.				S. Dak.				N. Dak.			Wis.			
	4b	5a	5b	1	2	3	4	1	2	3	4	A	B	C	1	2	3	4
Sharon	X	X	X															
Snow Famen	X	X	X															
Spartan	X	X		X				X	T						X	X	X	X
Spigold		X																
State Fair	X	X	T	X	X	X	X	X	X	T	T	T	T	T	X	X	T	T
Stayman		X													X	X		
Summer Treat	T	X	X															
Sweet Sixteen	X	X	T	X	X	X	X	X	X	T		X	X	X	X	X	X	T
Thorberg												T	T	T				
Wealthy	X	X	X	X	X	X	X	X	X	T		T	G	G	X	X	X	X
Whitney*	X	X	X	X	X	X	X								X	X	X	X
Winesap		X													X	T		
W. Viking	X	X	T	X	X										X	X	X	X
Wolf River	X	X	X	X	X										X	X	X	X
Yellow Transparent	X	X	X												X	X	X	X

X = recommended for planting; T = recommended for trial; G = recommended for planting but graft on branches of hardy tree such as Dolgo; * = crab apple. See zone map on page 20.

and subacid. In southern Iowa, this apple matures in early August and keeps only a short time in storage. The tree is susceptible to fireblight and intermediate in resistance to cedar–apple rust.

Selecting the Planting Site

Because of the harsh climate that prevails in most of the Upper Midwest, selecting the proper site is of utmost importance to successful apple production.

It is no accident that many of the most successful orchards are located near large bodies of water. Rivers or lakes usually have more protection from the frequency and severity of spring frosts. An early frost or freeze just before, during, or just after the blossoming stage can eliminate or severely reduce the crop. Near large bodies of water the air temperature during the day tends to be cooler, thus delaying the bloom. These bodies of water also create a warming effect at night, thus offering added protection.

In areas away from large bodies of water, the site selected should ideally be slightly elevated to provide good air movement. Because of its density, cold air tends to settle in low areas. Forshey et al. (1986) reported that on sites with good air drainage, night temperatures may be 5° F. or more above those of surrounding lowlands. This is also why depressions and areas that impede the movement of air should be avoided for orchards.

Apple orchards located on tops of ridges or in open, windswept areas are subject to winter injury, and even during the summer months, the wind may damage the trees or result in premature fruit drop. A natural windbreak on the north, south, and west sides of the orchard is ideal. If a windbreak or farm shelterbelt is planted, it should be located approximately 50 feet from the orchard to avoid root, nutrient, and sun competition. Likewise, avoid placing apple trees next to buildings where they are in shade the greater part of the day. Apples need full sun to develop properly.

Soil

Apples will grow on most reasonably fertile soil, but they will not survive on soils that become waterlogged and remain that way for an extended period. To develop properly, apple roots require good drainage and air movement. Likewise, very shallow or sandy soils, such as those in northern Minnesota and other areas of the Upper Midwest, should be avoided. Apples perform best on deep, well-drained soils with a pH of 6.0–6.5.

Spacing

Recommended spacing for each rootstock varies widely because of the difference in size of the various apple cultivars. For example, the spur 'Golden Delicious' is quite a small tree when grown on seedling rootstocks, but 'McIntosh', when grown on the same rootstock, is very large and takes up considerable space. Commercial growers should know the maximum size expected for each cultivar before establishing the orchard. Trees planted too closely will result in competition problems, and often every other tree may have to be removed. For the homeowner with only a few trees and lots of room, the recommended maximum spacing plan is the safest course to follow.

How to Plant

The secret to getting an apple tree to break dormancy or to bud quickly is to immerse the roots in a bucket of water for 4 to 6 hours before planting.

Table 6. Suggested spacing of apple trees (in feet)

Rootstock	Between plants	Between rows
M.9	6–12	14–20
M.26	8–14	16–22
M.7a	10–16	18–24
M.106	12–18	20–26
M.111	14–20	22–28
Standard	16–22	24–30

Source: Domoto and Nonnecke, 1988.

This gives all nursery stock a head start, and it is especially important if the roots have been treated with an antidessicant (drying) material as is the common practice of several mail-order nurseries. If weather conditions are unfavorable for planting when nursery stock arrives, store the plants in a cool place—basement or garage—out of the sun and keep the roots covered and moist at all times.

A messy cleanup problem can be avoided by placing a piece of plastic, canvas, or burlap near where the hole is to be dug. As the hole is dug, the soil is placed on this material.

The planting hole should be a foot wider and 6 inches deeper than the spread of the roots. When excavating, separate the sod (used later as mulch), topsoil, and subsoil so that there are three separate piles. In most soils suitable for growing apples, soil additives such as perlite, sand, peat, or manure are not required at planting time. Fertilizer should not be added at planting time except where a previous soil test has indicated a deficiency in phosphorus. One-half pound of superphosphate thoroughly mixed with the excavated soil will correct this deficiency. Organic gardeners can substitute bonemeal.

Depth of Planting

Standard Trees

Planting depth of trees grown on seedling rootstocks is not as important as for dwarf trees. Normally this type of tree is planted about 1 inch deeper than originally grown in the nursery. This height can be located by looking for the soil line on the stem. If the graft union is planted 1–2 inches below the soil line, some roots may form from the scion, but this is of no consequence.

Dwarfed Trees

Correct planting depth for dwarfed trees is critical to avoid disease problems and the loss of the dwarfing rootstock effect. The graft union must remain *above* the soil line. Ferree and Carlson (1987) recommend that on clay and silt

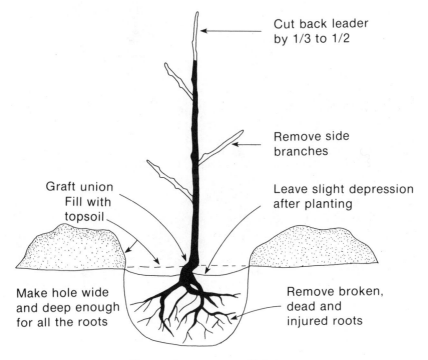

Cut back leader
by 1/3 to 1/2

Remove side
branches

Graft union
Fill with
topsoil

Leave slight depression
after planting

Make hole wide
and deep enough
for all the roots

Remove broken,
dead and
injured roots

How to plant a one-year-old fruit tree.

loam, trees not be planted more than 7–10 centimeters deeper than in the nursery. For the Upper Midwest, where extreme cold temperatures prevail, no more than 2 to 3 inches of the area below the graft union should be exposed. For specific recommendations on planting depths, refer to the section on rootstock descriptions.

Before planting, use sharp pruning shears to remove damaged or broken roots. Then add 4–6 inches of topsoil to the hole and position the plant so that it leans slightly toward the prevailing summer winds. Facing the bud union toward these winds will give added strength.

Next, spread out the roots evenly so that they do not overlap. Continue to add topsoil (use subsoil last), pressing with the hands to eliminate air spaces. When the hole is three-fourths full of soil, add three to five gallons of water. After the water has soaked in, add additional soil to fill the hole. To finish the planting, slowly add three to five gallons of additional water, allowing it to soak into the soil. Mulch with wood chips, peat, compost, or other suitable material.

*Young apple trees at the University of Minnesota Horticultural Research Center.
Note the guards to prevent girdling damage and the stakes to protect
the graft union from wind damage.*

Planting Container Stock

If planting container-grown stock, do not attempt to remove the plant if the soil has just been watered. With a dry container, it is usually easier to remove the entire soil ball in one piece. To facilitate this, gently pull on the stem while tapping the edge of the container on a hard surface. Some containers are narrower at the top or have an inward-projecting rim and will have to be cut apart.

Papier-mâché containers are sometimes planted directly, but I prefer to remove them. First, cut out the bottom and lower the container into the hole. Next, slit the sides in three to four pieces and carefully remove each piece so that the ball is left intact. The soil mix and the remaining planting are the same as for bareroot or other container-grown plants.

Staking

Many dwarf cultivars should be staked at planting time. There are multitudes of staking methods. The stake is usually positioned on the prevailing-wind side of the tree about 6 inches from the trunk. Steel fence posts can be used for durability or 2- × 2-inch wooden stakes. The stake should extend in the ground at least 24 to 30 inches. Tie the tree to the stake with strips of cloth or use an 8- to 10-inch piece of old garden hose. Run stiff wire through the hose and make sure only the hose comes in contact with the tree.

Before Pruning

Become familiar with the basic vocabulary involved in pruning and be sure to have a basic understanding of how the tree will respond to a specific pruning cut. Also, try to visualize how the tree will look at maturity. A standard apple tree may be 20 to 25 feet or taller. The limbs may carry hundreds of pounds of fruit, so it is important to build a strong framework to support the fruit crop.

Since pruning is a dwarfing process, it should be performed only when necessary. Likewise, excessive or haphazard pruning may delay the bearing age or result in reduced fruit productivity. The best time to prune is in late winter. Summer pruning may result in disease problems and fall pruning may delay dormancy or result in winter dieback.

Basic Pruning Terms

Crotch. An angle made by the attachment of a branch to the trunk or to another branch. Branches with narrow crotch angles tend to be weak and are prone to split or break under the weight of the fruit or during storms.

Heading back. Removal of the terminal portion of a branch. This stimulates branching on the remaining portion. Sometimes heading back is necessary when a side branch grows excessively, upsetting the overall symmetry of the tree, or when a side branch threatens to overtake the leader (the most prominent and upright branch extending through the center of the tree).

Scaffold limbs. The main branches that originate from the trunk and form the central framework of the tree.

Spur. A very short, lateral branch that has limited growth of not more than a few inches.

Sucker. A shoot of rapid growth which originates from the root or rootstock.

Thinning out. Cutting out whole branches at their point of origin.

Watersprouts. Like suckers, these are rapidly growing branches, but they develop from latent or adventitious buds on the scaffold limbs, the trunk, or the leader. These often form in the vicinity of pruning wounds.

Making the Cuts

When thinning out whole branches at their point of origin, *never leave stubs*. On older trees to avoid splitting, first undercut the branch 12 to 16 inches

Limb splitting caused by a narrow crotch angle.

from the trunk. Then cut from the top side an inch or two out from the undercut. Finally, prune the remaining stub flush with the trunk collar.

When heading back, make the cut just above a bud. The direction that growth will follow after the cut depends on the orientation of the bud, just below the cut. For example, if the bud is oriented downward, growth will follow that direction. By carefully observing the orientation of the buds, one can train the branches by proper pruning to grow in the direction desired.

Sealing Pruning Cuts

During the last few years, there has been a reevaluation of wound dressings used to seal pruning cuts. Some products formerly used have been shown to actually impede the healing process. The cheapest, and probably the best wound dressing, is water-soluble, exterior-grade white latex paint. Products containing creosote should not be used, and numerous aerosols and black pastes may contribute to excessive heat buildup.

Pruning cuts less than 2 inches in diameter require no treatment. Larger cuts treated with latex (if reapplied periodically to seal cracks) may impede entry of some wood-boring insects and disease (Domoto, 1987).

A good example of what can happen if apple tress are not pruned properly.

Pruning at Planting Time

If the tree is unbranched, use sharp pruning shears to cut off the top just above a bud to a height of 30 inches.

If the tree is well branched, shorten the leader by about 6 inches. If there are side branches long enough to threaten the growth of the leader, these should also be cut back to balance the growth of the tree. Approximately one-third to one-half of the side branches should be removed to balance the root loss. These should be cut flush with the main trunk—leave no stubs. Select for removal branches lower than 20 to 24 inches from the ground and leave only one branch at any one growing point on the trunk.

Training and Pruning Standard Apple Trees

Training standard apple trees to the form known as the central leader type is popular in the Upper Midwest, and it is also practical. This type of training attempts to produce a tree with a conic shape not unlike that of a Christmas tree. The shape is preferred for sunlight penetration since it prevents the upper branches from shading the lower ones. The central leader has well-separated scaffold branches. The scaffold branches are selected and trained to grow in an almost horizontal position from the main trunk. As might be ex-

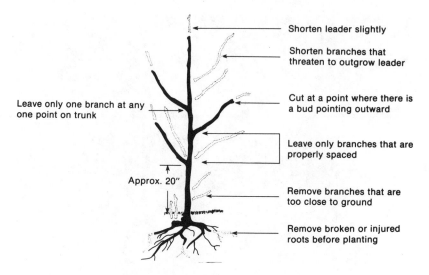

Shorten leader slightly

Shorten branches that
threaten to outgrow leader

Cut at a point where there is
a bud pointing outward

Leave only one branch at any
one point on trunk

Leave only branches that are
properly spaced

Approx. 20"

Remove branches that are
too close to ground

Remove broken or injured
roots before planting

Prune young fruit trees when you plant them.

pected, some selections are more difficult to train than others. For example, in some cultivars the scaffold branches have a natural tendency to grow upright in an almost vertical position. To achieve a horizontal angle, wooden spreaders of various lengths can be inserted between the trunk and the branch. Some growers use wooden clothespins for this purpose, and others prefer electrical tape or other tie-down methods.

Steps Involved in Training

First Dormant Pruning

1. Prune all branches lower than about 24 inches from the ground.
2. Select the scaffold branches. These should be wide-angled and separated 8 to 12 inches along the trunk. They should be well distributed around the tree at the desired height above the ground. Usually only two to three scaffold branches are suitable for selection during this first dormant pruning.
3. Thin out all upright shoots except the one to be saved for the leader.
4. Prune the tips of scaffold branches so that when holding them upright, their tips are 10 to 12 inches lower than the top of the leader.

Second Dormant Pruning

1. Examine the growth that has taken place from the leader during the previous summer. From the side branches that have developed on the leader

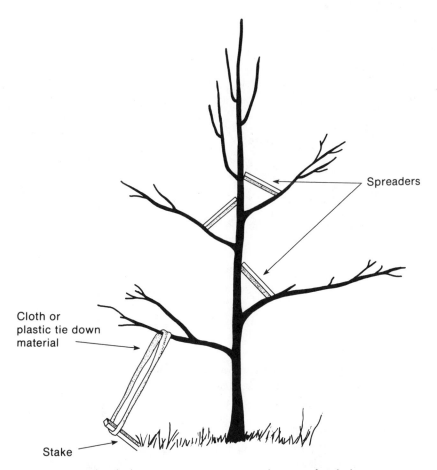

Spreading limbs to improve tree structure and promote fruit bud set.

    select two to three additional scaffold branches. Again, these should be wide-angled and well spaced.

2. Shorten the tips of the scaffold branches so that they are shorter than the leader.

3. Again, remove any upright shoots so that only one leader remains.

4. The scaffold branches selected after the first dormant pruning will now have branches. Remove all but two or three of the main branches but save the short twigs and spurs that develop on the inside of the tree. The branches that remain on the scaffold should be wide-angled and well spaced. Treat the development of the scaffold branches as if each

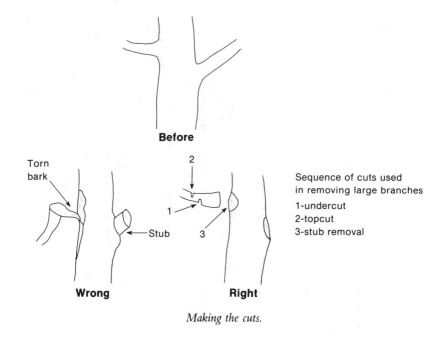

Making the cuts.

were a small tree. Head back any of the side branches of the scaffold that threaten to outgrow its leader.

5. Remove any suckers that may have developed.

Third Dormant Pruning

This is a repeat of the previous year's pruning. Additional scaffold branches are selected. The leader is maintained as are short twigs and spurs for fruiting.

Fourth Dormant Pruning

By now the tree should have developed its main framework and shape. There should be five to eight main wide-angled scaffolds and the tree should have the general conic shape. Branches of the scaffolds that rub or overlap may need to be removed or headed back if they threaten to outgrow the leader. Remove water sprouts now and in subsequent years since they produce no fruit and reduce the tree's vigor.

Subsequent Pruning

Some cultivars may produce fruit by the fourth or fifth year. The emphasis in pruning now shifts to thinning out to provide maximum light exposure. By thinning and cutting back the upper branches, the tree is kept fairly open and its size and shape can be maintained.

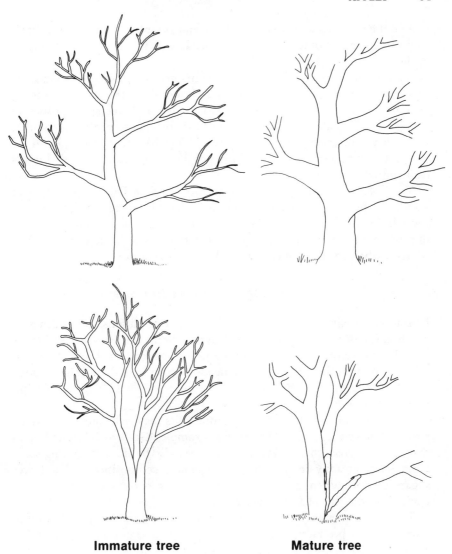

Immature tree   **Mature tree**

Correct (top) and incorrect (bottom) pruning.

Pruning and Training Dwarf Trees

Pruning dwarf trees that require some sort of support system is a most challenging and difficult procedure. Trees tied to a stake or post are usually trained to develop the central leader form, not unlike that of standard trees. In dwarf trees, more emphasis is on selecting scaffolds that are distributed around the tree so that an overall balance and symmetry can be maintained. In dwarfs, the scaffolds do not need to be as widely separated vertically as in the standard trees.

It is essential that a strong leader be maintained, and any upright vigorous branches that threaten to compete with the leader should be pruned. Heading back of the tips of the main scaffolds or their side branches is frequently necessary to maintain the conic shape of the tree and to protect the leader. In the small trees, such as those grown on M.7 or M.26 rootstocks, less thinning out may be necessary since all parts of the canopy usually receive abundant sunlight.

To protect the leader and to ensure its continued development, fruit should not be allowed to develop on the leader during the first few years of growth. In cultivars with a tendency to form narrow crotch angles, the use of spreaders or some sort of tie-down system is advised, and this should be started early, preferably during the first growing season.

Why Thinning of Fruit Is Important

During a year with extremely favorable weather conditions, the tendency to overbear can occur in most cultivars of apples. Some cultivars such as 'Haralson', 'Lodi', 'Mantet', and 'Wealthy' are notorious for their biennial bearing habits. One year they produce a tremendous crop with their branches sagging from the weight of all the fruit. The next year, few, if any, apples are produced.

When trees are overloaded, the mature fruits may lack some of the desirable characteristics of the cultivar. For example, 'Golden Delicious' apples may be more green than yellow and taste may also be affected. During some years one can readily detect a change in chemical composition such as lower sugar content. When trees are overloaded, a grower may harvest more apples, but the size of fruit is apt to be smaller.

There is no guarantee that annual thinning of the fruit crop will result in more uniform production from year to year, since an untimely frost, inactivity of pollinators, or other unfavorable conditions can all result in a diminished crop—but it is a step in the right direction.

How and When to Thin

Commercial growers often use chemical sprays to thin fruits, but for the person with just a few trees this method is not recommended. Most of the chemicals are not readily available and are costly and tricky to use.

In the hand-thinning method, the ideal is to produce one fruit for every 40 to 50 leaves. From a practical standpoint, rather than taking the time to count all the leaves, we can simply remove all but one fruit per every 3 to

5 blooming or nonblooming spurs. The remaining fruit should be the biggest and the healthiest, and free of damage from insects or disease. In the center of the tree, where sunlight penetration is at a premium, the fruits remaining after thinning should be spaced 5 to 8 inches apart.

Since formation of the flower buds, which will produce next year's crop, begins early in the summer growing season, it is important that thinning be performed within 30 to 35 days of full bloom to ensure flower buds for the next year and to have the greatest benefit on fruit size. Later thinning can be done to improve fruit size, but the benefit decreases as the growing season progresses.

Fertilization

When planning a large orchard, one should get a soil test through a private laboratory or the county extension agent. With just a few trees, a soil test is probably not necessary unless there has been difficulty growing a variety of plants in the past. In areas where the soil is known to be very acidic or alkaline, some soil modification may be necessary since the ideal soil pH for apples is 6.0 to 6.5.

On most sites, apple trees require regular fertilization to develop their full potential. In the Upper Midwest, the best time to fertilize is in the early spring before growth begins. For organic gardeners, a manure mulch or a compost combination around the base of the tree is recommended.

A good choice for inorganic fertilizers is an equal balance of nitrogen, phosphorus, and potassium. Fertilizers such as 10–10–10 or 12–12–12 are ideal and readily available in most areas. Commercial growers, based on soil tests and leaf analysis, usually employ single-element fertilizers because they are more economical for large acreages.

Fertilization the First Year

At planting time, no fertilization is advised. Usually growers wait 2 to 3 weeks after planting or until the soil has settled. At that time, ¼ pound of a balanced fertilizer such as 10–10–10 can be scattered in a circle extending 2½ feet from the trunk to just beyond the branch tips. Under drought conditions, additional fertilizer applied during the first year may cause extensive root injury.

Fertilization in Subsequent Years

How much to fertilize in subsequent years depends on the growth of the tree. Young trees should exhibit 15 to 30 inches of growth each year; bearing trees, 8 to 15 inches. 10–10–10 applied at an increasing rate of ½ pound per year to a maximum of 8 to 10 pounds at maturity should be sufficient.

Table 7. Indices for judging the nitrogen status of fruit trees

Index point	Low nitrogen	Normal nitrogen	Excessive nitrogen
Terminal shoot growth	Bearing: diameter less than 4 inches average length; nonbearing: less than 10 inches	Average 4 to 12 inches long; 10 to 24 inches long average	Average 12 to 20 inches long; 24 to 40 inches long average
Leaf size	Small, thin	Medium to average	Large, thick, often puckering at tip
Leaf color	Uniformly pale; yellowish green	Normal green	Very dark green
Fall leaf drop	Early; leaves show some red coloration in veins	Normal time; green to light green	Late; remain dark green until severe frost
Bark color	Light brown to reddish brown	Gray to dark gray-brown	Greenish gray to gray
Fruit set	Poor; June drop of young fruit usually heavy	Normal for the cultivar; apples have 1 to 3 fruits set per cluster	May have little or no effect; may reduce set somewhat
Fruit size	Per-tree average smaller than normal	Normal for the cultivar	Per-tree average larger than normal
Fruit overcolor	Highly colored, often earlier than normal	Average color for the cultivar at picking time	Poor color up to and after normal picking period
Fruit undercolor	Yellow color develops earlier than normal for the cultivar	Yellow green to yellow color develops normally for the cultivar	Green to greenish yellow at normal picking period for the cultivar
Fruit maturity	Somewhat earlier than normal for the cultivar	Normal picking dates for the cultivar	5 to 10 days later than normal for the cultivar

Source: Ohio State University Bulletin 458.

Nitrogen is the element needed most for growth, but if applied in excess, the results can be more damaging than not using enough. In lieu of a balanced fertilizer, commercial growers may supply actual nitrogen at a rate of 0.1 pound per year of tree age up to 10 years or 0.1 pound per inch of trunk diameter. Table 7 provides indices for judging the nitrogen status of fruit trees.

Preventing Winter Injury

Mulching

Mulching can be time-consuming and expensive, but it is recommended for all areas in the Upper Midwest where clonal dwarfing rootstocks are used. Mulching protects the shallow root system from temperature fluctuations and, of course, aids in water conservation during drought years. In addition, yield, especially on dwarf trees, may be increased. Many growers opt for a two-year replenishment program with a thin covering (straw or corncobs, for example) of continually decomposing material.

Protection from Wildlife

Just beneath the bark of young woody plants is a thin layer of meristematic cells called the cambium. The cambium produces xylem cells, which form wood, and phloem cells, which transport stored food up and down the tree.

When this transport system is interrupted by gnawing rodents, rabbits, or deer, we say that the tree has been *girdled*. When girdling occurs all the way around the tree, death will occur unless the damaged area is repaired. Perhaps the most common method of repairing girdled trees is by bridge grafting. This type of graft is used for trees with a trunk diameter of 2 inches or larger. On smaller trees, a different method called cleft grafting is usually employed. Details on the latter method will not be discussed here but are available from all county extension agents.

The best time to repair damaged trees is in April when the bark "slips" or peels readily. In the bridge-grafting method, some one-year-old water sprouts or scions are used to bridge the damaged area. The scions can be collected from branches of the damaged tree or from any other apple. As the accompanying diagrams illustrate, the first step is to trim back the bark to healthy tissue, using a razor-sharp knife to make clean, smooth cuts. Next, select the scions to be inserted into the damaged area. Each end of the scion should be cut back about 2 inches and it should be used as a pattern to determine where to make the notches in the damaged tree. When selecting a scion, be sure to mark the top and bottom. When inserted, the top should be pointed up and it should fit snugly into the notch. Scions should be spaced 2 inches apart.

Next, use small brads or No. 20 flathead ¾ " nails to tack the scion into position. Nail the top of the scion first, then flex the middle to position the lower part of the notch and finish nailing. The ends of the scions must be covered with a protective coating to prevent drying out. Commonly used sealers are grafting wax or asphalt-water emulsions.

The best protection against girdling damage is to use a cylinder of ¼-inch mesh hardware cloth. The hardware cloth is expensive, but for protection and durability it is probably the best choice. Plastic tree guards can be used, but they are effective only when the trees are small in diameter, and even then they may not be effective against mice. Plastic guards are not recommended for apples on dwarfing rootstocks because there may be a tendency to leave them on all year. This could create a pest haven and contribute to formation of burrknots.

When using hardware cloth, make a cylinder 6 to 8 inches in diameter and

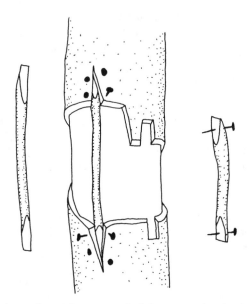

Two methods of bridge grafting. The scion on the left is inserted under the bark at each end; the scion on the right is inlaid in a groove at each end.

30 inches long. The cylinder should extend into the soil 1 to 6 inches (6 inches is more effective against rodents).

Poison baits can be used around the base of the trees, but I do not recommend these because of the possibility of accidental poisoning of children and pets. An effective mice and rabbit repellent can be made by dissolving 7 pounds of tree rosin in one gallon of denatured alcohol. Use warm water and stir occasionally while allowing the mixture to stand for 24 hours. This is enough to paint on the branches and trunks of 100 small trees.

Chicken wire or 1½-inch mesh wire can also be used to fence the orchard to provide protection from rabbits. The fence will need to be higher than the resulting snow cover. This method is expensive and if rabbits are a real problem, it may be necessary to reduce the population by trapping or hunting.

In many parts of the Upper Midwest, deer can cause serious damage to the orchard. Both apple buds and twigs are vulnerable since these are considered favored foods. Fencing an orchard for deer protection is an expensive proposition since the fence will need to be a minimum of 8 feet high. Some growers have used electric fences, but this is also expensive and to be effective must be constantly maintained.

Some success has been reported by spraying adjacent vegetation with a

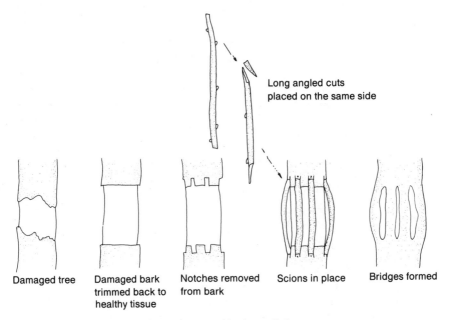

Long angled cuts
placed on the same side

Damaged tree

Damaged bark
trimmed back to
healthy tissue

Notches removed
from bark

Scions in place

Bridges formed

The proper way to bridge girdled trees.

sugar solution to attract the deer from the orchard. A small sock of mothballs tied in each tree may keep deer away for short periods. Blood meal or tankage from slaughterhouses may be diluted with water and sprayed on trees but repeated applications are necessary. An alternative is to hang blood meal in the tree in perforated plastic bags. In southern Minnesota, some growers have used soap as a deer repellent. Usually 4 to 6 bars of soap, such as Ivory, are tied to the main branches of each tree. Position the soap so that it does not run down the bark, because there is some evidence that it may attract rabbits. Caslick and Decker (1978) report that hanging kerosene-soaked rags in trees may be effective for short periods of time.

Burrowers like pocket gophers can often destroy the root system of apple trees. Where these animals are present in high numbers, trapping is probably the safest and most effective method of control.

Protection from Sunscald

Apple trees are particularly prone to sunscald damage, which occurs on the southwest side of the trunk and main branches. The warming effect of the sun during the day and the ensuing cold night temperatures often cause the bark to split. An open wound is an invitation to disease and damaging fungi.

To protect against sunscald, commercially available tree wrap can be used.

The wrap should extend from ground level to the first main branch. It should overlap so that the entire surface is covered. Tie the wrap securely in several places with twine. Remove the wrap during the summer months since it provides an excellent breeding ground for a multitude of pests.

An alternative to wrapping the tree is to cover the trunk with a white latex paint (50 percent paint in water mixture). In addition, boards are sometimes nailed onto the southwest side of the tree to prevent sunscald damage.

Physiological Protection

A lot of injury can occur if the tree is not physiologically (internally) prepared for the coming winter months. Sometimes winter damage is unavoidable, especially when the fall is warm and wet. When these conditions prevail, the tree often does not have time to reduce growth and to properly "harden up."

Any activity that encourages growth late in the fall is apt to be harmful to the tree. Thus, late cultivation, fertilization, and excessive irrigation should be avoided.

The choice of vegetation planted around apple trees or in the orchard row can also have an effect on fall dormancy. Members of the legume family such as clover and alfalfa should not be used. These plants, in association with bacteria, fix nitrogen. This nitrogen is beneficial to the plants during the normal growing season, but when legumes are present it is often produced in excess amounts late in fall and can clearly delay dormancy.

Pests and Diseases

Codling Moth. The adult moth appears just after the blossoms fall. These insects are grayish brown and may be seen crawling on the developing fruit. When the eggs are laid they hatch into larvae, which are often called apple worms. The apple worms burrow into the fruit and a brown excrement is usually visible at the point of entry. Larvae overwinter in silken cocoons under bark or in nearby sheltered locations. Infected apples do not keep long in storage. Chemical sprays are usually used when the larvae are crawling.

Baits, pheromones, or sex attractants may also help reduce the moth population, but they are used mainly to tell the grower when to initiate spraying. These are available from the National Gardening Research Center, Highway 48, P.O. Box 149, Sunman, IN 47041, and from other sources.

Apple maggot. The adult fly is somewhat smaller than the common housefly (about ½ inch long) and has clear wings with dark markings. The hind part of the body is dark-colored with light bands. The adults may be present from mid-June, or slightly later in northern regions, through

Apple-maggot damage. Photo courtesy of L. Hertz.

mid or late September, depending on the area and year. The flies lay their eggs under the apple's skin. When the larvae develop they feed on the flesh. In early stages of development their presence is difficult to detect unless the apple is cut open. These pests overwinter in the pupa form in the soil beneath apple, pear, and hawthorn trees. Removing all dropped fruit helps in control as does elimination of weeds, which this pest uses for resting and protection. Chemical sprays are used during the summer months when the adults are present. Apple-maggot bait traps are also available from the National Gardening Research Center. Homemade traps are discussed at the end of this section.

Apple and plum curculios. The adult forms which are commonly called snout beetles are ¼–½ inch long and dark-brown colored. The adults usually appear as the flower buds are expanding and they feed on leaves, flowers, and the young developing fruit. Eggs are laid on the fruit, where they hatch into feeding larvae. Fruit damaged by the beetles usually drops early or becomes distorted and scarred. A spray program timed to coincide with the presence of the adults can successfully control these pests, and it is important that fallen fruits be removed from the orchard.

Scale insects. These insects are easy to recognize because of a hard, protective waxy scale on twigs and branches. The protective scale allows the insect to overwinter on the tree. When infestation is heavy, entire branches may be covered with scale, which is sometimes present on the fruit as well. Young scale insects are called crawlers and may move on the branches for some time before choosing a permanent location. They suck nutrients from twigs and branches and fruit. In time they weaken the tree and injure the fruit. These insects may be controlled by using a commercial, dormant oil product or by spraying at the crawler stage.

Aphids. Close visual inspection of developing buds and leaves is necessary to detect these tiny sucking insects in the early stage of development. When large numbers are present, the leaves may curl and drop prematurely. Developing fruit may become deformed. Dormant oils may eliminate some overwintering eggs. A spray program early in the summer before the leaves are curled often is necessary to control large populations.

Mites. These pests are very difficult to observe without the use of a magnifying glass. They suck sap from the leaves and cause a general weakening of the tree. In heavy infestations, the leaves are speckled with minute bronze spots and appear leathery. Repeated sprays with a miticide (not an insecticide) are necessary early in the summer to control this pest.

Apple scab. This apple disease is serious in all parts of the Upper Midwest. The disease-causing organism is a fungus (*Venturia inaequalis*) that overwinters on fallen leaves. Spores from these leaves are spread by wind and rain early in the spring to young developing leaves on the tree. As the spores develop, they form rough, round scab lesions that vary in size from those of a pinpoint to ½ inch in diameter. At first the lesions are light green, but as they mature they become greenish black and velvety. In time the leaves turn yellow and drop off early in the season.

Scab lesions on the fruit are similar in appearance, and in time become corky and split, resulting in misshapen small fruit. During conditions that are favorable to apple scab, reinfection may occur from spores that develop during the current season's growth. A good sanitation program (removing fallen fruit and leaves) is essential for control of the disease. Since the spores are spread by wind, encourage nearby neighbors with apples to remove fallen debris to prevent spread of the disease. Chemical spraying with a fungicide in the early spring also helps check apple scab.

The severity of this disease varies from year to year. Severe outbreaks are more prevalent during years when the spring and early summer are

Cedar-apple galls on juniper.

wet. Most cultivars of apples are susceptible to scab, but some more so
than others. Refer to the section on cultivars for information on resistant types.

Cedar-apple and related rusts. Closely related species of the fungus genus *Gym-*
nosporangium cause disease problems not only in apples but also in a
number of other members of the rose family. Examples include flowering crabapple, hawthorns, pear, mountain ash, serviceberry, and
flowering quince. The fungus alternates parts of its life cycle with these
rosaceous plants and various species of the genus *Juniperus.* Besides the
red cedar, *Juniperus virginiana,* the fungus is also found on the Rocky
Mountain juniper *(J. scopulorum),* mountain juniper *(J. siberica),* horizontal juniper *(J. horizontalis),* dwarf juniper *(J. communis),* old field juniper
(J. communis), and Savin juniper *(J. sabina).*

On junipers the fungus produces brown galls (cedar-apples) that overwinter, and in the spring during wet periods they swell and form orange gelatinous structures that produce hornlike projections. At this
stage, the spores are shed and infect the apples and related hosts. Once
infection occurs, small yellow spots appear on the leaf surface, and
these gradually enlarge and turn orange. In time similar lesions appear
on the fruit, and at maturity, the fruit may be misshapened. Reinfection

of juniper trees occurs in late summer and early fall. The following summer the fungus begins further development and remains on the tree until the next spring. The life cycle requires two hosts and two years to complete.

Juniper trees seem less affected by the disease than do the alternate rosaceous hosts. In apples, the disease weakens the tree and seriously affects fruit quality. In time, fruit production may cease. In most cases, removing cedars, which are necessary for the completion of the life cycle, is impractical, since spores may be carried by the wind to a distance of 2 to 4 miles or more. On the other hand, where possible, avoid planting apples next to susceptible junipers. Planting resistant cultivars of apples is the best course to follow. Refer to the cultivar section for a comparison of cultivar resistance. A repeated fungicide spray program from bloom period until spore production ceases (usually sometime in June) can control the disease.

Fireblight. If left unchecked, this devastating disease can virtually kill apples and several other members of the rose family in a relatively short period of time. The disease was known simply as "blight" until Joseph C. Arthur, who received the first doctoral degree in the sciences at Cornell University, successfully demonstrated that it was caused by a bacterium. The disease-causing organism, *Erwinia amylovora,* can be disseminated by both insects and rain, and once a single tree in the orchard is infected, others are likely to follow.

Symptoms of fireblight include sudden wilting of leaves, followed by darkening of the flowers and young shoots. The affected branches on apples initially become brown (black in pears). Infection proceeds from the tip of the branches downward and eventually spreads throughout the tree. Cankered areas appearing on recently killed shoots, branches, and shoots of the trunk are often depressed and darker colored than healthy tissue. During wet periods, disease areas often produce a milky, sticky liquid which ultimately turns brown. This ooze may appear on blossoms, tips of branches, fruit, or the trunk. The presence of leaves still hanging on the tree during the winter months is another symptom of fireblight.

Halting the spread of the disease is essential, and with early detection the trees may survive. Infected areas should be pruned back to at least 12 inches of healthy tissue. After each cut, pruning equipment should be dipped in household bleach (Clorox) diluted 1:1 with water. This bleach solution will cause pruning equipment to rust, so after pruning, wash thoroughly with water, then oil.

Cankers that remain at the end of the growing season should be pruned out during the dormant season, preferably in February or early March.

This curved, dead branch, often called a shepherd's crook, is a common sight on trees infected with fireblight. Photo courtesy of L. Hertz.

Sometimes scraping the canker to remove infected tissue is all that is necessary. To do this, use a sharp knife to cut away the damaged bark, and the branch with healthy tissue may remain. Where cankers are severe, whole branches may need to be removed. To remove a branch, make the cut 12 inches below the canker margin in healthy wood. Bacterial chemical sprays applied early in spring and during bloom periods offer some control. As with scab and cedar-apple rust, the different cultivars of apples vary widely in their resistance to this disease.

Homemade Insect Traps

In the Upper Midwest, the most destructive pest of apples is the apple maggot, and without some method of control, 100 percent of the crop can be damaged. For decades the traditional method of controlling this pest was by repeated spraying of insecticides, but research now indicates that the pest can be controlled with trapping devices (Acuff, 1989; Foulk, 1989).

In the Upper Midwest, these pests emerge from the soil in mid-June or early July, depending on location, and then feed for seven to ten days on honeydew deposited by insects on apple leaves. After feeding, mating occurs, and the female begins depositing eggs beneath the skin of the developing apple. Larvae may spend 20 to 30 days burrowing through the fruit. Because adult flies continue emerging from the soil throughout August and September, the damage cycle continues until harvest.

During the seven- to ten-day feeding stage, Foulk (1989) reported that yellow rectangles are effective in attracting these pests. Size or shape of the traps does not seem to be so important as the glossy color of the paint. I have found that scraps of plywood (4 x 6 or 5 x 7 inches), painted yellow and sprayed with a sticky substance such as Tangle-Trap work fine.

After the feeding stage, the flies no longer seem attracted to yellow, but instead prefer other colors. Foulk (1989) reported that Tarter Red Dark and Black Gloss (from Sherwin-Williams) when applied to *spheres* proved to be powerful attractants. These painted spheres are also treated with Tangle-Trap. Spheres 7.5 centimeters (3 inches) in diameter seemed most effective throughout the season. The spheres can be wooden (old croquet balls), plastic, or rubber. I have found that solid rubber balls used with 1⅜-inch zinc-plated screweyes for anchorage work well.

Foulk (1989) reported that in trees 6 to 8 feet tall, traps hung at a height of 6 feet or more captured the most pests. It also appears that the traps are more effective if placed in the middle of the tree. It also apparently helps to remove a few of the leaves around the traps. In my own orchard I use three yellow rectangles and three or four spheres for each dwarf tree.

Another effective, homemade insect trap uses red, 5-ounce Solo drinking cups (uncovered) smeared with Tangle-Trap. The cups are filled with a homemade brew consisting of one cup of molasses, nine cups of water, and one package of yeast. Four to six traps are placed in each tree after the blooming period is completed. Many organic growers use one of more of these homemade traps as the only method of insect control. As might be expected, results are mixed and vary from year to year.

Care and Storage

One of the best keeping apples is 'Keepsake', but unless proper storage conditions are provided, it will last not months but just a few weeks or even days. The old adage that "one rotten apple can spoil the whole barrel" is not just folklore. Diseased, bruised, or otherwise damaged apples should be sorted, stored separately, and used first. Also, do not mix windfalls (fallen fruit) with fresh-picked fruit. Fallen apples generally give off more ethylene gas, which hastens the ripening process. In time all apples will give off this gas. Thus, to avoid rapid deterioration of other fruits and vegetables, store apples in a separate location.

Yellow rectangles and red spheres sprayed with Tangle-Trap are effective traps for the apple maggot.

Apples will last longer in storage if they are cooled immediately after harvest. With the exception of 'McIntosh', 'Northwestern', and 'Prairie Spy', which are stored at 36 to 38° F., most other Upper Midwestern cultivars store best at a temperature of 30 to 32° F. High humidity in the 80 to 85 percent range is also essential. Even slight variations in these standards can drastically affect storage life. For example, when apples are stored at 30° F., about 25 percent more time is required for ripening than at 32°. At 40°, apples ripen twice as fast as at 32°. At 60° the rate of ripening is three times faster than at 40°.

Few gardeners at home can duplicate the exacting storage conditions used by commercial orchards, but nevertheless, there are a number of home methods that work fine. The best storage area I have found is a well pit. High humidity plus just-above freezing temperatures allow most cultivars to keep near the maximum of their storage life. The next-best area is the home fruit cellar. Older homes lacking the insulation qualities of new construction usually work best. A dirt floor is preferred over concrete and an outside-air pipe where the incoming air flow can be regulated is ideal. To maintain high humidity, standing water can be added to old clay pots.

The home refrigerator also works for storage. Older, non-self-defrost models work best. Apples will keep longer there if stored in perforated plastic bags. Humidity can be increased by frequent misting.

Storage Disorders

Scald. This can affect all apple cultivars. The fruit has blisterlike or burnt areas on the surface, and the flesh beneath the skin may be soft and discolored. To minimize scald damage, harvest the fruit at minimum maturity. Wrapping individual fruits in newspaper moistened with mineral oil also helps prevent damage.

Watercore. Environmental conditions and overmaturity contribute to this disorder. Apples with watercore may have a glossy appearance near the core line. Some cultivars may taste sweeter than normal and others may develop a slight "off"-flavor. To help prevent watercore, harvest the fruit before it is overmature.

Jonathan spot. Harvest the fruit at minimum maturity and place it in cold storage immediately to prevent this problem. Apples with Jonathan spot develop dark, sunken spots on the skin. 'Jonathan' is particularly susceptible to this disorder, but it can also occur on other cultivars.

Internal browning. Brown streaks radiating from the core are typical of this disorder. To prevent this problem, store susceptible cultivars such as 'McIntosh' at 38° F.

Internal breakdown. Internal discoloration or breakdown of the flesh occurs when fruit has been stored too long or when overripe fruit has been harvested or improperly stored.

For more information on harvesting and storing apples, see Naeve and Domoto (1983).

SELECTED REFERENCES

Askew, R. G., R. L. Chaput, and E. N. Scholz. 1987. *Tree Fruit Culture for North Dakota.* North Dakota State University Coop. Ext. Ser. Cir. H-327.

Bittner, C. S., and R. M. Crassweller. 1985. *Pruning for Fruit.* Pennsylvania State University Ext. Ser. Special Cir. 126.

Bolluyt, K. 1982. Horticulture in Iowa and at Iowa State University. *HortScience* 17(3): 294.

Brooks, R. M., and H. P. Olmo. 1972. *Register of New Fruit and Nut Varieties.* 2nd ed. Berkeley: University of California Press.

Brown, G. A. 1975. Apples. In: *Advances in Fruit Breeding.* J. Janick and J. N. Moore (eds.). Lafayette, Ind.: Purdue University Press.

Brunner, R. F., and T. D. Johnson. 1976. *Apple Maggot Control in Backyard Situations.* Michigan State University Coop. Ext. Ser. Ag. Facts No. 72.

Carlson, R. F. 1978. *Budding and Grafting Fruit Trees.* Michigan State University Coop. Ext. Ser. Bull. 508.

Carlson, R. F., and J. W. Hull, Jr. 1978. *Rootstocks for Fruit Trees.* Michigan State University Coop. Ext. Ser. Bull. E-851.

Caslick, J. W., and D. J. Decker. 1978. *Control of Wildlife Damage in Orchards and Vineyards.* Cornell University Inform. Bull. 146.

Childers, N. F. 1983. *Modern Fruit Science.* Gainesville, Fla.: Horticultural Publications.

Dana, M., and G. Klingbeil. 1978. *Grafting and Budding.* University of Wisconsin Coop. Ext. Ser. Pub. A-1719.

Domoto, P. A. 1982. The Survival and Performance of Four Cultivars on Six Dwarfing Interstems. *Compact Fruit Tree* 15: 19-24.

Domoto, P. A. 1987. *Pruning and Training Fruit Trees.* Iowa State University Coop. Ext. Ser. Pub. PM780.

Domoto, P. A., and G. Nonnecke. 1988. *Planning and Managing a New Commercial Apple Orchard.* Iowa State University Coop. Ext. Ser. Pub. PM-672b (rev.)

Domoto, P. A., and L. E. Sweets. 1985. *Characteristics and Sources of Apple Cultivars.* Iowa State University Coop. Ext. Ser. Pub. PM1086.

Fear, C., and P. Domoto. 1986. The Delicious Apple. *Fruit Varieties Jour.* 40(1): 2-4.

Ferree, D. C., and R. F. Carlson. 1987. Apple Rootstocks. In: *Rootstocks for Fruit Crops.* R. C. Rom and R. F. Carlson (eds.) New York: Wiley-Interscience.

Forshey, C. G. 1986a. *Training and Pruning Apple Trees.* Cornell University Inform. Bull. 112.

Forshey, C. G. 1986b. *Cultural Practices in the Bearing Apple Orchard.* Cornell University Inform. Bull. 160.

Forshey, C. G., D. C. Elfving, and R. T. Lawrence. 1986. *The Planting and Early Care of the Apple Orchard.* Cornell University Inform. Bull. 65.

Foulk, D. S. 1989. Trap Apple Maggots. *American Fruit Grower* 109(3): 70, 72.

Frecon, J. L. 1979. One Hundred and Sixty-Three Years of Horticulture at Stark Brothers Nurseries and Orchard Company. *HortScience* 14(1): 95.

Gaus, A. E., and H. C. DiCarlo. 1987. *Home Fruit Production Apples.* University of Missouri Coop. Ext. Ser. Pub. G6021 (rev.).

Hedrick, U. P. 1922. *Cyclopedia of Hardy Fruits.* New York: Macmillan.

Heimann, M. F., and E. J. Stang. 1984. *Water Core of Apples.* University of Wisconsin Coop. Ext. Ser. Pub. A3280.

Hertz, L. B. 1987. *Fruit for the Home.* University of Minnesota Ext. Ser. Pub. AG-BU-0470.

Hertz, L. B., W. Steinstra, and D. Noetzel. 1987. *Commercial Apple Pest Control.* University of Minnesota Ext. Ser. Pub. AG-FO-0844 (rev.).

Hertz, L. B., and E. E. Hoover. 1987. *Dwarf Apple Trees.* University of Minnesota Ext. Ser. Pub. AG-FS-1109.

Hoover, E. 1986. *Before You Start an Apple Orchard.* University of Minnesota Ext. Ser. Pub. AG-FS-2837.

Hoover, E., and S. Munson. 1987. *Apples for Minnesota.* University of Minnesota Ext. Ser. Pub. AG-FO-1111 (rev.).

Klass, C., and D. L. Pinnow. 1977. *Disease and Insect Control in the Home Orchard.* Cornell University Inform. Bull. 124.

Klingbeil, G. C. 1977. *Dwarf Apple Trees.* University of Wisconsin Coop. Ext. Serv. Leaflet A2154.

Klingbeil, G. C., L. Hansen, M. Houland, L. Smith, and G. Thompson. 1976. *Growing Fruit for a Hobby.* University of Wisconsin Coop. Ext. Ser. Pub. A-2619.

Korban, S. S. 1986. Interspecific Hybridization in Malus. *HortScience* 21(1): 41-47.

Korban, S. S., and J. M. Morrisey. 1989. Scab-Resistant Apple Cultivars. *Fruit Varieties Jour.* 43 (2): 48-50.

Korban, S. S., and P. M. Skirvin. 1984. Nomenclature of the Cultivated Apple. *HortScience* 19 (2): 177-80.

Lamb, R. C., H. S. Adwinckle, and D. E. Terry. 1985. 'Freedom', a Disease-Resistant Apple. *HortScience* 20 (4): 774–75.

Lord, W. J., and D. W. Greene. 1982. Effects of Summer Pruning on the Quality of 'McIntosh' Apples. *HortScience* 17(3): 372–73.

Mahr, D. L., S. N. Jeffers, L. K. Binning, and E. J. Stang. 1986. *Apple and Cherry Pest Control.* University of Wisconsin Coop. Ext. Ser. Pub. A3314.

McGregor, S. E. 1976. *Insect Pollination of Cultivated Crop Plants.* USDA Agricultural Handbook No. 496.

Moorman, R. B. 1986. *Rabbit Damage to Tree Planting.* Iowa State University Coop. Ext. Ser. Pub. TS-5-86.

Naeve, L., and P. A. Domoto. 1983. *Harvesting and Storing Apples.* Iowa State University Coop. Ext. Ser. Pub. F-8-83.

Naeve, L., and P. A. Domoto. 1986. *Why Fruit Trees Fail to Bear.* Iowa State University Coop. Ext. Ser. Pub. F-10-83.

Peterson, R., and D. M. Martin.1979. *Apples 1979.* South Dakota State University Coop. Ext. Ser. Pub. FS-191.

Raese, J. T. 1981. Increasing Cold Hardiness of Apple Trees by Over-Tree Misting in Early Autumn. *HortScience* 16(5): 649–50.

Roach, F. A. 1986. History and Evolution of Fruit Crops. *HortScience* 23(1): 51–55.

Rom, R. C., and G. R. Motichek. 1987. Cultivar Effect on Adventitious Root Development of Clonal Apple Rootstocks. *HortScience* 22(1): 57–58.

Rupp, L. A., and J. L. Anderson. 1985. Growth and Fruiting Responses of Young Apple and Tart Cherry Trees to Weed Control. *HortScience* 20(4): 727–29.

Skroch, W. A., and J. M. Shribbs. 1986. Orchard Floor Management: An Overview. *HortScience* 21(3): 390–93.

Smock, R. M., and A. M. Neubert. 1950. Apples and Apple Products. In: *Economic Crops.* Vol. 2. Z. I. Kertsz (ed.). Danville, Ill.: Interscience Publishers.

Stack, R. W., and H. A. Lamey. 1985. *Diseases of Apples and Other Pome Fruits.* North Dakota State University Coop. Ext. Ser. Pub. PP-454 (rev.).

Stang, E. J. 1984. *Apple Cultivars for Wisconsin.* University of Wisconsin Coop. Ext. Ser. Pub. A2105.

Stang, E. J., and H. C. Harrison. 1987. *Home Fruit Cultivars for Southern Wisconsin.* University of Wisconsin Coop. Ext. Ser. Pub. A2582.

Stang, E. J., and G. C. Klingbeil. 1981. *Pruning Standard Apple Trees.* University of Wisconsin Coop. Ext. Ser. Pub. A1959.

Stang, E. J., and R. J. Tomesh. 1986. *Home Fruit Cultivars for Northern Wisconsin.* University of Wisconsin Coop. Ext. Ser. Pub. A2488.

Struye, Yves. 1981. Rootstocks and Varieties and Growing Problems in a Colder Climate. *Compact Fruit Tree* 14: 52–54.

Stushnoff, C., S. Munson, L. B. Hertz, W. Gray, and D. K. Wildung. 1980. 'State Fair', 'Sweet Sixteen', and 'Keepsake' Apples. *HortScience* 15(4): 542–43.

Taber, H. G., and C. Fear. 1986. *Fruit Cultivars for the Family.* Iowa State University Coop. Ext. Ser. Pub. PM 453.

Teskey, B. J. E., and J. S. Shoemaker. 1978. *Tree Fruit Production.* Westport, Conn.: AVI Publishing.

Upshall, W. H. (ed.). 1970. *North American Apples: Varieties, Rootstocks, Outlook.* East Lansing: Michigan State University Press.

Werner, R. 1980. Rating the Quality of Stored Minnesota Apple Varieties. *Minnesota Horticulturist* 108(6): 188.

Worf, G. L. 1986. *Apple, Flowering Crab, Hawthorn, Juniper Disorder, "Cedar Rust Complex".* University of Wisconsin Coop. Ext. Ser. Pub. A2598.

Chapter

3

Pears

Pears belong to the genus *Pyrus* and, like apples, are members of the family Rosaceae. Currently about 22 species are recognized and all are thought to have originated in either Asia or Europe (Lombard and Westwood, 1987).

The history of pear culture has been lost in antiquity, but Hedrick (1921) reported that the plants were known to the ancient Greeks and were discussed by Homer nearly 3,000 years ago. Centuries before Christ, several pear cultivars were described along with techniques for their propagation. Pear culture gradually expanded throughout central and western Europe, and by the early 1800s, there were 900 cultivars being grown in France (Layne and Quamme, 1975). In China, pears have been cultivated for more than 2,000 years (Pieniazek, 1966) and in Japan, since the eighth century (Kajiura, 1966).

Pears were introduced into this country by the European colonists, and according to Hedrick (1921), the first record of cultivation dates to 1629 in New England. The first pears grown here were the common European species, *Pyrus communis*. Most of the common cultivars grown today originated from this species.

In the 1800s, *P. communis* was hybridized with the Oriental pear *P. pyrifolia* to produce cultivars more resistant to *Erwinia amylovora*, the organism responsible for fireblight. Cultivars such as 'Kieffer', 'LeConte', and 'Garber', derived from these crosses, were more resistant to the disease, but the fruits were of lower quality (Layne and Quamme, 1975).

Toward the end of the 19th century, cold-hardy strains of *P. communis* and *P. ussuriensis* were imported from Russia for use in breeding work. Selections from *P. communis* and chance hybrids with *P. ussuriensis* proved very hardy and suitable for some of the colder areas of the Upper Midwest.

In the United States, 96 percent of the pear crop is confined to three states — California, Washington, and Oregon. 'Bartlett' is the leading cultivar in the Pacific Coast states and in 1989 accounted for 60 percent of production there. The value of the 1989 U.S. pear crop was $263,697,000. In the Upper Midwest, pear production is not economically significant and is largely confined to home gardens and small commercial orchards.

Pollination

The major pollinator of the pear, as with the apple, is the honeybee. Numerous investigators have shown that bees visit pear flowers mainly in search of pollen since the nectar produced has a low sugar content.

Fruit Set

In the literature, confusion exists as to whether two different cultivars are necessary for cross-fertilization and fruit set. For example, in some locations 'Bartlett' produces abundant fruit without the aid of pollen from another cultivar. In other areas, the absence of a suitable pollenizing cultivar results in little or no fruit production.

It appears that 'Bartlett' and certain other cultivars such as 'Parker' and 'Patten' will, in some locations and during favorable conditions, set fruit that is *parthenocarpic*. This type of fruit is seedless, or nearly so, and develops by self-fertilization.

The general conclusion is that the setting of fruit by nearly all pear cultivars will be enhanced by cross-pollination. Bud sports of a cultivar, of course, cannot be used to pollenize a similar cultivar. For example, 'Red Bartlett' cannot be used for 'Bartlett'. In addition, some other cultivars such as 'Bartlett' and 'Seckel' are cross-incompatible. Even when two cross-compatible cultivars are present, fruit set may be poor owing to nonoverlapping bloom times. For example, in some areas, 'Keiffer' blooms much too early to serve as a satisfactory pollenizer for 'Bartlett'. Ideally, the cultivars for cross-fertilization should be spaced no more than 50 to 100 feet apart. One pollenizer will be sufficient to fertilize seven or eight trees.

Standard Rootstocks

Seedlings of the French pear *P. communis* have been commonly used for rootstocks in the Upper Midwest, but they are not overly cold hardy and are susceptible to fireblight. For colder areas, seedlings of *P. ussuriensis*, which are more cold hardy and tolerant of fireblight, are preferred.

When clonal rootstocks are used, a selection called 'Old Home' is preferred. This rootstock, which is propagated vegetatively, is somewhat less hardy than *P. ussuriensis* but it is also very tolerant of fireblight. Some growers prefer trees where 'Old Home' is used to form the root, main trunk, and framework, and then they are budded with the preferred cultivar.

Dwarf Rootstocks

Dwarf pears are produced by grafting or budding desirable cultivars to rootstocks of the quince, *Cydonia oblonga*. Quince roots are shallow, lack cold hardiness, and are very susceptible to fireblight. A number of growers throughout the Upper Midwest have found these dwarf trees to be rather short-lived. They should be planted on a trial basis only.

Selection of Nursery Stock

Sizes of pear trees for purchase are basically the same as for apples. Unbranched one-year-old whips are preferred by commercial growers because they are cheaper and easier to train. Most retail stores and nursery catalogs that cater to the small grower feature two-year-old branched trees. Trees advertised as "jumbo" or "special select" grades are usually not worth the extra cost. Unless planting is delayed until late in the season, container-grown trees offer no advantage over bareroot stock.

Cultivars

Anjou. This 1823 Belgian introduction is considered intermediate in resistance to fireblight. The large fruit stores well and is primarily used for fresh eating. In Iowa, fruits are ready for harvest about October 1. This cultivar is considered a good pollenizer.

Bantam. Introduced in 1940 from Excelsior, Minnesota, this selection of unknown parentage has small green fruits that are blushed red. Harvested in North Dakota in early September, the tree has some resistance to fireblight. This cultivar has waned in popularity, and it may no longer be commercially available.

Bartlett. This is the most popular pear grown, accounting for over 75 percent of U.S. commercial production. Of unknown parentage, it originated in England about 1770 and is known as 'Williams' there. In 1817, Enoch Bartlett allowed the pear to be sold here under his name. This is a multipurpose pear considered excellent for canning. In Iowa, the fruits are harvested about September 1. The tree is susceptible to fire-blight and lacks hardiness in more northerly areas.

Bosc. This 1835 French introduction has large, gourd-shaped, russeted fruit that is considered of high quality for fresh use and canning. The fruit matures in early October in southern Iowa, and in Wisconsin it is recommended only for the southeastern counties. It is susceptible to fireblight.

Clapp's Favorite. According to Hedrick (1921), this pear was raised by Thaddeus Clapp of Dorchester, Massachusetts. The date of origin is uncertain, but it was mentioned at a meeting of the Massachusetts Horticultural Society in 1860. This is a large, high-quality pear, popular in southern Wisconsin, where it matures in late August. It must be harvested at the proper time or the fruit will deteriorate rapidly on the tree. It is best used fresh since storage is poor. This cultivar is susceptible to fireblight.

Ewart. Mortimer Ewart of Akron, Ohio, introduced this pear of unknown parentage in 1928. The fruit is medium size, greenish yellow, and has good quality and flavor. It ripens 10 to 20 days after 'Bartlett', which it resembles. The tree is somewhat more resistant to fireblight than 'Bartlett'. This selection may be difficult to locate.

Flemish Beauty. This 1810 European introduction has large, roundish fruit that ripens in late September. It is high quality and suitable for fresh eating and canning. Pear scab, which often blemishes the fruit, can be a serious problem with this cultivar, and the tree is also susceptible to fireblight.

Golden Spice. This cultivar of unknown parentage, introduced from Excelsior, Minnesota, in 1949, has waned in popularity. Today it is rarely planted and may be difficult to locate. The fruit is small, tart, spicy, and ready for harvest in midseason.

Gourmet. R. M. Peterson and J. R. Waples introduced this 'South Dakota F15' x 'Ewart' cross from Brookings, South Dakota, in 1988. The fruit ranges in color from greenish yellow to yellow and has numerous russet-colored dots. The flesh is crisp, juicy, and very sweet, with the rich flavor of European pears. Maturity time is the third week in September at Brookings. This pear is very cold hardy and is suggested for planting immediately north of areas where high-quality pear cultivars are generally grown. The trees are moderately productive and are apparently more tolerant to fireblight than most others.

Kieffer. An 1863 introduction from Pennsylvania, 'Kieffer' is generally rated as a poor quality pear that is suitable only for processing. The fruit is medium to large and ripens in late October. Positive features of this cultivar are its wide adaptability to different soils and intermediate resistance to fireblight.

Lincoln. This cultivar originated from an unknown seedling grown by Mrs. Maria Fleming of Corwin, Illinois, and was introduced about 1895. The medium to small fruit, which can be used for fresh eating and canning, matures in mid-September. The tree is rated as intermediate in resistance to fireblight.

Luscious. This 'South Dakota E31' x 'Ewart' cross was introduced from Brookings, South Dakota, in 1973. It is an excellent dessert pear adapted to parts of the northern Great Plains, which previously have been unable to grow high quality pears. The medium to medium-small fruits, which mature mid to late September, have a pleasant flavor similar to, but more intense than, 'Bartlett'. The tree is apparently more resistant to fireblight than most cultivars but is not immune.

Maxine. ('Starking Delicious'). Of unknown parentage, this pear was found as a seedling in Preble County, Ohio, and was propagated by E. M. Buechly of Greenville, Ohio, in about 1900. The fruit is medium size and rated fair to good in dessert quality. In Iowa, it matures about September 1. The trees are quite resistant to fireblight and may substitute for better-quality pears where fireblight is a serious problem.

Parker. This open-pollinated seedling of a Manchurian pear was introduced from Excelsior, Minnesota, in 1934. The fruit is medium to large and roundish. In Wisconsin, the fruit matures in mid-August and must be picked before it ripens. The tree is susceptible to fireblight.

Patten. This pear was developed by C. G. Patten of Charles City, Iowa, and was named and introduced by H. L. Lantz in 1922. In Iowa, the large fruit ripens in mid-September and has excellent quality for dessert but is rated only fair for canning. The tree is susceptible to fireblight.

Seckel. According to Hedrick (1921), sometime toward the close of the 18th century, this cultivar found growing on land near Philadelphia was named and introduced by a Mr. Seckel. The fruit is small, yellowish brown, and sometimes russeted. This multiple-use pear matures in Wisconsin in early October and is resistant, or intermediate in resistance, to fireblight.

Summercrisp. This cultivar was introduced in 1987 at Excelsior, Minnesota, from a seedling received in 1933 from John Gaspard of Caledonia, Minnesota. The plant flowers at the same time as 'Parker' and 'Patten' and 2 to 4 days earlier than 'Luscious'. The fruit is 3 to 4 inches long and 2½ to 3½ inches in diameter. It must be picked at the proper time or grit cells will form and a strong aroma will become apparent.

Tait-Dropmore. This open-pollinated seedling of 'Patten' was selected by David Tait in Cartertown, Ontario, Canada, and introduced in 1928 by Skinner Nursery. The fruit is small with greenish yellow skin blushed carmine. The tree is partially resistant to fireblight. This cultivar may be difficult to locate.

'Summercrisp' pear tree. Photo courtesy of J. Luby.

Selecting the Planting Site

Protection from frost should be given careful consideration in selecting a site for pear culture. Pears, like apples, can easily be injured by frost or cold temperatures during the blossoming state. However, pears are more susceptible to damage than apples since they bloom earlier, which makes their blossoms more likely to be exposed to cold.

The site should be elevated to avoid low spots where cold air settles. Pears planted in low areas also may do poorly because these sites may result in

Closeup of the fruit.

greater susceptibility to fireblight. Even on elevated sites, pears should not be planted with apples because of the possibility of the spread of fireblight.

Pears will grow on heavier, less-well-drained soils than apples, but they perform best on deep, fertile, well-drained sandy or clay loams. They perform poorly on shallow soils, and on light sandy soils supplemental moisture may be needed. The ideal soil pH for pears is 6.0 to 6.8.

Suggested Spacing

Standard cultivars require about 300 to 500 square feet of space per tree. Trees are commonly spaced 20 to 25 feet apart in rows 25 feet apart. Dwarf trees require 100 to 150 square feet of space. The plants are commonly planted 15 feet apart in rows 20 feet apart.

How and When to Plant

Pears, like apples, perform best if they are planted in the early spring as soon as the soil can be worked. Soaking bareroot stock in water several hours before planting will help break bud dormancy and speed up development. Root growth will begin when soil temperatures reach 40 ° F.

Fruit zones—
pears

Cultivar	Iowa			Minn.				S. Dak.				N. Dak.			Wis.			
	4b	5a	5b	1	2	3	4	1	2	3	4	A	B	C	1	2	3	4
Anjou		T	T												X	X		
Bantam												T	T	T				
Bartlett		T	T												X	X	T	X
Bosc		T	T												X	X		
Clapp's Favorite	T	T	T												X	X		
Ewart															X	X		
Flemish Beauty		T	T												X	X	X	X
Golden Spice	T	T	T	X	X	X			X	X	T	T	T	T	X	X	T	T
Gourmet	T	T	T	T	T	T	T	X	X	T		T	T	T	T	T	T	T
Kieffer	X	X	X					T							X	X		
Lincoln	X	X	X					X	T	T					X	X	X	X
Luscious	X	X	X	T	T	T		X	X	T	T				X	X	X	X
Maxine	T	X	X															
Parker	X	X	X	X	X			X	T	T		T	T	T	X	X	T	
Patten	X	X	X	X	X			T	T	T					X	X	T	
Seckel	X	X	X	X	X										X	X		
Summercrisp	T	T	T	X	X	X			T	T		T	T	T	X	X	T	
Tait-Dropmore												X	X	X				

X = recommended for planting; T = recommended for trial.
See zone map on page 20.

The trees should be planted slightly deeper than they were in the nursery. For dwarf pears with quince rootstocks, the graft union must remain above the soil line or the dwarfing effect may be lost. Root suckers on both types, and especially those on quince roots, are susceptible to fireblight. Because quince roots tend to be shallow, the plants should be mulched at planting time to conserve moisture. Mulching is also essential for winter because the quince rootstocks lack cold hardiness. Because the graft union on dwarfs is susceptible to breakage, these trees will need to be staked. At planting time, the lower branches should be cut off 18 to 24 inches above the ground, and the tree should be cut back to 30 to 36 inches. Select only one leader and remove any upright, vigorous-growing branches that threaten its development.

Select scaffold branches to remain that are 6 to 8 inches apart and wide-angled. Only one scaffold branch should remain at each growing point on the trunk. Shorten tips of scaffold branches that threaten to outgrow the leader.

Fertilization

Excessive nitrogen tends to stimulate young succulent growth, which is susceptible to fireblight; therefore, fertilizers in the pear orchard should be applied judiciously. In areas where a variety of cultivated trees and shrubs have been grown successfully in the past, a soil test is usually not necessary before planting.

During the planting year, fertilizer is not usually needed. In the early spring the year after planting, ⅛ to ¼ pound of a complete fertilizer like 10–10–10 or 12–12–12 can be scattered in a circle extending 2½ feet from the trunk to just beyond the drip line. After this initial fertilization, the amount of nutrients to apply in subsequent years should be based on the growth performance of the tree. For example, if the new growth of the main branches is averaging 6 inches or more a year and the leaves remain green with no signs of yellowing, additional fertilizer is probably not required.

In many cases, no additional fertilizer will be needed until the tree reaches bearing age. During the first few years of growth the trees are most susceptible to fireblight, and excessive nitrogen application during this time period compounds the problem. When trees reach bearing age, they should be fertilized every other year at the rate and dosage recommended for apples.

An estimated 50 percent or more of the pear trees planted in the Upper Midwest are lost to fireblight, and most are probably destroyed before they reach bearing age. A fertilization program designed to reduce the susceptibility of the trees to the disease is a necessary part of the overall cultural program required to successfully grow pears.

Thinning of Fruit

Brown and Childs (1929) reported that certain pear cultivars may produce as many as 8,000 fruit buds, and that each may produce at least seven flowers. The potential of 56,000 fruits per tree is enormous and, of course, far in excess of what the tree could support.

Naturally, not all of the flowers will develop into fruit, but during favorable seasons some thinning may be necessary. The goal to strive for is 30 to 40 leaves per fruit. Generally, during a favorable year when fruit set is heavy, remove all but one fruit per flower cluster. Thinning is usually done from mid-June to July. As with apples, chemical thinning agents are not recommended for the grower with just a few trees.

Pruning

Pruning and training of pear trees are basically the same as for apples except that less pruning is required. After the structural framework of the tree is established, only light pruning is required. Pruning should be largely restricted to removing branches that rub against other branches and to eliminating water sprouts and suckers. Exposed or wounded areas and young succulent growth are very susceptible to fireblight.

Pears are more difficult to train than most apple cultivars because the branches have a tendency to grow upward, forming narrow crotch angles. The use of spreaders or tie-downs should be employed during the first few years of growth.

Major pruning should be done in late winter, and should be completed by early March to minimize the spread of fireblight. To prevent the spread of disease, sterilize pruning equipment with household bleach after each cut. Fireblight-infected twigs and cankers should be removed in the same manner as for apples during the dormant period. Before the trees bloom, any new suckers, watersprouts, or short twiglike growth on the trunk should be removed.

Evidence of new infections of fireblight are likely to show up shortly after the bloom period. During this time through midsummer, trees should be inspected regularly, and if infected shoots are found they should be removed immediately. Make pruning cuts well below the diseased area into healthy tissue following the method described for apples.

Preventing Winter Injury

Pears, like apples, respond favorably to mulching, and for some cultivars and all dwarfs, it is necessary in most of the Upper Midwest. Pears must also be protected from wildlife. Basically, the cultural requirement described for apples can also be employed for pears. Pears should also be protected from sunscald. To minimize winter injury, avoid late-fall cultivation, pruning, excessive irrigation, and fertilization.

Pests and Diseases

Pears are subject to many of the same diseases and pests that affect apples. These include mites, scale, plum curculio, codling moth, and aphids. In cer-

Table 8. Days from flowering to harvest

Cultvar	Days
Clapp's Favorite	112–114
Parker	116–118
Bartlett	122–125
Flemish Beauty	126–129
Lincoln	132–136
Seckel	138–148
Kieffer	145–148

Source: Hansen et al., 1974.

tain areas, the pear psylla, which is a small insect similar in size to the adult aphid, may cause damage. This insect is a vector of a toxic mycoplasma responsible for "pear decline." This disease does not seem to be a problem in the Upper Midwest, but Childers (1983) reported that it has been responsible for the death of several hundred thousand pear trees in the Pacific Northwest.

Pears may also be infected with scab, which is caused by the fungus *Venturia pirina*. This disease, which shows up as dark moldy patches on fruit and leaves, is more likely to be a problem when spring rainfall is excessive.

In the Upper Midwest, the most destructive disease of pears is fireblight. Blossoms are usually infected first, then young shoots turn brown. In time, cankers appear on the structural framework of the tree.

Chemical and biological control measures for the insects, mites, and diseases are similar to those of apples. For specific information, contact the county extension agent or the state cooperative agricultural extension service.

Harvesting

Pears should be removed from the tree before they are fully ripened. If fully ripened, they tend to be gritty because of continued production of stone cells. The fruit also tends to become soft and deteriorates rapidly.

Harvest pears when the color begins to change to a lighter green, before a yellow color develops. Lenticels (tiny pores or spots) will change from white to brown, and the skin becomes waxy when the fruits are ready for harvest. At the time of harvest, the fruit, with a slight twist, should separate easily from the tree. Table 8 gives the average number of days from full bloom to harvest for selected cultivars.

Storage

Pear cultivars vary widely in storage qualities. Most cultivars are taken directly from the orchard and stored at 30 to 32° F. with a relative humidity of 90 percent. After removal from storage, they ripen quickly at a room temperature of 60 to 70° F. Because they emit ethylene gas, pears should not be stored with other fruits and vegetables.

SELECTED REFERENCES

Batjer, L. P., H. A. Schomer, E. J. Newcomer, and D. L. Coyier. 1967. *Commercial Pear Growing.* USDA Agricultural Handbook 330.

Brooks, L. 1984. History of the Old Home x Farmingdale Pear Rootstocks. *Fruit Varieties Jour.* 38: 126–28.

Brooks, R. M., and H. P. Olmo. 1972. *Register of New Fruit and Nut Varieties.* 2nd ed. Berkeley: University of California Press.

Brown, A. G. 1943. The Order and Period of Blossoming in Pear Varieties. *Jour. Pomology* 20: 107–10.

Brown, G. G., and L. Childs. 1929. *Pollination Studies of the Anjou Pear in the Hood River Valley.* Oregon Agr. Exper. Stat. Bull. 239.

Carlson, R. F., and J. Hull, Jr. 1978. *Rootstocks for Fruit Trees.* Michigan State University Coop. Ext. Ser. Bull. E–851.

Childers, N. F. 1983. *Modern Fruit Science.* Gainesville, Fla.: Horticultural Publications.

Crane, M. B. 1949. Genetical Studies in Pears. 5. Vegetative and Fruit Characters. *Heredity* 3: 85–97.

Dana, M. N., E. J. Stang, and D. L. Mahr. 1985. *Pear Production in Wisconsin.* University of Wisconsin Coop. Ext. Ser. Pub. A2072.

Domoto, P. A., and L. E. Sweets. 1986. *Characteristics and Sources of Pear Cultivars.* Iowa State University Coop. Ext. Ser. Pub. PM–1117.

Faust, M. 1976. *Dwarf Fruit Trees.* USDA Ag. Research Ser. Leaflet No. 407.

Gorter, C. J., and R. Visser. 1958. Parthenocarpy and Pears and Apples. *J. Hort. Sci.* 33: 217–27.

Griggs, W. H., and B. T. Iwakiri. 1969. Effect of Rootstock on Bloom Periods of Pear Trees. *Proc. Am. Soc. Hort. Sci.* 94: 109–11.

Hansen, L. C., M. J. Houland, G. C. Klingbeil, L. C. Smith, and G. S. Thompson. 1974. *Harvesting and Storing Pears.* University of Wisconsin Coop. Ext. Ser. Fact Sheet A2621.

Hayden, R. A., and J. Janick. 1978. *Growing Pears.* Purdue University Coop. Ext. Ser. Pub. HO–122.

Hedrick, U. P. 1921. *The Pears of New York.* New York State Dept. Agr. 29th Annual Report. Vol. 2. Albany: J. V. Lyons.

Hertz, L. B. 1974. *Apple-Crabapple-Pear Varieties for Minnesota.* University of Minnesota Ext. Ser. Pub. 303.

Johnson, H. G. 1978. *Fireblight.* University of Minnesota Ext. Ser. Plant Path. Fact Sheet No. 17.

Kajiura, M. 1966. The Fruit Industry of Japan, South Korea and Taiwan. *Proc. 17th Internat. Hort. Congr.* 4: 403–25.

Larsen, R. P. 1976. *Pear Culture in Michigan.* Michigan State University Coop. Ext. Ser. Bull. E–519.

Layne, R., and H. Quamme. 1975. Pears. In: *Advances in Fruit Breeding.* J. Janick and J. N. Moore (eds.). Lafayette, Ind.: Purdue University Press.

Lewis, L. N., and A. L. Kenworthy. 1962. Nutritional Balance as Related to Leaf Composition and Fireblight Susceptibility. *Proc. Amer. Soc. Hort. Sci.* 81: 103–15.

Lombard, P. B., and M. N. Westwood. 1976. Performance of Six Pear Cultivars on Clonal Old Home, Double Rooted and Seedling Rootstocks. *J. Amer. Soc. Hort. Sci.* 101: 214–16.

Lombard, L. N., M. N. Westwood, and R. L. Stebbins. 1984. Related Genera and *Pyrus* Species for Pear Rootstocks to Control Size and Yield. *Acta Hort.* 146: 197–202.

Lombard, L. N., and M. N. Westwood. 1987. Pear Rootstocks. In: *Rootstocks for Fruit Crops.* R. C. Rom and R. F. Carlson (eds.). New York: Wiley-Interscience.

Lutz, J. M., and R. E. Hardenburg. 1969. *The Commercial Storage of Fresh Fruits and Vegetables, and Florist and Nursery Stocks.* USDA Agricultural Handbook 336.

McGregor, S. E. 1976. *Insect Pollination of Cultivated Crop Plants.* USDA Agricultural Handbook No. 496.

Oberly, G. R., R. C. Lamb, and C. G. Forshey. 1981. *Pear Culture.* Cornell University Inform. Bull. 126.

Patterson, J. V. 1957. *Growing Pears.* Ohio Agr. Exper. Stat. Bull. 359.

Pieniazek, S. A. 1966. Fruit Production in China. *Proc. 17th. Internat. Hort. Congr.* 4: 427–56.

Rubzov, G. A. 1944. Geographical Distribution of the Genus *Pyrus* and Trends and Factors in Its Evaluation. *American Naturalist* 78: 358–66.

Teskey, B. J. E., and J. S. Shoemaker. 1978. *Tree Fruit Production.* Westport, Conn.: AVI Publishing.

van der Zwet, T., W. A. Oitto, and R. C. Blake. 1974. Fireblight Resistance in Pear Cultivars. *HortScience* 9(4): 340–41.

van der Zwet, T., D. Stankovic, and B. Ristevski. 1987. Collecting *Pyrus* Germplasm in Yugoslavia. *HortScience* 22(1): 15–20.

Westwood, M. N. 1978. *Temperate Zone Pomology.* New York: Freeman.

Westwood, M. N. 1982. Pear Germplasm of the New National Clonal Repository: Its Evaluation and Uses. *Acta Hort.* 124: 57–65.

Westwood, M. N., and P. B. Lombard. 1982. Rootstocks for Pear. *Proc. Oregon Hort. Soc.* 73: 64–79.

Westwood, M. N., and P. B. Lombard. 1983. Pear Rootstocks: Present and Future. *Fruit Varieties Jour.* 37(1): 24–28.

Chapter

4

Peaches

The peach, *Prunus persica,* is also a member of the rose family. The species is thought to have originated in China and has been cultivated in Asia and Europe for well over 2,000 years. The peach was disseminated by seed throughout Asia, Europe, and finally the New World. From China, it was carried to Persia and then to the Mediterranean Basin, where it was introduced to the Romans and Greeks. The Romans, in their travels and conquests, were probably responsible for distributing the peach throughout much of Europe (Hesse, 1975).

The peach was introduced to America by the Spanish conquest of Mexico and appeared in Florida as early as 1565. The American Indians, followed by the early colonists, spread the peach practically to the limits of its present culture (Hesse, 1975).

Over 40 percent of the U.S. peach crop is produced in California. South Carolina ranks second with about 14 percent of production. Other major peach-producing states include Georgia, New Jersey, Pennsylvania, Washington, and Michigan. The value of the 1989 crop was $360,377,000 (*Noncitrus Fruits and Nuts,* January 1990).

Let the Buyer Beware

Despite the fact that the entire Upper Midwest area is unsuitable for growing peaches, thousands of new trees are planted each year. Most of the trees are probably planted by unsuspecting growers who have been lured by flashy-colored nursery catalogs espousing claims about super-hardy, subzero-tolerant cultivars. Of course, a few have been planted by growers who knew the risks but welcome a challenge.

Certainly, of the peach trees planted in all five states some have borne fruit, but even when fruit is produced, the crop is usually inferior. Most trees are killed before they reach bearing age.

Even in southern Iowa, in fruit zones 5a and 5b where climatic conditions are better for peach production than in most other areas of the Upper Midwest, crop production is usually a frustrating experience. There, Taber and Fear (1986) cautioned that peaches should not be grown with any expectation of producing a crop more than once every four to five years. This is very disappointing since the trees are very short-lived, often surviving only six to eight years. They are very susceptible to attacks by insects, viruses, and bacterial diseases. To check these pests, a comprehensive spray program must be undertaken each year, even before bearing age.

Bud Injury in Winter

The major limiting factor to peach culture in the Upper Midwest is injury by cold temperatures. Teskey and Shoemaker (1978) reported that a temperature of $-10°$ F. is near the minimum for bud survival in most cultivars. Most areas of the Upper Midwest experience temperatures lower than this nearly every winter and often for prolonged periods of time.

Wood Injury in Winter

Teskey and Shoemaker (1978) report that although no precise low temperatures can be given that will cause injury to peach wood, temperatures of $-18°$ to $-20°$ F. may cause damage. They add that even high temperatures have been known to cause injury to trees that were not fully dormant or hardened. In my own experience in Minnesota, I have seen three-year-old trees in reasonably healthy condition killed back to the ground after a severe winter.

In most areas of the Upper Midwest, the best chance for success with peaches is probably to grow the plants in large tubs or containers. For winter protection, the plant should be tipped and completely covered with straw, hay, or other mulch material.

Selecting Plants

Because peaches are self-fruitful, only one cultivar is needed. Peaches grown on dwarfing rootstocks are available, but they are not recommended since even in more favorable growing areas such as Missouri, they have proved unsatisfactory. Standard-size peach trees have been grown on a number of

This southern Minnesota peach harvest was deemed rare enough to warrant a photo in the Mankato Free Press. *Photo by J. Cross.*

seedlings and clonal rootstocks, but more information is needed on which are the best choices for the Upper Midwest. The best course is to purchase No. 1, one-year-old standard trees from a northern nursery.

In general, the selection of nursery stock, methods of planting and pruning, and cultural requirements described for apples and pears can also be applied to peaches. Differences in the details will not be presented here because these plants are not recommended for culture in any of the regions of the five-state area.

For those living in zone 5a in Iowa, the cultivars 'Polly', 'Sungold', and 'Reliance' may be suitable on a trial basis. Besides these, Iowa growers in zone 5b might consider 'Champion', 'Hale Haven', and 'Red Haven'. In most other areas of the Midwest, 'Reliance' is probably the best cultivar to consider.

SELECTED REFERENCES

Anonymous. 1967. *Growing Peaches East of the Rocky Mountains.* USDA Farmer's Bulletin 2205.

Brown, D. S., and R. W. Harris. 1958. Summer Pruning of Early Maturing Peach Varieties. *Proc. Amer. Soc. Hort. Sci.* 72: 79–84.

Buchanan, D. W., R. H. Briggs, and J. F. Bartholic. 1974. Cold Hardiness of Peach and Nectarine Trees Growing at 29–30 Degrees Latitude. *Jour. Amer. Soc. Hort. Sci.* 99(3): 256–69.

Campbell, R. W. 1948. More Than Thirty Peach Varieties Survived − 32 Degrees F. *Proc. Amer. Soc. Hort. Sci.* 52: 117–20.

Gaus, A. E., and R. R. Rothenberger. 1986. *Peaches.* University of Missouri Coop. Ext. Ser. Bulletin.

Hayden, R. A., and Frank H. Emerson. No date. *Peach Varieties.* Purdue University Coop. Ext. Ser. Bull. HO-106.

Hedrick, U.P. 1917. *The Peaches of New York. Part 2.* Geneva, N.Y., Agr. Exper. Stat.

Hedrick, U.P. 1950. *A History of Horticulture in America to 1860.* New York: Oxford University Press.

Hesse, Claron O. 1975. Peaches. In: *Advances in Fruit Breeding.* J. Janick and J. N. Moore (eds.). Lafayette, Ind: Purdue University Press.

Knowlton, H. L. 1937. Hardiness of Peach and Apple Buds. *Proc. Amer. Soc. Hort. Sci.* 34: 238–41.

Lantz, H. L. 1948. *Improved Varieties of Peaches with Special References to Hardiness.* Iowa Agr. Exper. Stat. Report 1948. Pp. 277–78.

Layne, R. E. C. 1987. Peach Rootstocks. In: *Rootstocks for Fruit Crops.* R. C. Rom and R. F. Carlson (eds.). New York: Wiley-Interscience.

McGregor, S. E. 1976. *Insect Pollination of Cultivated Crop Plants.* USDA Agricultural Handbook No. 496.

Taber, H. G., and C. Fear. 1986. *Fruit Cultivars for the Family.* Iowa State University Coop. Ext. Ser. Pub. PM 453.

Teskey, B. J. E., and J. S. Shoemaker. 1978. *Tree Fruit Production.* 3rd ed. Westport, Conn.: AVI Publishing.

Chapter

5

Cherries and Cherry Plums

Worldwide, pie or tart cherries, *Prunus cerasus*, and sweet cherries, *P. avium*, are the two most important cherry species used commercially (Perry, 1987). The ground cherry, *P. fruticosa*, indigenous to south central Europe and Asia, is considered the probable parent of both tart and sweet cherries (Olden and Nybom, 1968). So-called Duke cherries are hybrids of *P. avium* and *P. cerasus*.

Hedrick (1915) suggested that cherries were first cultivated in Greece and were probably seed disseminated by man and birds throughout continental Europe. The early settlers introduced cherries to this country in 1629, and they were distributed only by seed until about 1767. By then, people were starting cherries, and the early pioneers could carry both seeds and trees as they moved west (Fogle, 1975).

In the Upper Midwest, cherry production is limited largely to tart cherries, *P. cerasus*; Nanking cherries, *P. tomentosa*; sand cherries, *P. besseyi*; and cherry-plum hybrids. In addition to the major *Prunus* species already mentioned, several other species are used primarily for landscaping, windbreaks, food for wildlife, or other purposes. For details on using the following species see Snyder (1980): *P. x cistena*, Purpleleaf Sand Cherry; *P. fruticosa*, European Dwarf Cherry; *P. japonica*, Japanese Bush Cherry, Korean Cherry; *P. maackii*, Amur Cherry; *P. padus*, European Bird Cherry; *P. pensylvanica*, Wild Red Cherry, Pin Cherry; *P. pumila*, Sandcherry; *P. sargentii*, Sargent Cherry; *P. serotina*, Black Cherry; and *P. virginiana*, Chokecherry.

Sweet Cherries

The following states, listed in order of importance, are the major sweet cherry producers: Washington, Oregon, California, and Michigan.

Sweet cherries are not recommended for any of the five states in the Upper Midwest, with the possible exception of the southern portions of Iowa and Wisconsin. In Iowa, Taber and Fear (1986) have cautioned growers not to attempt planting sweet cherries north of Highway 30, and that a good crop is seldom produced. In the most favorable areas, one or two of the yellow-fruited cultivars, such as 'Yellow Glass', would be the best choice for trial.

In Wisconsin, some growers report success with the cultivar 'Cavalier' and some have experimented with 'Gold' and 'Van'. All of these cultivars should be planted on a trial basis only.

Tart Cherries

Michigan is the top producer of tart cherries followed by New York, Utah, Oregon, Wisconsin, Pennsylvania, and Colorado.

Door County, with 332,013 trees, has 94 percent of Wisconsin's cherry trees on 3,348 acres (Wisconsin Agr. Stat. Ser., 1987). During the last few years, cherry production in Wisconsin has been erratic because of unfavorable weather conditions and market factors. In 1984 the value of the utilized cherry crop was $2,922,000, but in 1987 it was only $295,000. In 1988 there was some improvement but only to a level of $973,000 (*Fruit Situation and Outlook Yearbook*, July 1987; *Noncitrus Fruits and Nuts*, January 1990).

Horticultural Groups

Tart cherries are separated into two distinct horticultural groups based on the color of the juice. The amarelle group, which includes 'Meteor' and 'Montmorency', has colorless or very light red juice. The morello type, typical of the cultivars 'North Star' and 'English Morello', has dark red flesh and reddish juice.

Pollination and Fruit Set

All the tart cherry cultivars are self-compatible; that is, they will set fruit with their own pollen, and thus only one cultivar is required. On the other hand, the pollen must be transmitted to the stigma by some means. If the cherry blossom is not fertilized by pollen, the fruit fails to develop properly and will drop off before maturity. Numerous investigators have established that the honeybee is the major pollinator of cherries. In commercial orchards, colonies of bees should be present at flowering time.

Rootstocks

Tart cherries, like the other fruits discussed, are propagated by grafting or budding the desired cultivar (scion) onto a hardy rootstock. The two most common rootstocks used for cherries are mazzard *(P. avium)* and mahaleb *(P. mahaleb)*. In the Upper Midwest, mahaleb is usually preferred because it is more vigorous, productive, drought tolerant, and cold hardy (Bryant, 1940; Coe, 1945; Perry, 1987). In a 1984–85 survey in Michigan, Wisconsin, and other eastern states, Perry (1987) estimated that 90 percent of the tart cherry trees were being grown on mahaleb rootstocks, and only 10 percent on mazzard. The hardiest rootstock for sour cherries is *P. cerasus*, which Price and Little recommended for Iowa in 1903. This rootstock is also recommended for tart cherries in the Ukraine (Tarasenko, 1958). Dwarfing rootstocks and interstem trees are not recommended for the five-state region. For growers desiring small trees, a natural dwarf cultivar such as 'North Star' would probably be the best choice.

Selection of Nursery Stock

As with the other fruit trees, selection of northern-grown stock obtained from reputable local sources is highly recommended. Sizes of nursery stock are generally the same as for the other fruit cultivars; however, with cherries, peaches, and pears, availability of sizes is generally more limited than for apples. For cherries, 1- or 2-year nursery trees may be used. Branched trees 4 to 5 feet high and $9/16$ to $11/16$ caliper are economical and will perform well with proper care. Bareroot stock is preferred over container-grown plants.

Tart Cherry Cultivars

English Morello. According to Hedrick (1922), this cherry probably originated in Holland or Germany, then was introduced into England and finally America. The cultivar matures 10 to 14 days after 'Montmorency', and the fruit is of the morello type. The trees are more spreading than upright, and in most areas suitable for this cultivar, 'Montmorency' is the preferred choice. The fruit is multiple use.

Mesabi. This cultivar was selected by Chris Knutson of Duluth, Minnesota, and was introduced by Farmer Seed and Nursery in 1964. The hybrid of 'Bing' x a chance seedling is considered a tart cherry, but the sugar content of the fruit is midway between sweet and tart. The fruit resembles 'Meteor', but the pit is smaller. The 10- to 14-foot tree grows slowly but is reported to be a good producer.

Meteor. This is a University of Minnesota introduction released in 1952 from a cross of 'Montmorency' x a Russian type tracing back two or more generations to the cultivars 'Vladimir' and 'Shubianka'. It is generally

**Fruit zones—
tart cherries**

Cultivar	Iowa			Minn.				S. Dak.				N. Dak.			Wis.			
	4b	5a	5b	1	2	3	4	1	2	3	4	A	B	C	1	2	3	4
English Morello		X	X															
Mesabi				X	X	X	T	T	T			T	T	T	X	X	T	T
Meteor	X	X	X	X	X	X		X	X	T	T	T	T	T	X	X	X	X
Montmorency	T	X	X	T	T										X	X	T	
North Star	X	X	X	X	X	X		X	X	X	T	T	T	T	X	X	X	X

X = recommended for planting; T = recommended for trial.
See zone map on page 20.

regarded as slightly hardier than 'Northstar' and the amarelle-type fruit ripens 7 to 10 days later. This later ripening date usually means less damage by birds. Owing to pit breakage, the cultivar is not suitable for commercial processing. The tree is semidwarf (8 to 14 feet).

Montmorency. The most widely grown tart cherry in the U. S., this is the principal cultivar of commercial orchards in Wisconsin. The cultivar lacks hardiness and should be grown only in more temperate areas of the Upper Midwest. In favorable areas the 12- to 18-foot trees are vigorous and highly productive. This European introduction produces fruit of the amarelle type, which has multiple use.

North Star. This 'English Morello' x 'Serbian Pie I' hybrid was introduced in 1950 at Excelsior, Minnesota. The morello-type fruit is small (about 3/4 inch in diameter) and at maturity is very dark red. It is of good quality for sauce and pies. The tree is small (6 to 10 feet high) and very ornamental.

Site Selection

Because cherries bloom quite early, the site selected for planting should be chosen with frost protection in mind. Site selection near large bodies of water is ideal. In other areas, upland sites where good air movement and soil drainage are adequate should be selected.

Cherries will grow in a wide range of soil types, but they will not survive long in heavy soils where water accumulates for an extended period of time. Likewise, they will also do poorly on shallow or very sandy soils. Teskey and Shoemaker (1978) report that the ideal soil for cherries is a gravelly or sandy loam that is deep, warm, easy to work, and well drained. To minimize

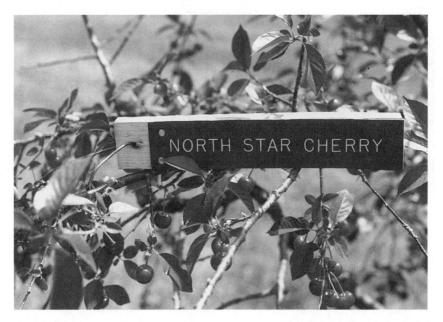

'Northstar' is a very ornamental cherry developed by the University of Minnesota.

verticillium wilt, do not plant cherries on soils where tomatoes, potatoes, or other solanaceous crops have been grown during the previous five years.

Spacing and Yield

Sour cherries for small home orchards are commonly spaced 15 feet apart in rows separated by 15 feet. Natural dwarfs like 'North Star' are occasionally spaced closer. In large commercial orchards, trees are commonly spaced 18 to 22 feet apart with rows 22 to 24 feet apart. Most cultivars reach bearing age in three to five years, and three-quarters to one bushel of fruit per tree is considered a good yield. In favorable areas, however, 'Montmorency' is much more productive.

How and When to Plant

Planting cherries in the fall is not advised. For best results plant early in the spring as soon as the soil can be worked. At planting time, buds should be dormant. Bareroot trees with greatly expanded buds are very difficult to get established. The general method for planting is the same as that described for apples. Cherries are normally planted about 1 inch deeper than they grew in the nursery. In more northerly areas, it may be advisable to plant the graft union 2 to 4 inches below the soil surface.

Pruning at Planting Time

Trees of $\%_{16}$ to $^{11}\!/_{16}$ inch caliper are usually well branched. Select the *three* strongest scaffolds that are wide-angled and evenly spaced around the tree. The lowest scaffold should be no less than 2 feet from the ground. The other scaffolds should be spaced a minimum of 6 inches apart. Select a central leader and remove any branches that compete with it. Prune back the tips of the selected scaffolds so they are shorter than the tip of the leader. If the tree is weak and spindly, cut the scaffolds back to one bud and allow a new scaffold system to develop. If the leader is more than 12 inches longer than the tips of the scaffold branches, it should be shortened.

Subsequent Pruning to Select Scaffolds

Dormant pruning in late winter or early spring before growth begins should be directed to selecting two or three additional scaffolds to form the main framework of the tree. The total of five to six scaffolds selected should be evenly distributed over 3 to 4 feet of the trunk. Only scaffolds with wide angles should be selected. The central leader is maintained, and no heading back of the scaffolds is necessary unless they threaten to outgrow the leader or grow so vigorously that they upset the balance or symmetry of the tree. Other pruning should be limited to removing branches that cross, rub, or otherwise cause crowding.

Pruning after Scaffold Selection

After the main scaffolds are selected, pruning should be kept to a minimum since this activity has a dwarfing effect and will delay blooming. Maintain the symmetry of the tree by heading back vigorously growing tips of scaffolds. If the leader exhibits vigorous growth, it may be shortened to keep the tree from getting too tall. In most cases, the leader is normally shortened after four to five years of growth. Remove watersprouts, suckers, and branches that are crowded or rub. After trees reach bearing age, occasional thinning may be necessary to allow penetration of sunlight. Heavily shaded portions of the tree will produce few fruits, and these are generally of poor quality.

Mulching

Mulching not only protects cherry rootstocks from winter injury, it also helps to eliminate competing weeds and to conserve moisture. In the home garden, a 3-square-foot area around the trunk of each tree should be mulched, especially during the first few years of growth.

Fertilization

No fertilizer should be applied at planting time, and the amount to apply in subsequent years depends on the initial fertility of the soil and, of course, the overall growth response of the trees. Cherries should exhibit 6 to 12 inches of new growth of the terminal branches each year. The leaves on a tree receiving proper nutrient levels should remain green through the growing season with no signs of yellowing, leaf curl, or early drop.

For the grower with just a few trees, a readily available, complete fertilizer such as 12-12-12 is probably the easiest to use. When fertilizer is needed, the method of application and the rate suggested for apples can be followed. For commercial growers, a soil test and leaf analysis are recommended.

Preventing Winter Injury

Any activity that encourages late fall growth is apt to result in some winter injury. For example, summer pruning, fall fertilization, late cultivation, or excessive irrigation late in the growing season should be avoided. Sometimes new succulent growth occurs in the fall in spite of good cultural practices. This is probably most evident during a wet summer or fall. When these types of climatic conditions prevail, the grower can do little.

Cherries, like the other fruits, should be wrapped, painted with white latex, or given some other means of protection against fluctuating, diurnal winter temperatures. In addition, the trunk should be encased in a mesh-wire cylinder to prevent girdling damage by rabbits and rodents.

Pests and Diseases

Birds

Damage to cherry fruit by birds is a serious problem in all areas of the Upper Midwest. Early protection is essential since birds frequently damage fruit long before it is fully ripe.

Homemade repellents of a visual and auditory nature can offer some protection, but most are ineffective. Scare devices such as aluminum-foil streamers, various types of whirlers, spinners, scarecrows, or plastic hawks

*'Meteor' cherry in full bloom (top) and
the same plant covered with netting for protection from birds (bottom).*

and owls have all been used. Caslick and Decker (1978) advise that scare devices should be changed daily to prevent the birds from learning that they pose no threat. Sound devices such as automatic exploders and those that emit electronic sounds or bird alarm calls are often used by commercial growers, but the degree of protection varies considerably.

For the grower with just a few trees, using a protective netting to cover the entire tree is probably the best course to follow. There are a number of plastic-impregnated paper, nylon, cotton, and polyurethene netting types available which offer effective control. Most netting can be used for several years if it receives proper care and is stored in a dry place out of sunlight.

Chemical bird repellents are also used by commercial growers, but because of a number of factors such as potential damage to the birds and other organisms, as well as the cost, these are not recommended.

Insects

Black cherry aphid. This tiny, black, shiny insect causes the leaves to curl on cherry trees, and when infections are severe, it may check growth. Black eggs may be present on twigs and small branches during the dormant season, and when these hatch in the spring, the young aphids may be found in clusters on opening buds.

Cherry fruit fly. This pest overwinters in an immature form in the soil. In spring or early summer, the female adult lays eggs in the fruit. The white larvae hatch from the eggs and tunnel into the flesh of the fruit. After about two weeks, the larvae fall to the ground and pupate. Chemical sprays are usually applied shortly after the emergence of the adults and then periodically until about two weeks before harvest.

Curculios. Worms that appear in the fruit at harvest time are usually the white larvae of the plum curculio. The adults, which are dark brown snout beetles about ⅕ inch long, make a crescent-shaped slit in the fruit where they deposit eggs. These insects hibernate in trash in the orchard or near it.

Pear slug. The pear slug or cherry slug is a slimy, dark-colored worm (larva) that feeds as a skeletonizer on the upper side of the leaf. These pests do not require chemical control since they can easily be washed from the leaves with a strong jet of water from a garden hose. The slugs, once on the ground, cannot return to the tree.

Peach tree and American borers. These borers attack the trunk and lower limbs and can be detected by the presence of gum and sawdust, which collect at the wound opening and at the base of the tree. Some types of tree wrapping, especially plastic guards, tend to encourage borer problems. These should be removed each year in the spring and stored until growth ceases in the fall. Recent studies have shown that borer problems in old tree wounds can be reduced by sealing damaged areas with tree paint. This prevents new borer larvae from entering.

Other insects. Cherries are occasionally attacked by the eyespotted bud moth, fruit tree leafroller, green fruitworm, redbanded leafroller, and a variety of other pests. For identification and current pest-control recommendations, contact the county extension agent or the state agricultural extension service.

Fungal Diseases

Cherry leaf spot. This disease seems more prevalent in years when the spring and early summer are wet. The fungus overwinters in dead leaves on the ground. In the spring, spores are produced and transmitted by wind to the leaves. Initially, small purple spots appear on the upper surfaces of the leaves. These gradually increase in size and number until the centers fall out. The leaves at this stage have a shot-hole appearance, and before maturity they turn yellow and prematurely drop. The fungus causes a gradual weakening of the tree, and in time death may result. For control, a repeated fungicide spray program is essential. For details, follow local recommended spray programs. In addition, follow a good orchard sanitation program by raking and destroying fallen leaves.

Black knot. This fungal disease attacks a number of *Prunus* species including wild and cultivated plums and cherries. Initially, the fungus shows up on new or one-year growth as small, light brown knots on one side of the twigs. About a year later, the knots swell, turn light green, and develop a velvety texture. By the end of the growing season, the knots turn black and have increased in both length and width. This cycle continues, and in subsequent years their growth increases. Often two or more infected areas may fuse.

Dormant pruning of infected areas is essential on young shoots. Prune to 4 to 6 inches below the infected area into healthy wood. On larger limbs and branches, the infected parts can sometimes be dissected out. In these cases, the cut should be made well into healthy tissue. Since wild cherries and plums can spread the disease, infected trees growing in the vicinity should also be pruned during the dormant season. All parts removed in the pruning should be raked and destroyed. As with cherry leaf spot, a repeated fungicide spray program may be necessary for protection against additional infection.

Brown rot. Occasionally, cherry fruits are damaged by a fungal disease called brown rot. Brown spots form initially on the fruit, which gradually enlarge and become covered with masses of brown or gray spores. This disease is more prevalent in plums, and additional details and control measures are discussed in that chapter.

Perennial canker. Two species of fungi belonging to the genus *Valsa* cause cankers on cherry, apricot, plum, and chokecherry. The cankers start small and gradually enlarge over the year so that affected branches are completely girdled. Infected areas may secrete gum (gummosis), but this can also occur when borers are present or when the tree has been wounded. Canker-affected areas should be pruned and destroyed. Sealing wounded areas with tree paint helps prevent infection by the fungal spores.

Verticillium wilt. This soil-borne fungus causes the leaves to be pale and often to drop prematurely. Symptoms usually show up at the bases of affected branches, and the disease progresses upward toward the tips of the branches. Trees affected for several seasons often lack vigor and appear stunted. There are no effective sprays for verticillium wilt. Removal of affected branches and good cultural practices are the only recommended treatment. Do not replant cherries in the same spot where verticillium wilt is suspected, and avoid areas where vegetables susceptible to the disease have been planted in the previous five years. This disease is common on apricot, tart cherry, plum, and more than 300 other species of cultivated plants.

Powdery mildew. This fungal disease affects apricots, pin cherry, chokecherry, plum, flowering almond, and black cherry. Affected leaves are covered with a whitish "bloom," and when infection is severe, the leaves may become curled and misshapen. In most areas this disease is a minor problem that rarely warrants control measures.

Bacterial Diseases

Bacterial spot. At least two bacterial species may cause leaf diseases on apricot, plum, chokecherry, flowering almond, and tart cherries. Commonly called shothole or bacterial spot, the disease first causes water-soaked spots on the undersides of the leaves. In time, the spots turn brown to black and fall out, causing the shothole effect. Seriously affected leaves may turn yellow and drop prematurely. Occasionally, the spots may also show up on the fruit. Good cultural practice is the best preventive measure for this disease.

Crown gall. This is another soil-borne disease caused by the bacterium *Agrobacterium tumefaciens.* Common symptoms include a large corky tumor or gall on the stem just above or below the soil line. In some cases, galls may also be present on the roots or higher on the stem. Nursery stock exhibiting these symptoms should not be planted since there is no effective control for the disease. To minimize possible infection, use care in cultivation or mowing so that the trunk area near the soil line is not injured.

X-disease and viruses. A number of virus diseases may affect cherries by causing leaf and fruit discoloration and deformation, lack of vigor, general decline, and death. Other than removal of diseased trees there are no effective control measures. Purchasing virus-free planting stock is the safest course to follow. X-disease, which is caused by a viruslike organism called a mycoplasma, has been a serious problem in Michigan cherry orchards and in some other areas of the Upper Midwest. Symptoms range from sudden collapse of the foliage to a general decline over several years. When individual branches are affected, growers remove these to prevent spread of the disease. Apparently both X-disease and some of the virus diseases can be transmitted from chokecherries to the tart cherry. Where practical, cherries should not be planted within 500 feet of chokecherries.

Harvesting

Care must be exercised in picking cherries since it is relatively easy to damage the fruit spur, which will form next year's crop. Taste is the best guide for determining when to harvest the crop.

If the fruit is to be used right away, it is probably best to pick only the fruit, leaving the stem attached to the tree. When cherries are to be sold on the local fresh-fruit market or shipped to a distant location, the stems should be attached to the fruit.

To maintain fruit quality and color, cherries should be processed as soon as possible after harvest. Commercial processing plants usually require that growers deliver the crop no more than six to nine hours after harvest. In commercial orchards, immediately after harvest, cherries are placed in water-cooled tanks maintained at about 50 to 54° F.

Sand Cherries

In areas where cold hardiness and drought are problems, the native western sand cherry, *P. besseyi*, is sometimes grown for ornament, windbreaks, hedges, and fruit. In its growth habit, the plant is a spreading shrub reaching a height of 4 to 4½ feet. The small, purplish black fruits rarely exceed ¾ inch in diameter, and they are most frequently used for jelly and jams, and in combination with apples for making pies.

Named cultivars such as 'Black Beauty', 'Sioux', and 'Brooks' are propagated vegetatively, and all the named selections are self-sterile. Thus, two or more cultivars should be planted for cross-pollination. The species

Nanking cherry, Prunus tomentosa.

can also be grown from seed and is most frequently offered by nurseries simply as "Hansen bush cherry," a name that unfortunately is also used for the Nanking cherry, *P. tomentosa*.

The seed-grown selections are quite variable and also may be partially self-sterile, thus two or preferably several plants should be purchased to ensure effective cross-fertilization. Sand cherries are hardy and can be grown throughout the Upper Midwest. Because of the minor differences among the cultivars, no attempt has been made to identify distinguishing characteristics.

Bareroot plants, 18 to 24 inches, are economical and large enough for good growth without special care. Plants should be spaced 6 feet apart in rows 6 feet apart. At planting time (early spring), prune the plants back one-half; after that, little additional pruning is required. Sand cherries grow best on well-drained soil in full sun.

Nanking Cherries

Another dwarf species is the Nanking, Chinese bush, or Hansen bush cherry, *P. tomentosa*. This Asian native is a spreading shrub reaching 5 to 7 feet tall. The most productive stems are two to four years old. Older, nonproductive stems should be cut back to the ground each year. The bright red fruit is small

Table 9. Cherry-plum cultivars

Cultivar	Place and year of introduction	Probable parentage	Color and size of fruit	Other characteristics
Compass	Minnesota, early 1900s	*Prunus besseyi* *P. hortulana*	Small, medium	Good pollenizer
Deep Purple	Minnesota, 1965	*P. besseyi* x *P. salicinia*	Dark purple, large	Used mostly for processing
Dura	Canada, 1940	Open-pollinated seedling of Sapa	Medium, purple	Less clingstone than Sapa
Hiawatha	N. Dakota, 1957	Open-pollinated seedling of Sapa	Fairly large, mottled purple	Fruit superior to Sapa
Oka	S. Dakota, 1924	Open-pollinated seedling of Champa	Small, purplish red	Resembles Compass
Opata	S. Dakota, 1911	Sand cherry x *P. munsoniana* x *P. salicinia*	Medium, purple	Fair for eating, good for cooking
Red Diamond	Minnesota, 1979*	Unknown	Medium to large, reddish purple	Hardy, disease resistant, good multiple use
Sacagawea	N. Dakota, 1957	Open-pollinated seedling of Sapa	Large, mottled purple	Very hardy, makes excellent jam
Sapa	S. Dakota, 1908	Sandcherry x *P. salicinia*	Medium, dull reddish purple	Multiple use for fruit
Sapalta	Canada, 1941	Open-pollinated seedling of Sapa	Medium, dull reddish purple	Sweeter and less clingstone than Sapa

*LeRoy Moling of Fergus Falls, Minn., who developed 'Red Diamond', recommends 'Oka' as a pollenizer.

(½ inch in diameter) and is somewhat intermediate in flavor between the sweet and tart cherries. The quality is good for fresh eating, sauce, pies, or jelly.

From the species, the cultivar 'Drilea' was selected and released by the Canadian Morden Research Station in 1938. In 1948, the University of Minnesota released the cultivar 'Orient'. Many Midwestern nurseries also offer the species simply as "Nanking bush cherries." These latter selections are usually grown from seed, and though they may produce a satisfactory plant,

Cherry plums like this 'Red Diamond' cultivar are frequently used in areas where sour cherries are difficult to grow.

the named cultivars generally give the best results. These plants may be grown throughout the five-state area.

Nanking cherries, like the sand cherries, may be self-sterile; thus, several selections should be planted to ensure cross-pollination and fruit set. Bareroot nursery stock, 12 to 18 inches tall, is preferred. The plants should be spaced 8 feet apart in rows 6 feet apart. Each plant should yield two to four quarts of fruit.

Cherry Plums

This remaining group is a hybrid complex involving the sand cherry, *P. besseyi,* and some of the plums or tree cherries or both (see Table 9). These cherry-plum hybrids are small trees or large shrubs, and they are frequently used in areas where sour cherries are difficult to grow. The fruit is cherry-size, about 1 inch in diameter, and is considered excellent for juice, canning, jams, and preserves.

Cherry plums are commonly trained as spreading shrubs. At planting time, very closely spaced branches that are crowded or rub should be eliminated. Heading back of the remaining branches will encourage new growth

Fruit zones—
cherry-plum hybrids
(pollenizer required)

Cultivar	Iowa			Minn.				S. Dak.				N. Dak.			Wis.			
	4b	5a	5b	1	2	3	4	1	2	3	4	A	B	C	1	2	3	4
Compass*				X	X	X	X	X	X	X	X	X	X	X	X	X	X	X
Deep Purple				X	X	X	X					T	T	T	X	X	T	
Dura												X	X	X				
Hiawatha												T	T	T				
Oka*	X	X	X	T	T										T	T		
Opata				X	X	X	X	X	X	X	X	X	X	X	X	X	X	X
Red Diamond				T	T	T	T					T	T	T	X	X	T	T
Sacagawea												T	T	T				
Sapa	X	X	X	T	T			X	X	X	X	X	X	T	X	X	X	X
Sapalta				X	X	X	X	X	X	X	X	X	X	T	X	X	X	X

X = recommended for planting; T = recommended for trial; * = good pollenizer. See zone map on page 20.

and compensate for root loss. In general, about one-third of the wood should be removed at planting time.

These plants produce their best fruit during the first few years of growth; thus, excessive pruning in the early years will diminish the crop. As the plants mature, old nonproductive wood should be removed to stimulate new growth. Generally, the bearing life can be extended if one-quarter of the old wood is removed each year.

These plants are commonly spaced 15 feet apart in rows 15 feet apart. The time from planting to fruiting is two to four years, and during the most productive years, each plant should yield about one bushel of fruit. Plants $7/16$ to $9/16$ inch caliper or those 3 to 4 feet are preferred. Cherry plums are commonly budded on hardy *P. americana* rootstocks.

SELECTED REFERENCES

Alderman, W. H. 1926. *New Fruits Produced at the University of Minnesota Fruit Breeding Farm.* Minnesota Agr. Exper. Stat. Bull. 230.

Anonymous. 1966. *Cherry Leaf Spot.* Purdue University Coop. Ext. Ser. Pub. BP–3–7.

Anonymous. 1977. *Growing Cherries East of the Rocky Mountains.* USDA Farmer's Bulletin 2185.

Askew, R. G., L. J. Chaput, and E. N. Scholz. 1987. *Tree Fruit Culture for North Dakota.* North Dakota State University Coop. Ext. Ser. Cir. H–327.

Banta, E. S., F. S. Howlett, and R. G. Hill. 1977. *Pruning and Training Fruit Trees.* Iowa State University Coop. Ext. Ser. Pub. PM 780.

Brooks, R. M., and H. P. Olmo. 1972. *Register of New Fruit and Nut Varieties.* 2nd ed. Berkeley: University of California Press.

Bryant, L. R. 1940. Sour Cherry Rootstocks. *Proc. Amer. Soc. Hort. Sci.* 37: 322–23.

Carlson, R. F., and J. Hull, Jr. 1978. *Rootstocks for Fruit Trees.* Michigan State University Coop. Ext. Ser. Bull. E–851.

Caslick, J. W., and D. J. Decker. 1978. *Control of Wildlife Damage in Orchards and Vineyards.* Cornell University Inform. Bull. 146.

Coe, F. M. 1945. *Cherry Rootstocks.* Utah Agr. Exper. Stat. Bull. 319.

Cullinan, F. P. 1937. Improvement of Stone Fruits: Cherries. *USDA Yearbook of Agriculture* 1937: 724–37.

Fogle, Harold W. 1975. Cherries. In: *Advances in Fruit Breeding.* J. Janick and J. N. Moore (eds.). Lafayette, Ind.: Purdue University Press.

Hayden, R. A. 1977. *Growing Cherries in Indiana.* Purdue University Coop. Ext. Ser. Pub. HO–9.

Hedrick, U. P. 1915. *The Cherries of New York.* Geneva, N. Y., Agr. Exper. Stat.

Hedrick, U. P. 1922. *Cyclopedia of Hardy Fruits.* New York: Macmillan.

Hertz, L. B. 1977. *Pruning Fruit Trees.* University of Minnesota Ext. Ser. Folder 161.

Hertz, L. B. 1978. *Plum, Cherry and Apricot Varieties for Minnesota.* University of Minnesota Ext. Ser. Hort. Fact Sheet No. 43 (rev.).

Hertz, L. B. 1981. *Growing Stone Fruits.* University of Minnesota Agr. Ext. Hort. Fact Sheet No. 42.

Johnson, W. T., and H. H. Lyon. 1976. *Insects that Feed on Trees and Shrubs.* Ithaca, N. Y.: Cornell University Press.

Jones, A. L., and T. B. Sutton. 1984. *Diseases of Tree Fruits.* North Central Regional Ext. Pub. No. 45.

Judkins, W. P. 1940. Sites and Soil Management for Sour Cherries. *Ohio Farm Home Res.* 34: 167–69.

Kask, K. 1989. The Tomentosa Cherry, *Prunus tomentosa* Thunb. *Fruit Varieties Jour.* 43(2): 50–51.

Kesner, C. D., and J. E. Nugent. 1984. *Training and Pruning Young Cherry Trees.* Michigan State University Coop. Ext. Ser. Bull. E–1744.

Koval, C. F., and E. K. Wade. 1978. *Plum, Cherry and Peach Pest Control for Home Gardeners.* University of Wisconsin Coop. Ext. Ser. Pub. A–2130.

Lamey, A. H., and R. W. Stack. 1985. *Disease Control in Plums, Cherries and Other Stone Fruits.* North Dakota State University Coop. Ext. Ser. Pub. 689 (rev.).

Mahr, D. L., S. N. Jeffers, L. K. Binning, and E. J. Stang. 1986. *Apple and Cherry Pest Control.* University of Wisconsin Coop. Ext. Ser. Pub. A3314.

McGregor, S. E. 1976. *Insect Pollination of Cultivated Crop Plants.* USDA Agricultural Handbook No. 496.

Mitchell, A. E., and J. H. Leven. 1969. *Tart Cherries, Growing, Harvesting and Processing for Good Quality.* Michigan State University Coop. Ext. Ser. Bull. E–654.

Olden, E. J., and N. Nybom. 1968. On the Origin of *Prunus cerasus* L. *Hereditas* 59: 327–45.

Ourecky, D. K. 1977. *Minor Fruits in New York State.* New York State College of Agriculture and Life Sciences Inform. Bull. 11.

Perry, R. L. 1987. Cherry Rootstocks. In: *Rootstocks for Fruit Trees.* R. C. Rom and R. F. Carlson (eds.). New York: Wiley-Interscience.

Peterson, R., and D. Martin. 1976. *Fruit Cultivars for South Dakota.* South Dakota State University Coop. Ext. Ser. Pub. FS–398.

Price, H. C., and E. E. Little. 1903. *Cherries and Cherry Growing in Iowa.* Iowa State College Exper. Stat. Bull. No. 73.

Roberts, R. H. 1922. *Better Cherry Yields.* Wisconsin Agr. Exper. Stat. Bull. 344.

Shoemaker, J. S. 1928. *Cherry Pollination.* Ohio Agr. Exper. Stat. Bull. 422.

Snyder, L. C. 1980. *Trees and Shrubs for Northern Gardens.* Minneapolis: University of Minnesota Press.

Stang, E. J., and H. C. Harrison. 1981. *Home Fruit Cultivars for Southern Wisconsin.* University of Wisconsin Coop. Ext. Ser. Pub. A2582.

Taber, H. G., and C. Fear. 1986. *Fruit Cultivars for the Family.* Iowa State University Coop. Ext. Ser. Pub. PM–453.

Tarasenko, M. D. 1958. Change in Certain Characters of Cherry Caused by the Rootstock. *Agrobiologija* 5: 127–29.

Teskey, B. J. E., and J. S. Shoemaker. 1978. *Tree Fruit Production.* 3rd ed. Westport, Conn.: AVI Publishing.

Tukey, H. B. 1927. *Responses of the Sour Cherry to Fertilizers and to Pruning.* New York State Agr. Exper. Stat. Bull. 541.

Wade, E. K. 1974. *Plum (Prunus) and Cherry (Prunus) Disorder: Black Knot.* University of Wisconsin Coop. Ext. Ser. Fact Sheet A–2588.

6

Plums

Plums, like almonds, apricots, cherries, nectarines, and peaches, belong to the genus *Prunus*. Today, plums are widely grown throughout the world, but they were domesticated originally in three separate areas.

Domestication Centers

Europe

The most important European domesticate is *P. domestica*. This species has been cultivated in Europe for over 2,000 years, and Hedrick (1911) suggested it originated in the Caucasus Mountains near the Caspian Sea. Crane and Lawrence (1952) proposed that the species arose from hybridization of *P. cerasifera* and *P. spinosa* followed by the development of polyploidy or chromosome doubling. But more recently, Salesses (1977) has uncovered genetic evidence suggesting that more research is needed before the exact origin of *P. domestica* can be firmly established.

The major plum types that originated from this species include:

Prunes. In the United States this term is used loosely for any plum that can be dried with the pit intact. In Europe, prunes may be any number of large blue-purple freestone types (Okie, 1987).
Green Gage or Reine Claude. These plums are greenish yellow.
Lombard. The fruit is purplish red.
Yellow Egg. Both the skin and flesh are usually yellow.

The other European domesticate, *P. insititia*, is native to Europe or western Asia. Weinberger (1975) reported that pits of this plum have been found in ancient ruins, and thus this species is considered older than *P. domestica*. Popular types derived from the species include the Damson and Mirabelle plums.

Asia

The most important Asiatic species is *P. salicina*, native to China. According to Hedrick (1911), members of this species were brought to Japan 200 to 400 years ago and subsequently were distributed to other parts of the world as "Japanese plums." Luther Burbank imported *P. salicina* seedlings from Japan in 1884 and 1885 and bred them with several American species and the apricot plum, *P. simonii* from northern China (Weinberger, 1975).

North America

When the European settlers arrived and began to explore, they found a number of native plum species distributed throughout the New World. Most of these species were of inferior quality, and until the 19th century, plum culture was confined largely to species imported from Europe. One of the first attempts to improve native American species was initiated in 1860 by H. A. Terry of Crescent, Iowa. He used the selection method of cross-pollination to produce over 50 named cultivars (Cullinan, 1937). By 1915, over 600 cultivars using native American breeding stock had been developed (Wright, 1915). For the Upper Midwest, plum-breeding programs using native American and Japanese species to produce cold-hardy hybrids were initiated in Iowa, Minnesota, and South Dakota. More than 2,000 cultivars of plums have been grown in the United States, but as with the other fruits, the number of cultivars has steadily declined.

Today, plums are grown in practically every state, but about 90 percent of commercial production is in California. Other important plum-producing states include Oregon, Washington, Michigan, and Idaho. The total value of the 1988 plum and prune crop in the U.S. was $222,451,000 (*Noncitrus Fruits and Nuts*, January 1990).

Pollination and Fruit Set

All the European cultivars grown in the Upper Midwest are self-fruitful. In contrast, hybrid plums require a pollenizer, but the European cultivars cannot be used. Good pollenizers for hybrid plums are 'South Dakota', 'Toka', and 'Kaga'. The honeybee is the principal pollinator for all plums.

Rootstocks

Fruit trees are no hardier than their rootstocks, and this is certainly true for plums. Plums are grown on a number of rootstocks including *P. cerasifera* ('Myrobalan'), peach, apricot, cherry, almond, and a number of other *Prunus* species (Okie, 1987). For the Upper Midwest, where cold hardiness is of primary concern, the native *Prunus* species are the best choice for plum rootstocks. For example, *P. americana* (wild plum) is a very hardy and satisfactory rootstock for European, native, and hybrid plums. Trees advertised as dwarf are frequently budded on *Prunus* St. Julien rootstocks, but cold hardiness may be a problem in some areas.

Selection of Nursery Stock

Plants should be obtained from reliable, Upper Midwest nurseries to ensure that the scion is budded to a hardy native species.

The size of available plum stock is commonly listed as follows:

Height	*Caliper (diameter)*
4½ feet and up	$^{11}/_{16}$ and up
4 feet and up	$^{9}/_{16}$ to $^{11}/_{16}$
3 feet and up	$^{7}/_{16}$ to $^{9}/_{16}$
2 feet and up	$^{5}/_{16}$ to $^{7}/_{16}$

For plums, the $^{9}/_{16}$ to $^{11}/_{16}$-inch size is a good selection. These are usually two-year-old, branched trees. Larger sizes are rarely worth the additional cost, and smaller sizes may require special care. Bareroot stock is preferred over packaged or container-grown plants.

European Plums

Damson. There are several types of Damson plums, and all are regarded as tender. It is essential to select a cultivar adapted to local conditions. The most popular is 'Shropshire', which originated in England sometime in the 17th century. Damson plums are purplish black with golden yellow flesh. The fruit is juicy, tart, and excellent for processing.

Dietz. This plum of uncertain parentage was imported from Germany by August Dietz. It was later brought to the attention of C. Edwin Swenson of St. Peter, Minnesota, who developed the cultivar. Years ago it was popular in Minnesota, not only for its fruit but also for its use as a windbreak. Its popularity declined until about ten years ago when it was featured by one of the larger nurseries. The blue, medium-size fruit is good for fresh eating and canning. In Minnesota, a good crop is

'Mount Royal' is one of the best European-type blue plums for the Upper Midwest.

produced only about every four years because the plant has a tendency to bloom very early and is damaged by spring frost.

Green Gage ('Reine Claude'). According to Hedrick (1911), these were imported to France from Italy about 1500 by Queen Claudia, wife of Francis I. The name Reine Claude was given in her honor. This greenish yellow, medium-size fruit is clingstone, firm, juicy, sweet, and of excellent quality for multipurpose home use. Trees may have a tendency to overbear, and the fruit is susceptible to brown rot.

Italian (Italian Prune, 'Fellenburg', 'York State'). This is an old European cultivar, long a favorite for canning and drying. The medium-size fruit is purplish black with greenish yellow flesh that is freestone. These plums are apparently resistant to brown rot.

Lombard. Hedrick (1911) reported that this plum was grown from seed by Judge Platt of Whitesboro, New York. It was named by the Massachusetts Horticultural Society after a Mr. Lombard of Springfield, Massachusetts, who introduced it to that state. The plum is purple or reddish violet with yellow cling-type flesh and is considered good for canning.

Mount Royal. One of the hardiest of the European cultivars—and in many areas, including Minnesota and Wisconsin—'Mount Royal' is regarded

Fruit zones—
European plums
(no pollenizer required)

Cultivar	Iowa			Minn.				S. Dak.				N. Dak.			Wis.			
	4b	5a	5b	1	2	3	4	1	2	3	4	A	B	C	1	2	3	4
Damson		X	X															
Dietz								T	X	X								
Green Gage			X												X	X	T	
Italian															X	T	T	T
Lombard		X	X												X	T		
Mount Royal	X	X	X	X	X			X	T						X	X	T	T
Stanley	X	X	X	X	X			T	T						X	X	T	

X = recommended for planting; T = recommended for trial.
See zone map on page 20.

as the best blue cultivar. The less-than-medium-size fruit is bluish black with freestone, tender, juicy flesh. This plum has very good qualities for dessert or culinary use and is excellent frozen.

Stanley. This 'Agen' x 'Grand Duke' hybrid was introduced in 1926 by Richard Wellington at Geneva, New York. The cultivar is regarded as slightly less hardy than 'Mount Royal'. The medium-size, dark blue fruit has juicy yellow flesh that is semifreestone. It is a leading cultivar in Michigan and is considered good for fresh eating, sauce, and other culinary purposes. The trees may have a tendency to overbear and require thinning.

Hardy Native and Hybrid Plums

Alderman. This 'Burbank' x 'Older' cross was introduced in 1986 at Excelsior, Minnesota. It was named in honor of W. H. Alderman, former University of Minnesota professor who made the original cross in 1937. The large fruit is burgundy red with golden yellow, sweet, juicy clingstone flesh. The tree is very attractive and is valued as an ornamental. It is very precocious, bearing fruit as early as one year after planting. 'Alderman' is a hardy plum, and it fruited consistently every year at Excelsior, Minnesota, from 1972 to 1985.

Chinook. W. P. Baird introduced this open-pollinated seedling of *P. nigra*

'Ojibwa' at Mandan, North Dakota, in 1957. For a native plum, the fruit is quite large, averaging about 20 per pound. The skin is bright red with juicy, sweet flesh. The tree is a heavy annual bearer, and in North Dakota the fruit usually ripens in late August. 'Chinook' may be difficult to locate.

Ember. This 'Shiro' x 'South Dakota 33' cross was introduced in 1936 at Excelsior, Minnesota. The medium to large fruit has yellow skin with a red blush. The yellow flesh is sweet and clingstone. This plum is excellent for fresh eating and has good culinary qualities. The tree is only moderately productive, and in Minnesota the fruit ripens in early September.

Fiebing ('Fiebing Prize', 'Phoebe'). Charles Haralson introduced this 'Wickson' x 'Kaga' cross at Deephaven, Minnesota, in 1929. The large fruit has dark red skin with yellow, sweet flesh and is considered to be of very good quality. The tree is vigorous and productive, and its fruit ripens in early September. Over the years this cultivar has waned in popularity.

Gracious. This open-pollinated seedling of 'Emerald' was introduced by W. P. Baird in 1957 at Mandan, North Dakota. The skin is mottled red, and the flesh is yellow, sweet, juicy, and freestone. The plum was rated good in cooking tests. This cultivar was originally recommended for planting in most areas of the northern Great Plains, but it may be difficult to locate.

Hanska. N. E. Hansen introduced this native 'plum' x 'chinese apricot' cross from Brookings, South Dakota, in 1908. *Hanska* is the Sioux Indian word for tall. The fruit is medium size and bright red. The flesh is reddish, firm, and semi-freestone.

Kaga. This plum originated from the same pedigree as 'Hanska' and was introduced by N. E. Hansen at Brookings, South Dakota, in 1909. *Kaga* is the Sioux Indian term for "pitch a tent." The fruit is very similar to 'Hanska'.

LaCrescent ('Golden LaCrescent', 'Golden Minnesota'). Introduced at Excelsior, Minnesota, in 1923, this plum is a cross of 'Shiro' *(P. americana* x *P. salicina)* x 'Howard yellow' *(P. americana)*. The fruit is small to medium, and the skin is yellow, sometimes with a light blush. The flesh is yellow, sweet, juicy, freestone, and somewhat suggestive of apricots. The fruit quality is excellent for fresh eating, good for jam, and fair to good for jelly. The tree is vigorous but only moderately productive.

Monitor. W. H. Alderman introduced this 'Burbank' x *P. americana* hybrid at Excelsior, Minnesota, in 1920. The skin is bronze red and the yellow flesh is sweet, juicy, and clingstone. The medium–size fruit is considered multipurpose but may have a tendency to crack in rainy weather. This cultivar is no longer as popular as it once was.

Pembina. Introduced about 1923 from Brookings, South Dakota, this plum was selected from a cross of 'Red June' *(P. salicina)* x *P. nigra.* The large fruit has red skin with yellow, juicy, sweet flesh. It is good quality for fresh use but only fair for canning. In South Dakota, the fruit ripens in late August.

Pipestone. This 'Burbank' x *(P. salicina* x 'Wolf') cross, released in 1942, is another University of Minnesota introduction. The large red fruit has yellow flesh that is sweet, juicy, and clingstone. The fruit is very good for fresh use, jam, and jelly. The tree is productive and produces ripe fruit in midseason.

Premier. Walter D. Krause of Merced, California, introduced this 'Burmosa' x 'Santa Rosa' Japanese-type plum in 1963. The tender cultivar has large red fruit with amber clingstone flesh. It may be somewhat self-fruitful, but another cultivar should be planted for cross-pollination.

Redcoat. Excelsior, Minnesota, is the home of this 'Burbank' x 'Wolf' hybrid introduced in 1942. The fruit has red skin, and the flesh is yellow, somewhat juicy, mildly subacid, and freestone. It is used for canning and other culinary purposes. This cultivar is not as popular as it used to be.

Redglow. This plum is a 'Burbank' *(P. salicina)* x 'Jewell' *(P. munsoniana)* hybrid introduced in 1949 at Excelsior, Minnesota. The large red fruit has orange, juicy, sweet, clingstone flesh. The quality is good for fresh use, jelly, and jam. When cooked, the fruit becomes acidic, owing to its medium-astringent skin.

South Dakota. N. E. Hansen introduced this American-Japanese hybrid of unknown parentage at Brookings, South Dakota, in 1949. The medium-size fruit has red-over-yellow skin. The flesh is tender, juicy, and freestone. The overall quality is not outstanding. It is good for fresh eating and jelly but only fair for jam. The tree is hardy and is an excellent pollenizer.

Superior. Introduced at Excelsior, Minnesota, in 1933, this plum originated from a cross of 'Burbank' x 'Kaga' *(P. simonii).* The fruit is large with dark red, russet-dotted skin. The flesh is yellow, juicy, sweet, and clingstone. The quality is good for fresh eating, jelly, and jam. This tree lacks hardiness in more northerly areas, and in favorable areas it has a tendency to overbear.

Tecumseh. N. E. Hansen introduced this 'Shiro' x 'Surprise' hybrid at Brookings, South Dakota, in about 1923. The medium-size fruit has bright red skin with yellow, subacid, juicy flesh. The fruit quality is rated good, and it ripens in South Dakota in mid-August.

Toka. This plum originated from the same pedigree as 'Kaga' and 'Hanska' and was introduced at Brookings, South Dakota, by N. E. Hansen in

'Waneta' plum in bloom.

1911. *Toka* is the Sioux Indian word for adversary. This cultivar is very similar to 'Kaga', and both are regarded as good pollenizers.

Underwood. This 'Shiro' x 'Wyant' *(P. americana)* hybrid was introduced from Excelsior, Minnesota, in 1921. The flesh of this medium–large, red fruit is golden yellow, juicy, sweet, and clingstone. This plum ripens very early and is good quality for fresh use and jam.

Waneta. N. E. Hansen introduced this 'Terry' *(P. americana)* x 'apple plum' (large Japanese type) cross from Brookings, South Dakota, in 1912. According to Hansen, Waneta was a "Yankonais" boy from the wilds of the James River who won fame in the war of 1812. This is a large (2 inches in diameter) red plum with yellow flesh. It is sweet, juicy, and very good quality.

Spacing and Yield

For the European and hybrid plum cultivars, a spacing of 20 feet between rows and 20 feet between plants in the row gives very satisfactory results. The time from planting to fruiting is usually three to five years, and each tree should yield one to two bushels of fruit.

**Fruit zones—
hardy native and hybrid plums
(pollenizer required)**

Cultivar	Iowa			Minn.				S. Dak.				N. Dak.			Wis.			
	4b	5a	5b	1	2	3	4	1	2	3	4	A	B	C	1	2	3	4
Alderman	X	X	X	X	X	T		X	X	T		T	T	T	X	X	T	T
Chinook*												T	T	T				
Ember															X	X		
Fiebing												T	T	T				
Gracious												T	T	T				
Hanska								X	X	X	T							
Kaga*								X	X	X	T	X	X	X	X	X		
LaCrescent				X	X	X		X	X	X		X	X	X	X	X	T	
Monitor	X	X	X															
Pembina												X	X	X				
Pipestone				X	X	X		X	X	T		X	T	T	X	X	T	T
Premier		X	X															
Redcoat		X	X					X	X	T		X	X	X	X	X	T	T
Redglow				X	X	X									X	X	T	
S. Dakota*				X	X	X	X	X	X	X	X	X	X	X	X	X		
Superior	X	X	X	X	X	X		X	X			T			X	X	X	X
Tecumseh								X	X	X	X	X	X	X				
Toka*	X	X	X	X	X	X	X	X	X	X	T	X	X	X	X	X	X	X
Underwood		X	X	X	X	X	X	X	X	X	X	X	X	X	X	X	X	X
Waneta	X	X	X					X	X	T		X	X	X				

X = recommended for planting; T = recommended for trial; * = good pollenizer.
See zone map on page 20.

Location of the Planting Site

Plums require full sun, and they will grow in a variety of soil types, but they will not survive for long in heavy soils where there is poor drainage. The best soils for most cultivars are sandy or gravelly loams.

When choosing a planting site, keep frost protection in mind. Avoid low-lying areas and tops of hills or knolls where cold and wind injury is likely to occur. The best sites are located in close proximity to large bodies of water or on slopes where good air movement is possible. A northern or north-eastern slope may help retard bloom until danger of frost is past.

How and When to Plant

Planting plums is advised only in spring. Planting should be early, as soon as the soil can be worked. When planting, the trees should be set slightly deeper than originally growing in the nursery. The general method of planting is the same as that described for the other fruit trees.

Pruning at Planting Time

European and hybrid plums are commonly trained using the modified leader method. If smaller, unbranched trees are selected, cut off the whip to a height of 30 inches above the ground.

If larger sizes are selected (which is recommended), the trees are usually branched. In these trees, two to three strong scaffolds with wide crotch angles should be selected. Other branches and all limbs lower than 2 feet above the soil surface should be removed. The central leader is maintained, and the selected scaffolds should be spaced a minimum of 5 inches apart. The tips of the scaffold branches should be shortened if they threaten to outgrow the leader. If the leader is too weak and spindly, it too may be shortened if it is more than 12 inches longer than the tips of the closest lateral.

Subsequent Pruning

In European and hybrid plums, pruning is directed toward maintaining a central leader with six to eight evenly spaced scaffolds at maturity. Pruning, as with the other fruits, should be done during the dormant season, preferably in very early spring.

After three years with proper pruning, the main structural framework consisting of six to eight evenly spaced scaffolds can usually be established. Scaffolds with wide angles should be spaced 5 to 10 inches apart. Other pruning activities should be confined to thinning excessive growth or occasional heading back of the tips of scaffolds that threaten the leader. Avoid severe pruning in these cultivars.

Fertilization

No fertilizer is recommended at planting time. In subsequent years the amount of nutrients to apply depends on the fertility of the soil. Trees exhibiting less than 6 inches of new growth each year may require additional nutrients, which should be applied in the very early spring.

In very young trees, well-rotted manure spread evenly at depths of 2 to 4 inches may be used. For trees of bearing age, apply two to four bushels of well-rotted manure for each plant.

When inorganic fertilizers such as 10–10–10 are selected, the amount to use depends on the age and size of the tree. Generally ½ pound for each year of tree age is sufficient, with a maximum of 6 pounds per plant. The nutrients should be spread in a circle extending one foot from the trunk to the dripline.

Thinning of Fruit

Both European and hybrid plums may require fruit thinning. Thinning during over-productive years may reduce the chances of limb breakage and improve fruit quality. In addition, since crowded fruits are more subject to certain fungal diseases, thinning may be viewed as a way to prevent disease. And, cultivars with a tendency to produce biennially may, with proper thinning, bear fruit on an annual basis.

The best time for hand thinning is just after the last "June drop." This is the time period shortly after bloom when a number of flowers that did not get pollenized, or otherwise have defective fruit, start to fall from the tree. This abscission or fruit drop continues into June, then terminates. When the June drop is completed, excess fruit can be removed by hand. Thinning should be directed toward removing crowded fruits that are likely to touch each other when they mature. After thinning, remaining fruits should be spaced 1 to 3 inches apart.

Additional Cultural Practices

As with the other fruit cultivars, plums thrive when mulched. The mulch should be 6 to 8 inches deep and extend in a circle from the trunk to the dripline. This mulch is particularly beneficial during the first five years of growth while the root system is being established. In subsequent years, the mulch can gradually be replaced with sod or lawn grass.

European and hybrid plums should be given winter protection from potential girdling damage by rabbits and mice. The trunks of European and hybrid plums should be wrapped, painted with white latex, or protected by other methods against winter temperature fluctuations.

Pests and Diseases

Many of the pests and diseases that affect plums also cause problems in other fruits. Cherries, in particular, suffer from many of the same pests and

Black knot, a fungal disease, on a species of wild plum.

diseases—for additional information, refer to that chapter. The most frequent insect pests are plum curculio, peach borers, and American borers. The most common fungal diseases are brown rot and black knot. Plums are occasionally damaged by mites, scale insects, aphids, green fruitworm, and tarnished plant bug and plum gouger.

An additional disease that has not been discussed is "plum pockets," caused by fungal species belonging to the genus *Taphrina.* These fungi produce hollowed-out pockets on the fruit of wild plum, plum hybrids, sand cherry, Nanking cherry, wild black cherry, and chokecherry (Lamey and Stock, 1985). In addition to causing serious fruit damage, the fungi may also cause enlarged and deformed shoots and curled leaves on several *Prunus* species. Lime sulfur applied just before bud break effectively prevents infection.

Many pest and disease problems can be minimized by following a good management and sanitation schedule. For example, the brown-rot fungus survives the winter in diseased fruit (mummies) on the tree and on the ground, and in twig cankers. Mummies should be removed in the fall and destroyed. All diseased limbs and twigs should be pruned and destroyed during the late winter or early spring pruning season.

In addition, many insect and disease pests may come from nearby wild plums and cherries. Where practical, these plants should be removed.

Caution with Herbicides

All fruit cultivars can be damaged with careless use of herbicides, and plums are particularly sensitive. Use extreme caution when applying broadleaf weed killers such as 2,4-D to the home lawn to prevent accidental drift to nearby plum trees.

Harvesting and Storing

Most plum cultivars do not ripen evenly, so it may be necessary to pick the fruit in stages. The European cultivars are especially good for drying, and instructions for drying fruit are available from most county agents.

Plums can rarely be stored longer than three to four weeks. For some cultivars the storage life is considerably less. A storage temperature of 31 to 32° F. and a relative humidity of 80 to 90 percent is best, but since few growers can provide these exacting conditions, the home refrigerator is commonly used for storage. Here, many of the cultivars will remain in good condition for one to two weeks if they are stored in polyethylene bags without holes to reduce moisture loss.

SELECTED REFERENCES

Alderman, W. H., and E. Angelo. 1933. Self and Cross Sterility in Plum Hybrids. *Proc. Amer. Soc. Hort. Sci.* 29: 118–21.

Alderman, W. H., and T. S. Weir. 1951. *Pollination Studies with Stone Fruits.* Minnesota Agr. Exper. Stat. Tech. Bull. 198.

Anderson, E. T., and T. S. Weir. 1967. *Prunus Hybrids, Selections and Cultivars at the University of Minnesota Fruit Breeding Farm.* Minnesota Agr. Exper. Stat. Tech. Bull. 252.

Anonymous. 1977. *Black-Knot of Plums.* Purdue University Coop. Ext. Ser. Pub. BP–3–4.

Askew, R. G., L. J. Chaput, and E. N. Scholz. 1987. *Tree Fruit Culture for North Dakota.* North Dakota State University Coop. Ext. Ser. Cir. H–327.

Brooks, R. M., and H. P. Olmo. 1972. *Register of New Fruit and Nut Varieties.* 2nd ed. Berkeley: University of California Press.

Brown, A. G. 1951. Factors Affecting Fruit Production in Plums. *Fruit Yearbook* 1950(4): 12–18.

Buchanan, R. E. 1903. Contribution to our Knowledge of the Development of *Prunus americana. Proc. Iowa Academy Sciences* 77–93.

Carlson, R. F., and J. W. Hull, Jr. 1978. *Rootstocks for Fruit Trees.* Michigan State University Coop. Ext. Ser. Bull. E–851.

Craig, J. 1900. *Observations and Suggestions on the Root Killing of Trees.* Iowa Agr. Exper. Stat. Bull. 44: 179–213.

Crane, M. B., and W. J. C. Lawrence. 1952. *The Genetics of Garden Plants.* 4th ed. London: Macmillan.

Cullinan, F. P. 1937. Improvement of Stone Fruits. *USDA Yearbook of Agriculture* 1937: 703–23.

Domoto, P. A. 1987. *Pruning and Training Fruit Trees.* Iowa State University Coop. Ext. Ser. Pub. PM780.

Dorsey, M. J., and J. Bushnell. 1925. *Plum Investigations II. The Inheritance of Hardiness.* Minnesota Agr. Exper. Stat. Tech. Bull. 32.

Hedrick, U. P. 1911. *The Plums of New York.* Geneva, N.Y., Agr. Exper. Stat. Report 1910.

Hertz, L. B. 1977. *Pruning Fruit Trees.* University of Minnesota Ext. Ser. Pub. 161.

Hertz, L. B. 1978. *Plum, Cherry, and Apricot Varieties for Minnesota.* University of Minnesota Ext. Ser. Hort. Fact Sheet 43.

Hertz, L. B. 1981. *Growing Stone Fruits.* University of Minnesota Ext. Ser. Hort. Fact Sheet 42.

Hertz, L. B. 1987. *Fruit for the Home.* University of Minnesota Ext. Ser. Pub. AG–13U–0470.

Kinman, C. F. 1943. *Plum and Prune Growing in the Pacific States.* USDA Farmer's Bulletin 1372.

Koval, C. F., and E. K. Wade. 1978. *Plum, Cherry and Peach Pest Control for Home Gardeners.* University of Wisconsin Coop. Ext. Ser. Pub. A–2130.

Lamey, A. H., and R. W. Stack. 1985. *Disease Control in Plums, Cherries and Other Stone Fruits.* North Dakota State University Coop. Ext. Ser. Pub. 689 (rev.).

Layne, R. E. C., and W. B. Sherman. 1986. Interspecific Hybridization of *Prunus. HortScience* 21(1): 48–51.

Luby, J. J., W. H. Alderman, S. T. Munson, D. K. Wildung, W. H. Gray, and E. E. Hoover. 1980. Alderman Plum. *HortScience* 21(2): 327–28.

McGregor, S. E. 1976. *Insect Pollination of Cultivated Crop Plants.* USDA Agricultural Handbook No. 496.

Okie, William R. 1987. Plum Rootstocks. In: *Rootstocks for Fruit Crops.* R. C. Rom and R. F. Carlson (eds.). New York: Wiley-Interscience.

Peterson, R., and D. Martin. 1976. *Fruit Cultivars for South Dakota.* South Dakota State University Coop. Ext. Ser. Pub. FS–398.

Salesses, G. 1977. Research About the Origin of Two *Prunus* Rootstocks, Natural Interspecific Hybrids: An Illustration of a Cytological Study Carried Out in Order to Create New *Prunus* Rootstocks (in French). *Ann. Amel. Plantes* 27: 235–43.

Stang, E. J., D. C. Ferree, and F. O. Hartman. 1978. *Fruit Tree Propagation.* Ohio State University Coop. Ext. Ser. Bull. 481.

Stang, E. J., and G. C. Klingbeil. 1987. *Plums for Wisconsin.* University of Wisconsin Coop. Ext. Ser. Fact Sheet A–2581.

Taber, H. G., and C. Fear. 1986. *Fruit Cultivars for the Family.* Iowa State University Coop. Ext. Ser. Pub. PM 453.

Teskey, B. J. E., and J. S. Shoemaker. 1978. *Tree Fruit Production.* 3rd ed. Westport, Conn.: AVI Publishing.

Wade, E. K. 1974. *Plum (Prunus) and Cherry (Prunus) Disorder: Black Knot.* University of Wisconsin Coop. Ext. Ser. Fact Sheet A–2588.

Weinberger, J. H. 1975. Plums. In: *Advances in Fruit Breeding.* J. Janick and J. N. Moore (eds.). Lafayette, Ind.: Purdue University Press.

Winklepleck, R. L., and J. A. McClintock. 1939. The Relative Cold Resistance of Some Species of *Prunus* Used as Stocks. *Proc. Amer. Soc. Hort. Sci.* 37: 324–26.

Wright, R. C. 1963. *Commercial Storage of Fruits, Vegetables and Nursery Stocks.* USDA Agricultural Handbook 66.

Wright, W. F. 1915. *The Varieties of Plums Derived from Native American Species.* USDA Bulletin 172.

Chapter

7

Apricots

Worldwide, all commercially important apricot cultivars belong to *Prunus armeniaca*, a species thought to be indigenous to the mountains of northeast China. From its ancestral home, where it has been cultivated for over 3,000 years, the species spread slowly through Asia, finally reaching Armenia. Bailey and Hough (1975) have suggested that the species name, *armeniaca*, was derived from the Armenian merchants who first introduced the plant to Europe. Cross-Raynaud and Audergon (1987) place the date of introduction to Italy and Greece at about 70–60 B.C. They believe additional seedlings were imported from Iran through North Africa and Spain by Arabs in the seventh century A.D.

P. *armeniaca* is a variable species, and currently three common varieties are recognized. Variety *armeniaca* is the source of all the commercially important cultivars. The other two varieties, *sibirica* and *mandshurica*, are the principal apricots suitable for most areas of the Upper Midwest. The Russian apricot, variety *sibirica*, has been used as a source for cold-hardy breeding stock, but its fruit is small and inedible. Variety *mandshurica*, also called the Manchurian apricot, "makes a fine ornamental, and its fruits make excellent preserves" (Snyder, 1980). This latter variety has been selected and crossed with the species to produce the cold-hardy cultivars suitable for the five-state area.

According to Gourley and Howlett (1941), the first apricots imported to this country were brought to California from Spain by the early Mission Fathers in the 18th century. Today, California is still the leading producer with nearly 95 percent of U.S. production. The other major apricot-producing states are Washington and Utah. The total value of the U.S. apricot crop in 1989 was $38,349,000 (*Noncitrus Fruits and Nuts*, January 1990).

Rootstocks

Seedlings of 'Myrobalan' *(P. cerasifera),* cherry plum, peach, 'Greengage' plum, and of domestic cultivars have been commonly used as rootstocks for apricots. For the Upper Midwest, seedlings of the cold-hardy Manchurian apricot are preferred. Trees advertised as dwarf should be budded on *P. besseyi* rootstocks.

Pollination

The literature on pollination requirements for apricots is meager, but McGregor (1976), after a thorough review, concluded "some cultivars must be cross pollinated and other cultivars are benefited by cross pollination." To be safe, the general recommendation here is to plant two or more seedlings or different-named cultivars to ensure cross-fertilization. As with all the other fruits, honeybees are the chief pollinators.

Apricot Cultivars

Goldcot. This open-pollinated seedling of 'Perfection' was introduced from South Haven, Michigan, in 1967. The fruit is golden and medium to large. During favorable years, thinning of fruit may be necessary to produce larger, better-quality fruit.

Manchu. N. E. Hansen introduced this cultivar in 1936 at Brookings, South Dakota, from seed obtained from northern Manchuria. The fruit quality is rated fair to poor.

Mantoy. W. P. Baird introduced this Manchurian seedling in 1957 at Mandan, North Dakota. The flesh is golden yellow, freestone, and the size is large (about 22 fruits per pound). At Mandan, fruit buds are sometimes winter injured, and late-spring frosts frequently injure flowers. This cultivar may be difficult to locate.

Moorpark. This is an old, English cultivar that is thought to have been introduced from France to England, but the exact date of introduction is uncertain. The large fruit has a red blush and is freestone; the flesh is yellow, mild, and sweet.

Moongold. This cultivar and 'Sungold' are sister siblings introduced in 1961 from 'Superb' x 'Manchu' crosses made by A. N. Wilcox, T. S. Weir, and S. Trantanella at Excelsior, Minnesota. The skin is orange, and the flesh is orange yellow, sweet, and freestone. Fruit quality is good, but it tends to ripen unevenly, and there may be some splitting and premature fruit drop. 'Moongold' and 'Sungold' are self-unfruitful.

Scout. This cultivar was introduced in 1937 at Morden, Manitoba, from seed

Row of 'Sungold' and 'Moongold' apricots.

sent from Manchuria. The skin is bronzy golden and the flesh is deep yellow and freestone. The dessert quality of the fruit is rated fair to good and it is generally regarded as good for canning and jam.

Sungold (see 'Moongold'). The fruit skin is golden orange, and the flesh is clear orange. In Minnesota the very good fruit is ready for harvest in early August, somewhat after 'Moongold'. 'Sungold' and 'Moongold' are the two most popular apricot cultivars grown in most areas of the Upper Midwest.

Selecting Nursery Stock

Two-year-old, branched trees are preferred over one-year whips. Caliper sizes from $9/16$ to $11/16$ and those ranging in height from 4 to 4½ feet are good choices. Trees under 3 feet and $9/16$-inch stem diameter require special care.

When choosing plants, select those in which the buds are still dormant. Bareroot stock is preferred, but plants with enlarged buds often become weakened before the root system and the energy-producing mechanism are fully operational. Purchasing northern stock budded on hardy Manchurian rootstocks is advised.

**Fruit zones—
apricots**

Cultivar	Iowa			Minn.				S. Dak.				N. Dak.			Wis.			
	4b	5a	5b	1	2	3	4	1	2	3	4	A	B	C	1	2	3	4
Goldcot															X	X		
Manchu									X	X								
Mantoy												T	T	T				
Moorpark		T	T															
Moongold	T	T	T	X	X			X	X			T	T	T	X	X		
Scout				T	T							T	T	T	T	T		T
Sungold	T	T	T	X	X			X	X			T	T	T	X	X		

X = recommended for planting; T = recommended for trial. * = In addition to the named cultivars, many nurseries also offer the Manchurian apricot. These plants are almost always grown from seed and are quite variable. The seedlings are hardy in all zones but the fruit, when produced, is a surprise. It may be sweet and juicy or inedible. See zone map on page 20.

Location of the Planting Site

Apricots are often erroneously considered drought-resistant species, but in many respects they are more sensitive to soil-moisture conditions than the other tree fruits. They will tolerate very low atmospheric humidity and are often grown in dry areas, but they have a shallow root system. Apricots grown on very sandy soils frequently need supplemental irrigation. Likewise, apricots do very poorly on heavy soils where water stands or is poorly drained. Deep, fertile, well-drained soils are best.

Because apricots bloom so early, frost damage is likely to be the major factor limiting fruit production. Elevated, frost-free sites with good movement of air are preferred. Sites in close proximity to large bodies of water are ideal. A northern exposure is also preferred since in these locations blooming may be delayed. Apricots need full sun to develop properly. Avoid shaded areas next to buildings, trees, and windbreaks.

Spacing and Yield

If space is a premium, apricots can be planted as close as 14 feet apart in the row and 18 feet between rows. For more efficient management and harvesting, the trees are more commonly spaced 20 to 25 feet in each direction. The plants will start to bear fruit two to four years after planting, and the approximate yield per plant for most cultivars is one to two bushels.

How and When to Plant

Apricots planted in the fall are frequently injured during the first winter after planting—thus, only spring planting is advised. Because delayed planting in the spring diminishes the chances for success, apricots should be planted as soon as the soil is dry and can be worked.

When planting standard trees, the graft union should be 2 to 3 inches below ground level. If suckers start to develop from the scion during the growing season, they should be promptly removed. Dwarf trees should be planted with the graft union just above the soil surface.

Pruning at Planting Time

Most trees of the size recommended for planting are branched, but if unbranched whips are selected, these should be cut back to 30 to 36 inches. Apricots are commonly trained to the modified central-leader system. At planting time, select two or possibly three strong scaffolds with wide angles at the point of attachment to the trunk. The lowest scaffold should be no closer than 24 inches to the ground. The next scaffold should be spaced 8 to 10 inches from the first and preferably originate from the opposite side of the trunk. If a third scaffold is selected it should be 8 to 10 inches from the second. The leader should be maintained and shortened only if it is 12 inches longer than the tips of the scaffolds. Shorten the tips of the scaffolds if they threaten to outgrow the leader. After pruning, the tree should consist of the straight trunk with its leader and two to three scaffold branches.

Subsequent Pruning

Very late winter or preferably early spring after planting is the time for the first dormant pruning. Select one or two additional scaffolds to remain and prune the other branches originating from the trunk. Head the scaffolds back if they are long or willowy, and especially if they threaten to overtake the leader. In subsequent years, direct pruning efforts toward removing old wood that has fruited, stimulating new growth, thinning, and shaping.

Apricots produce fruit on one-year-old shoots and on short spurs. Normally, the productive life of a spur is one to three years. Thus, remove old spurs that are no longer productive and head back long branches to ensure continued fruit production. Once the tree reaches a desirable size for harvesting the fruit, the leader may be headed back to limit upward growth of the tree.

Fertilizing

Occasionally, in some areas apricots are deficient in zinc, iron, manganese, and boron. These are rarely lacking in soils of the Upper Midwest, and the nutrient requirement can usually be supplied with a complete fertilizer such as 10–10–10 or with well-rotted manure.

During the first few years of growth, it is especially important that the fertilization program be carefully monitored to prevent excessive growth. Trees supplied with excess nitrogen often grow rapidly and fail to mature or harden properly before winter arrives.

On reasonably fertile soils, fertilizer may not be needed until the tree reaches bearing age. On most soils, nitrogen is the first element likely to show up as a deficiency. Trees lacking adequate amounts of nitrogen may exhibit terminal growth of less than 8 to 10 inches per year and have pale green or yellowing leaves or small, premature fruit.

When nutrients are needed, spread evenly one bushel of well-rotted manure per square yard beneath each tree or use 10–10–10 at the rate recommended for plums. All nutrients should be applied before growth begins in the early spring.

Thinning of Fruit

Apricots rarely produce fruit on an annual basis. The reason for this is twofold. First and foremost, early frosts frequently destroy the blossoms. Second, in years when the blossoms escape frost, the trees sometimes have a tendency to overbear. Because of the heavy energy drain, the trees the following year produce few and sometimes no fruits.

The fruits can be hand thinned when they are about the size of a dime. Remove the excess fruits so that those remaining are spaced 3 to 4 inches apart. Where tight clusters of fruit are formed, remove all but the healthiest one.

Additional Cultural Practices

Because of their shallow root systems, apricots may need supplemental water during droughts. A lack of sufficient soil moisture in the very early summer when the fruit buds are forming may limit the crop the following year. Mulching helps conserve moisture, and it is highly recommended. Spread the mulch evenly to a depth of 6 to 8 inches or more from the trunk to just beyond the tips of the branches.

Avoid cultivating beneath the tree after mid-July since late cultivation stimulates excessive growth, which may be injured by low winter tempera-

Brown rot on apricots. Photo courtesy of L. Hertz.

tures. As with the other tree fruits, give the trees adequate winter protection against rabbits and rodents. A white latex paint (do not use paint containing turpentine or oil) applied around the trunk up to the first scaffold will help keep the bark from splitting during the winter.

Just before the ground freezes in the fall, inspect the trees to see that no soil depressions have formed around the trunk. Water accumulates in such depressions, and the resulting ice may injure or completely girdle the tree.

Pests and Diseases

Because the apricot is closely related to the other stone fruits of the genus *Prunus*, it is also susceptible to many of the same pests and diseases. Refer to earlier chapters for detection and control methods for scab, scale, apple maggot, fruitworm, mites, peach-tree borers, aphids, plum curculio, and brown rot. Plum curculio and brown rot are likely to cause the most serious problems in most areas of the Upper Midwest.

Harvesting and Storage

Apricots are normally harvested during July and August. The fruit may be used fresh, canned, frozen, or dried. Even under ideal storage conditions of

31 to 32° F. and 85 to 90 percent relative humidity, ripe, freshly picked fruit rarely stores in good condition for longer than one to two weeks. In the home refrigerator, the fruit deteriorates rapidly after a week.

SELECTED REFERENCES

Anonymous. 1977. *Growing Apricots for Home Use.* USDA Home and Garden Bulletin No. 214 (rev.).

Bailey, C. H., and L. F. Hough. 1975. Apricots. In: *Advances in Fruit Breeding.* J. Janick and J. N. Moore. (eds.). Lafayette, Ind.: Purdue University Press.

Brooks, R. M., and H. P. Olmo. 1972. *Register of New Fruit and Nut Varieties.* 2nd ed. Berkeley: University of California Press.

Carlson, R. F., and J. W. Hull, Jr. 1978. *Rootstocks for Fruit Trees.* Michigan State University Coop. Ext. Ser. Bull. E–851.

Carlson, R. F., J. Hull, Jr., and J. E. Moulton. 1977. *Growing Apricots in Michigan.* Michigan State University Coop. Ext. Ser. Bull. 533. (rev.).

Coe, F. M. 1934. *Apricot Varieties.* Utah Agr. Exper. Stat. Bull. 251.

Cross-Rynaud, P., and J. M. Audergon. 1987. Apricot Rootstocks. In: *Rootstocks for Fruit Crops.* R. C. Rom and R. F. Carlson, (eds.). New York: Wiley-Interscience.

Cullinan, E. P. 1937. Improvement of Stone Fruits. *USDA Yearbook of Agriculture* 1937: 665–748.

Gourley, J. H., and F. S. Howlett. 1941. *Modern Fruit Production.* New York: Macmillan.

Harvey, J. M., W. L. Smith, and J. Kaufman. 1972. *Market Diseases of Stone Fruits: Cherries, Peaches, Nectarines, Apricots, and Plums.* USDA Agricultural Handbook 414.

Hertz, L. B. 1977. *Pruning Fruit Trees.* University of Minnesota Ext. Ser. Pub. 161.

Hertz, L. B. 1978. *Plum, Cherry, and Apricot Varieties for Minnesota.* University of Minnesota Ext. Ser. Hort. Fact Sheet 43.

Hertz, L. B. 1981. *Growing Stone Fruits.* University of Minnesota Ext. Ser. Hort. Fact Sheet 42.

Hertz, L. B. 1987. *Fruit for the Home.* University of Minnesota Ext. Ser. Pub. AG–BU–0470.

Hesse, C. O. 1952. *Apricot Culture in California.* University of California Agr. Exper. Stat. Cir. 412.

McGregor, S. E. 1976. *Insect Pollination of Cultivated Crop Plants.* USDA Agricultural Handbook No. 496.

Paunovic, S. A. 1964. Apricot Growing: Its Problems. Measures for Their Solution. *Sixteenth International Horticulture Congress* 1962. (5): 492–501.

Schultz, J. N. 1948. Self Compatibility in Apricots. *Proc. Amer. Soc. Hort. Sci.* 51: 171–74.

Slate, G. L. 1970. Apricots, Nectarines, and Almonds. *Horticulture* 48(5): 42, 47–48.

Snyder, L. C. 1980. *Trees and Shrubs for Northern Gardens.* Minneapolis: University of Minnesota Press.

Teskey, B. J. E., and J. S. Shoemaker. 1978. *Tree Fruit Production.* 3rd ed. Westport, Conn.: AVI Publishing.

Watkins, R. 1976. Cherry, Plum, Peach, Apricots, and Almond-*Prunus* spp. Rosaceae. Pp. 242–47 in: *Evolution of Crop Plants.* N. W. Simmonds (ed.). New York: Longman.

Chapter

8

Grapes

Grapes, which belong to the genus *Vitis*, a member of the family Vitaceae, have the unique distinction of being the most widely grown fruit crop in the world. They are cultivated on every continent and Howell (1987) has estimated world planting at over 10 million hectares (24,710,000 acres). In the United States nearly 30 native species and four basic groups of grapes are grown commercially. California leads all states in grape production, and the value of the 1989 crop was $1,544,350,000. Other major grape-producing states include Washington, New York, Arizona, Pennsylvania, Michigan, Oregon, Ohio, Georgia, Arkansas, Missouri, North Carolina, and South Carolina. Total U.S. grape production in 1989 exceeded $1.7 billion (*Noncitrus Fruits and Nuts*, January 1990).

European Grapes

Commercially, the most important species is *Vitis vinifera*, the old-world or European-type grape. This species is indigenous to the region between the Black and Caspian seas and has been cultivated for millennia. Einset and Pratt (1975), in tracing the historical development of the species, reported that it was cultivated in Egypt 5,000 to 6,000 years ago. The authors traced the species from its original home to the Mediterranean region, first from coastal areas, then inland.

In this country the early settlers tried repeatedly to establish the old-world grape in eastern North America but did not succeed. Gourley and Howlett (1941) reported that *V. vinifera* was brought to Virginia in 1619 but later

Grape leaf infected with phylloxera.

failed throughout the colonies from New England to Georgia. The *vinifera* grapes lacked cold hardiness and were attacked by a variety of diseases and soil pests.

A major pest affecting the *vinifera* grapes in the East was the phylloxera aphid. This insect can attack both leaves and roots, but immature forms that feed on the latter are of more serious concern. Although the mode of entry is unknown, phylloxera were accidentally introduced into Europe in the 1860s (Johnson, 1971). Shortly thereafter, symptoms that led to the demise of the *vinifera* grapes in the eastern United States began showing up in French vineyards. Little (1963) estimated that almost one-third of all French grapes were destroyed, but Johnson (1971) suggested the pest had a far greater impact, killing "virtually every vine in France." Relief was found in phylloxera-resistant rootstocks imported from America, but as Howell (1987) has pointed out, the effect on the French wine industry was devastating and the land in grapes is less today than during the pre-phylloxera period.

Although there were problems with phylloxera , the failure of the *vinifera* grapes in the eastern United States was not repeated in the West. These wine grapes were introduced to California from Mexico in the late 18th century (Einset and Pratt, 1975). There, Spanish missionaries assisted in the art of winemaking and helped to distribute the species throughout California during the 19th century. Rapid expansion took place between 1860 and 1900, and the foundation for today's modern wine industry was firmly established. These grapes are grown mainly in California, Arizona, and Washington, and during the last few years there has been a renewed interest in cultivating *vinifera* grapes in some eastern states.

American Grapes

The second important group involves mainly the native American species. Nearly all of the principal cultivars have been derived from *V. labrusca* or from hybrids of *labrusca* with one or more species such as *V. aestivalis, V. riparia, or V. vinifera*. Selections that contain all or some element of *labrusca* are commonly referred to as American grapes.

These grapes are characterized by having thick skins that readily slip from the flesh (slip-skinned) and are grown primarily around the Great Lakes; in the west central region consisting of Arkansas, Missouri, Iowa, Illinois, Kansas, and Nebraska; and on the Pacific coast in Washington. Although some wine is made from the *labrusca*-type grapes, most are used for juice ('Concord' is the leading cultivar), jellies, and table grapes. The top four states, in 1989, producing American grapes were Washington, New York, Pennsylvania, and Michigan (*Noncitrus Fruits and Nuts*, January 1990).

Muscadine Grapes

The Muscadine or Southern Fox grape, *V. rotundifolia,* is grown primarily in the southeastern United States, where it is native. Commercial production is limited almost exclusively to North Carolina, South Carolina, Georgia, Mississippi, Alabama, Tennessee, and Florida (Shoemaker, 1978). These grapes are also slip-skinned and have many characteristics of the northern grapes, but they are very tender and are often injured or killed when the temperature drops below 5° F.

Interspecific (French hybrid) Grapes

The remaining grapes of commercial importance in this country are the interspecific hybrids. These were developed by crossing various cultivars of the old-world species *V. vinifera* with several hardy, disease-resistant, native American species. These hybrids are grown primarily for wine, and for this purpose are considered superior to the American grapes, which produce a wild or "foxy" flavor.

Most of the original breeding work on the hybrids was done in France, and until recently most of the cultivars produced were grown there or elsewhere. The interspecific hybrids are often called French hybrids.

In this country, interest in these grapes began shortly after World War II, and today they are considered commercially important throughout the eastern wine-grape region.

Grapes in the Upper Midwest

Over a hundred years ago, there was a strong interest in growing grapes in many areas of the Upper Midwest. In Minnesota, for example, some pioneer sodbusters grew grapes not only for their own use but also for cash income. *The History of the Minnesota Horticultural Society* (1873) provides a glimpse of the importance of grapes to the early settlers.

As early as 1860, one grower had planted 37 cultivars, and he reported, "27 have fruited." In the same year, Truman M. Smith, a former president of the Minnesota Horticultural Society, had an acre of grapes. In 1866, members of the society agreed that there was a good show of grapes, and the most prominent and successful cultivars grown in Minnesota were 'Concord', 'Delaware', 'Hartford Prolific', 'Northern Muscadine', 'Clinton', and 'Creveiling'. By 1873, there was a report that a German grower in Brownsville, Houston County, had produced 2,000 gallons of wine.

In 1885, the *Mankato Review* carried an advertisement to sell Minneopa Falls (now in Minneopa State Park) with a tract of 15 acres and "one block of about six acres, *splendid for grape growing.*" The same year the *Mankato Review* advertised another farm that included a vineyard of 1½ acres with 700 bearing vines producing 5,000 to 6,000 pounds annually.

In 1887, 25,000 to 30,000 pounds of 'Delaware' grapes were sold at the Minnetonka, Minnesota, farmer's market and by 1900, state production had reached 600,000 pounds per year. Interest in grape growing in Minnesota and in other areas of the Upper Midwest continued until the turn of the century and then gradually waned.

Interest in grape growing probably declined because of economics and convenience. The advent of refrigeration and improved rail traffic brought competition with imported grapes from California. The labor for grape culture and the tedious task of protecting grapevines from winter injury could now be diverted to other areas. Grapes no longer had to be grown at home; they could be purchased over a longer time span at the supermarket.

In the Upper Midwest most grapes grown in home gardens are American types that originated in the East. Detailed historical accounts of the development of these grapes have been provided by Hedrick (1908) and Snyder (1937). For our region, breeding work in Wisconsin, Minnesota, and South

Grape breeder Elmer Swenson.

Good-quality wine is now being produced at several wineries in the Upper Midwest.

Dakota has produced several cultivars that are better adapted to the North than the tender eastern types and the European-developed French hybrids.

One of the pioneers responsible for a renewed interest in grape growing in the Upper Midwest is Elmer Swenson of Osceola, Wisconsin. For more than 40 years Swenson has bred eastern cultivars, hardy wild grapes, and French hybrids to develop cultivars suitable for the North. His grapes, known to the trade as Swenson hybrids, are suitable for wine, fresh eating, and culinary purposes.

In addition to American grapes, Swenson hybrids, and small trial plantings of *vinifera*, the only other grapes grown in the five-state area are the French hybrids. Interest in growing French hybrids has developed principally during the last two decades. Some states formerly considered too cold to grow good wine grapes are now sporting new wineries. For example, at the Wollersheim Winery in Wisconsin, French hybrid wines such as Baco Noir, Foch, and Seyval are available.

Even Minnesota, a state where until just a few years ago interest in grape growing had waned and commercial wine production seemed out of the question, now sports four new wineries. Today, Minnesota has a wine competition at the state fair, and a Minnesota Grape Growers Association boasts more than 200 members.

In Wisconsin, Wollersheim, located at Prairie du Sac, is the largest winery, with over twenty acres of grapes. About eleven other small wineries, which often utilize imported juice from grapes and other types of fruit, are scattered throughout the state. Iowa has about fifteen wineries that purchase grapes, and most are located in the Amana area. One commercial winery has been recently established in South Dakota, but there and in North Dakota, wine production is limited largely to home use.

Interest in French hybrid grapes is also increasing in other midwestern states. The grapes are now very important in Michigan, Illinois, Indiana, and Ohio.

Flowers and Pollination

Most grape cultivars grown in the Upper Midwest have bisexual flowers and are completely self-fertilizing or are cross-pollinated by wind — thus, usually only one cultivar is needed for fruit production. In some cultivars, like 'Worden', the crop will be improved if pollinated by a different cultivar. Also, 'Brighton' is pollen sterile and must have a pollen-producing neighbor for fruit set.

Very few cultivars have only female flowers and are described in nursery catalogs as *pistillate*. In order to get fruit production, a second pollen-producing (bisexual) cultivar must be planted in close proximity. Most non-pistillate cultivars will work as pollenizers.

The role that bees and other insects play in pollination of grapes has still not been firmly established. In the past, it was assumed that their role was negligible, but some scientists (McGregor, 1976) are calling for a reappraisal of the bee's role in pollination. At any rate, contrary to popular opinion, bees do not injure the fruit of grapes unless the skin has been broken by insects, wind, or other causes.

Rootstocks

Most grapes planted in the Upper Midwest are grown on their own roots. The few that are grafted onto a hardy rootstock should be planted so that the graft union is approximately the same depth as it was originally in the nursery. For details on planting depths of other types, see the section on planting.

Selecting Nursery Stock

As with all nursery stock, beware of cheap, bargain plants since these are frequently nursery culls with poorly developed root systems. Usually the best results are obtained by purchasing barerooted, one- or two-year-old plants

Potted grapes ready for spring planting.

labeled as No. 1. Plants labeled as No. 2 are not recommended. Likewise, potted plants, which are usually more expensive, offer no advantage over bareroot stock. Quite often, potted material is merely leftover stock that did not sell the previous year.

When purchasing plants from a local nursery, examine the root and shoot system carefully. Roots should be long, well branched, vigorous, and protected from drying out. Beware of packaged plants that are located in areas exposed to the sun. The buds on the canes should still be dormant, with little or no signs of expansion.

Availability of Cultivars

With the exception of a few select cultivars such as 'Foch', 'Cascade', and 'Aurore', French hybrid grapes are not readily available from most upper midwestern nurseries. Eastern nurseries such as Boordy Vineyard, Box 39, Riverwood, MD 21139, and Foster Nurseries, Fredonia, NY 14063, carry many of the cultivars.

How Many Plants?

How many vines to plant depends on the needs of the grower and the cultivars selected. Most American cultivars will yield four to six quarts of fruit or more per plant. For wine production, ten to twenty pounds of fruit are needed for each gallon of wine. Each vine should produce enough fruit to make approximately one-half to one gallon of wine.

Table, Juice, and Jelly Grapes (seeds present)

Beta. This is supposedly a *riparia* x 'Concord' hybrid introduced from Minnesota by Louis Suelter in 1881, but there is considerable confusion about the parentage. It is one of the hardiest grapes available and can be grown in most areas without winter protection. The fruit is somewhat acidic and is used primarily for making jelly.

Bluebell. Introduced from the University of Minnesota in 1944, this grape is a cross of 'Beta' x an unknown eastern cultivar. It resembles 'Concord' in size, use, and color, but the skin is much more tender. It also has better table quality than 'Concord' but produces a lighter juice. In Minnesota, the fruit is ripe in early to mid-September. The vine is regarded as quite hardy.

Brighton. Jacob Moore introduced this 'Diana Hamburg' x 'Concord' selection at Brighton, New York, in 1872. The red fruit ripens a few days before 'Concord'. For production, another cultivar must be planted for cross-pollination. Good for fresh use, the fruit deteriorates quickly after harvest. 'Brighton' may be difficult to locate.

Buffalo. Geneva, New York, is the home of this 'Herbert' x 'Watkins' cross introduced in 1938. The blue fruits are noted for their excellent fresh-eating qualities. This cultivar matures mid-season about three weeks before 'Concord'. Vines are vigorous but require winter protection in more-northerly areas.

Clinton. This cultivar of unknown parentage was named by L. B. Langworthy from New York in 1835. Pioneer sodbusters to the five states in the 1800s grew this cultivar, but it is no longer popular and may be difficult to locate. 'Clinton' is quite hardy and the fruit resembles 'Beta'.

Concord. This is the most popular juice cultivar grown in the U.S., but because of the long season required for maturity (155 to 160 days), it is not the best choice for most upper midwestern areas. 'Concord' is a seedling of a wild *labrusca* found by Ephriam Bull of Massachusetts in 1849. The vines are half hardy and in many areas winter protection is advised.

Edelweiss. This 'Minnesota 78' ('Beta' x 'Witt') x 'Ontario' cross released in 1980 is one of seven hybrids introduced during the last decade by Elmer Swenson of Osceola, Wisconsin. 'Edelweiss' is a white table grape that has proved hardy and popular in southern Minnesota. It has survived temperatures lower than − 30° F. without winter protection. Fruit clusters sometimes weigh a pound or more. One disadvantage is that the fruit does not handle or store well. Wine from this cultivar has been described as "pleasant." If wine is made from very ripe fruit, it usually has a very foxy flavor.

Fredonia. F. E. Gladwin introduced this 'Champion' x 'Lucile' cross at Fredonia, New York, in 1927. The black fruit ripens in mid–September but may have a tendency to shatter at maturity. For fresh eating, the fruit is usually rated fair to good. Unfermented juice is excellent, but wine from this cultivar has a strong *labrusca* flavor. The vine is hardy to about − 25° F. and is susceptible to downy mildew.

Lucile. According to Hedrick (1908), J. A. Putnam of Fredonia, New York, selected this supposed seedling of 'Wyoming', which it resembles in both fruit and vine characteristics. It was introduced by Lewis Roesch in 1899. The red fruit ripens earlier than 'Concord' and is good quality but may have a tendency to crack at maturity.

Mandan. N. E. Hansen introduced this 'Wilder' x North Dakota wild selection in 1925 at Brookings, South Dakota. The small black fruit has been described as having a "fair flavor." The vine is quite hardy, vigorous, and a heavy producer. 'Mandan' has waned in popularity, and it may be difficult to locate.

Moore Early. Captain John B. Moore selected this seedling of 'Concord' at Concord, Massachusetts, in 1871. This cultivar resembles 'Concord' in nearly all characteristics except that it matures earlier. In most areas of the Upper Midwest, it is superior to 'Concord'.

New York Muscat. Introduced from New York in 1961, this is a 'Muscat Hamburg' x 'Ontario' hybrid. The fruit is reddish black to black with a flavor combining muscat and American fruitiness. In Minnesota, the fruit ripens midseason. Vines are tender and require winter protection.

Niagara. According to Hedrick (1908), C. L. Haag and B. W. Clark of Lockport, Niagara County, New York, selected this 'Concord' x 'Cassady' hybrid. It was introduced about 1882 by the Niagara Grape Company. The white green berries are larger than 'Concord' and ripen at about the same time, but the vine is not as hardy. This cultivar is suitable for fresh use, wine, and fresh juice.

Portland. This 'Champion' x 'Lutie' cross originated in New York in 1912. It is another white, early, dessert cultivar with a sweet, foxy flavor. Vines are tender and will require protection in most areas.

Red Amber. From unknown parentage, this seedling was introduced at Excelsior, Minnesota, in 1944. The small, reddish amber berries are sweet and of good dessert quality. The fruit matures in early September. 'Red

**Fruit zones—
table, juice, and jelly grapes**

Cultivar	Iowa 4b	5a	5b	Minn. 1	2	3	4	S. Dak. 1	2	3	4	N. Dak. A	B	C	Wis. 1	2	3	4
Beta	X			X	X	X	P	X	X	X	X	X	X	X	X	X	X	X
Bluebell				X	X	P									X	X	P	P
Brighton															X			
Buffalo		X	X									P			X	X	P	
Clinton		X	X									P	T	T				
Concord	P	X	X	X	P										X	X	P	
Edelweiss	X	X	X	X	X	P	P					T	T	T	X	X	P	P
Fredonia	X	X	X	X	P	P		P	P			T		T	X	X	P	P
Lucile			X															
Mandan												P	T	T	X	X	X	P
Moore Early		X	X												X	X	P	
New York Muscat				T	T										X	X	P	
Niagara			X	P	P								T		X	P	P	
Portland															X			
Red Amber								T	T						X			
Schuyler															X	X	P	
Stueben		X	X	T											X	X	P	
Swenson Red	X	X	X	X	P	P						T	T	T	X	X	P	P
Valiant	X	X	X	X	X	X	P	X	X	X	X	X	X	X	X	X	P	P
Van Buren			X	T											X	X	P	P
Worden				X	X	P						T	T	T	X	X	P	P

X = recommended for planting; P = recommended for planting, but winter protection advised; T = recommended for trial, winter protection advised.
See zone map on page 20.

Amber' is extremely rare today and is no longer available commercially.

Schuyler. Originating in New York in 1947, this is a 'Zinfandel' x 'Ontario' hybrid. The black fruit is a European type described as very sweet with a vinous tang. It ripens in midseason. The vines lack cold hardiness.

Steuben. This is a 'Wayne' x 'Sheridan' hybrid introduced from New York in

1946. The medium, blue black fruit is sweet and ripens late with 'Concord'. Winter protection is advised for most areas.

Swenson Red. One of the best Swenson hybrids for table use, it was introduced in 1980 from 'Minnesota 78' x 'Seibel 11803' crosses made at Osceola, Wisconsin. The fruit has excellent flavor and good storage quality. The vines require winter protection in most areas and are susceptible to mildew.

Valiant. R. M. Peterson introduced this 'Fredonia' x *Vitis riparia* cross in 1982 at Brookings, South Dakota. The blue fruit matures early and is considered excellent for juice. The vine is vigorous, productive, and very hardy.

Van Buren. Fredonia, New York, is the home of this 'Fredonia' x 'Worden' cross introduced by F. E. Gladwin in 1935. The medium, blue black fruit resembles 'Worden' in many respects but is smaller and does not hang on the vine or store well. This cultivar matures early, a month before 'Concord'.

Worden. Like 'Moore Early' and 'Fredonia', this is an old 'Concord' type that performs better in many areas of the North than 'Concord'. It was introduced from seed of 'Concord' planted by Schuyler Worden of Oswego County, New York, in 1863. In the North the fruit ripens one to two weeks before 'Concord' and usually reaches full maturity before frost in the southern part of the Upper Midwest region. 'Worden' is mildew resistant.

Seedless Cultivars

With the possible exception of southern Iowa and southern Wisconsin, none of the seedless cultivars have proved reliably hardy in the five-state area without winter protection.

Canadice. One of the more hardy of the seedless cultivars, but winter injury can be expected if the temperature drops much below −20° F. This is a 'Bath' x 'Himrod' cross introduced in 1977 at Geneva, New York. The fruit ripens very early and has a flavor similar to 'Delaware'.

Himrod. An 'Ontario' x 'Thompson seedless' cross introduced in 1952 from New York, this is probably the best-quality seedless grape for the North. The fruit is yellow with sweet flesh.

Interlaken Seedless. This cultivar was developed from the same parentage as 'Himrod' and was introduced from New York in 1947. The small, golden fruit is sweet and good quality. The vine is not quite as hardy as 'Himrod'.

Reliance. J. N. Moore introduced this 'Ontario' x 'Suffolk Red' cross in 1982 at Clarksville, Arkansas. This is probably the hardiest of the seedless

**Fruit zones—
seedless-grape cultivars**

Cultivar	Iowa			Minn.				S. Dak.				N. Dak.			Wis.			
	4b	5a	5b	1	2	3	4	1	2	3	4	A	B	C	1	2	3	4
Canadice			T	X	X	T									X	T	T	
Himrod			T	X	X	T						T			X	T	T	
Interlaken												T			X	T	T	
Reliance		T	T	X	X	T									X	T	T	T
Seedless Concord			T	X	X	T									X	T	T	T
Suffolk Red															X	T	T	T
Vanessa		T	T	T	T	T									X	T	T	T

X = recommended for planting, winter protection advised; T = recommended for
trial, winter protection advised.
See zone map on page 20.

cultivars but injury can be expected if the temperature drops much below − 20° F. The red, medium fruit is sweet and has good storage quality. This cultivar is tolerant of several fungal diseases.

Seedless Concord. This is a mutation of 'Concord' which originated in Maryland. It ripens about one week after 'Concord'. The best use is probably
for pies.

Suffolk Red. Introduced in 1972 from New York, this is a 'Fredonia' x 'Russian
Seedless' cross. The large, red fruit has excellent quality as a table grape.
Ripening time is early to midseason.

Vanessa. 'Seneca' pollinated by N.Y. 45910 is the parentage of this cultivar
released from the Vineland Ontario Station in 1984. The medium,
bright red fruit is a good-quality table grape. The vines are not quite
as hardy as 'Canadice'.

Wine Cultivars

Aurore (Seibel 5279). The date of introduction of this S788 x S29 hybrid from
France is unknown. The fruit is pinkish white and the wine from it has
been described as a neutral delicate white of fair quality. The plant is
susceptible to black rot and powdery mildew.

Baco Noir (Baco No. 1). Francois Baco developed this 'Folle Blanche' x *Vitis
riparia* hybrid in France, and it was introduced to the United States in
1951. Berries are small and black produced in long clusters. Wine from

A sample of the different types of wine grapes now being grown in Minnesota.

this cultivar is red, fruity, and light. The plant is quite vigorous and resistant to mildews but is very susceptible to cold injury.

De Chaunac (Seibel 9549). This is another important French hybrid in New York State. It was selected from a cross of S5163 x S793 made in France. The berries are blue black borne in medium size clusters. The red wine produced from this cultivar has been described as pleasant with good tannin and color. The plant is vigorous with good disease resistance.

Delaware. According to Hedrick (1908), this cultivar of unknown parentage was brought to the attention of Abram Thompson, editor of the *Delaware Gazette* of Delaware, Ohio, in 1849. It was later named by A. J. Downing and introduced in 1856. The small, pink to red berries produce a light golden wine that is often used in blending to make champagne.

Esprit. Elmer Swenson of Osceola, Wisconsin, introduced this 'Edelweiss' x 'Villard Blanc' cross in 1986. The plant is quite vigorous but less hardy than 'Edelweiss'. The fruit is as large as 'Edelweiss' but is produced in a more compact cluster and the ripening time is 10 to 14 days later. The berries are soft and susceptible to cracking. The white table wine produced from this cultivar is mild and fruity.

Foch (Marechal Foch, Kuhlmann 188–2). This *(riparia* x *rupestris)* x 'Gold-riesling' hybrid was introduced from France. This has been a very successful cultivar at wineries in Minnesota and Wisconsin, and some award-winning, red burgundy-type wine has been made from it. The berries are small and black, and are borne in small clusters. The plants are vigorous with good resistance to disease. 'Foch' is one of the hardiest French-hybrid cultivars available.

Kay Gray. This is another Swenson hybrid introduced from Wisconsin in 1981. The open-pollinated seedling of Swenson 217 produces white, juicy berries borne in small clusters. The white wine from this cultivar is mild and fruity. The plant is quite vigorous and is perhaps the most hardy of the Swenson hybrids. This cultivar was named to honor Kay Gray, wife of Dick Gray, a Minnesota supporter of the Swenson research.

LaCrosse. A Swenson hybrid selected from Swenson 114 x 'Seyval' and introduced in 1983. The berries are white and medium size. The white wine from this cultivar is somewhat suggestive of 'Seyval'. The plant has medium vigor and productivity.

Leon Millot. This is a sister seedling of 'Foch'. Berries and wine are similar to 'Foch', but 'Leon Millot' is earlier ripening, less hardy, and more susceptible to mildew.

St. Croix. Of the Swenson hybrids, this cultivar ranks second after 'Kay Gray' with respect to hardiness. It is very productive and, without proper pruning, will overbear. The berries are low in acid and are similar to 'Beta' in color and size. Wines from this cultivar tend to be bland or neutral in character. 'St. Croix' was introduced in 1981 from Swenson 283 x Swenson 193.

St. Pepin. This selection is pistillate, which means another cultivar will have to be planted for cross-pollination. Swenson introduced this sister seedling of 'LaCrosse' in 1984. It is similar to that cultivar but is more vigorous, slightly less hardy, and sweeter, and has twice the cluster size. According to the Minnesota Grape Growers (1986), this cultivar produces wine that blends well with 'LaCrosse' to make a good German-style wine.

Seyval (Seyval Blanc). Another French hybrid selected from a cross of S4995 x S4986. The berries are white and make a good-quality, white wine. The plants have medium vigor with good resistance to disease.

Ventura. Introduced in 1974, this is a 'Chelois' (Seibel 10878) x 'Elvira' selection from Ontario, Canada. The small, white berries, which resist cracking, are produced in medium-size clusters. This cultivar reportedly makes a good-quality, dry white wine. The plants are vigorous and tolerant to mildew.

Fruit zones—
wine cultivars

Cultivar	Iowa			Minn.				S. Dak.				N. Dak.			Wis.			
	4b	5a	5b	1	2	3	4	1	2	3	4	A	B	C	1	2	3	4
Aurore			P	P	P										X	P	P	
Baco Noir			P	T	T										P	P		
De Chaunac			P	P	P										X	P	P	
Delaware			P	X	P										P	P	P	
Esprit				P	P										X	P	P	
Foch		X		X	P	P							T		X	P	P	P
Kay Gray			P	X	X	P							T		X	X	P	P
LaCrosse			P	P	P										X	P	P	
Leon Millot		X		P	P										P	P	P	
St. Croix	X	X		X	X	P							T		X	X	P	
St. Pepin	P	P		P	P										X	X	P	
Seyval			P	P	P										X	P	P	
Ventura				T	T										T	T		

X = recommended for planting; P = recommended for planting, winter protection advised; T = recommended for trial, winter protection advised.
See zone map on page 20.

Selection of the Planting Site

Grapes can be successfully grown in a wide variety of soil types ranging from gravelly loams to heavy clay. The principal requirements of the soils are good internal drainage and a moderate water-holding capacity. Grapes do poorly on waterlogged soils and on very sandy soils, which dry out quickly. Soil modification may be necessary if the soil pH is below 5 or above 7. Grapes seem to perform best when the pH is between 5 and 6.5.

Grapes need full sun to develop properly. They will do poorly if they compete with the roots of nearby trees and shrubs. The plants are subject to frost injury in both spring and fall. The site should give maximum frost protection. Locations on the south and east sides of larger lakes and rivers are ideal, along with elevated slopes with good air movement.

Even though north slopes have cooler temperatures in the spring, thereby delaying growth, the Minnesota Grape Growers Association recommends,

152 GRAPES

Table 10. Other wine cultivars grown by the Minnesota Grape Growers* (all should be considered trial and will require winter protection in most areas)

Cultivar	Fruit	Wine
Cascade (Seibel 13053)	Small, black	Rosé or light red
Cayuga white	Golden, yellow	White, resembles Riesling
Chancellor (Seibel 7053)	Blue black, medium-large, loose clusters	High-quality red
Chelois	Medium, blue black	Good red table
Joffre (Kuhlmann 187–1)	Small, black	Burgundy-type red
Rayon d'or	Golden, medium-size cluster berries	Fruity, white
Siegfried (Siegfriedrebe)	White	White, similar to Riesling
Veeblanc	Large, compact white berries	White, table
Vignoles (Ravat 51)	Yellow, white, small compact clusters, small berries	Good-quality white
Vivant	Small, translucent yellow-tan	White, delicate, fruity, crisp

*In addition to the cultivars listed here, Private Stock Winery, Boone, Iowa, has four acres of 'Rosette' (Seibel 1000). This cultivar, known for its ability to withstand very low winter temperatures, produces a light-bodied rosé wine.

for reasons of heat accumulation and air movement, that grapes be planted on slopes facing south, southeast, and southwest.

Spacing and Orientation of Rows

Where mechanical tilling, spraying, or harvesting operations using large tractor-type equipment are anticipated, the vines should be spaced 8 to 10 feet apart in the rows with a space of 9 to 10 feet between rows. For the home gardener with just a few vines, a closer spacing of 5 to 8 feet between plants and 8 feet between rows is satisfactory.

For maximum penetration of sunlight, the rows should be oriented in a north–south direction; however, if the vineyard is located on a slope where erosion is likely to be a problem, the rows should run in contour fashion across the slope.

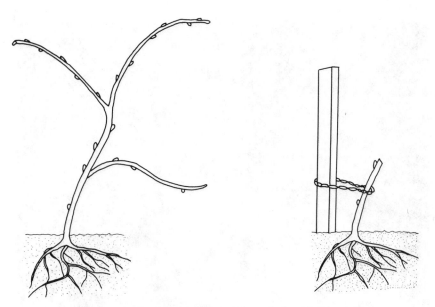

*A newly planted grapevine before (*left*) and after (*right*) pruning.*

Planting

Dormant, bareroot stock seems to benefit from being planted as soon as the soil can be worked in the early spring. For green-growing vines, delay planting until danger of frost has passed.

The roots on bareroot stock should be kept moist at all times, but do not soak in water for longer than four hours. A brief period in water (two to three hours) before planting will help break dormancy and speed up initial establishment of roots and vines.

A vigorous grape plant has a root system that is quite long and extensively branched, so it is important that the hole for planting be large enough so the roots can be properly spaced and spread out without overlapping. On reasonably fertile land where the soil is easily worked, the hole for planting should be one-third wider and deeper than the root system. On poorer or compacted soils, it is advisable to remove the soil to a depth of 2 feet in a 3-foot radius. In all plantings, the fertile topsoil should be placed in the bottom of the hole first and the subsoil added last.

The most common way to plant grapes is to evenly spread out the roots and to position the plant *upright* so that the lowest bud is close to ground level. In most cases this means that the vine is planted slightly deeper than it originally grew in the nursery. After planting and watering, the vine should be pruned back to a single cane so that only three to five buds remain.

Newly planted grapevine using the "Alma" method.

An alternative to the upright planting method is to position the plants in the hole so that the cane is at a *30-degree angle* from the soil surface. The reasons for choosing this planting method are discussed in the next section.

Care during the First Season

In most areas, many of the grapes grown in the Upper Midwest will need some form of winter protection. For most cultivars, this means the vines will need to be removed from the trellis or wires and covered with soil or an appropriate mulch. This is a simple task when the plants are young, but as they mature it becomes increasingly more difficult to "bend" the woody trunk so that all parts are protected. For this reason, growers in the North have originated special training and pruning methods so that the trunk grows parallel to the ground for a short distance.

One technique that has been particularly effective is the "Alma" method, named after Alma Eisert, who with her husband, Jerry, owned and operated for many years the showplace of Minnesota vineyards near Hastings.

In this technique, the vines are planted at a 30-degree angle, and during the first year, the first 12 to 24 inches of trunk originating from the ground is trained by means of a stiff, wire wicket to grow parallel to the soil surface.

Subsequent growth beyond the first 2 feet can be supported by means of twine attached to a stake or overhead wires. If the rows are oriented north-south, the vine should be trained to grow south.

For cold-hardy cultivars, the vines may be left attached to the wires or trellis during the winter months. In this case, the shoot is allowed to grow upright and is tied loosely to a stake or overhead wire.

Growth during the first season may range from a few inches to several feet, depending on growing conditions and the inherent vigor of the cultivar. In slower-growing cultivars, the training of the trunk may take two to three years or longer. To facilitate development of the trunk, allow only one terminal shoot to develop. When side branches develop, the end or terminal bud of these branches should be removed after three to four leaves have formed.

These side branches will continue to develop through the summer, and the terminal bud of each should be removed. The goal is to produce one vigorous trunk with short side branches.

In most cultivars that must be laid down and given winter protection, more pruning is required in the fall after the first hard frost. Hardy cultivars like 'Beta' and 'Valiant' are exceptions. These are normally pruned in March.

In the fall pruning, remove a third of the main stem and all side branches. After the leaves have fallen, the trunk can be laid down and covered with a mound of soil or with 6 or more inches of a mulch such as straw. In the Eisert Vineyard in Minnesota, the vines are pinned to the ground with wire wickets and completely covered with corn straw. During the winter of 1976, when outside air temperatures registered $-43°$ F., the temperature under the mulch was $-8°$ F. Without the mulch, few, if any, cultivars would have survived, but with it, even the tender French-hybrid cultivars survived with no damage.

Cultivation

Grapevines thrive under clean cultivation. Ideally, a strip the entire length of the row, 18 to 24 inches wide, on each side of the plants should be kept free of weeds and grass during the growing season. If time does not permit clean cultivation, the entire length of the row should be mulched. Uncultivated areas between rows should be mowed regularly.

Cultivation of grapes is not recommended after August 1. Cultivation after this date is likely to promote new growth, which may not harden properly before winter arrives.

Caution with Herbicides

Grapes are extremely susceptible to damage from many of the common herbicides. 2,4-D, which is the main ingredient in most home lawn-weed-

Early spring in a Minnesota vineyard (top).
The same vineyard just before the fall harvest (bottom).

control sprays, is particularly detrimental and accidental drift can severely injure, or in some cases kill, grapevines. No herbicide should be used in the vineyard unless it is specifically approved for use on grapes.

Weed control is essential, but for small plantings, hand or mechanical tillage is probably the best course to follow. Even many commercial vineyards have shunned the use of herbicides, and instead have developed specially designed rotary hoes for weed control and cultivation. Too often, the mulch used to cover grapes in the winter is overlooked as a weed-control method. Additional mulch can be added in the growing season and has the added benefit on lighter soils of water conservation during dry periods in the summer.

Care during the Second Season

Begin the second season by removing the soil or mulch placed over the vines for winter protection. This should not be attempted until after the soil has thawed and can be worked.

It is important to tie the vine to the trellis as soon as possible. Evidence from Minnesota suggests that vines left on the ground in the spring may be injured or are slower to develop than those tied to the trellis immediately. This is apparently a result of cold air settling near the soil surface, causing stress from temperature fluctuation. Wire should not be used to tie the vine to the trellis since it may girdle the stems. Binder twine is acceptable but is difficult to remove. Two-ply twine is probably the best and least expensive to work with. When tying, secure all the vine parts to minimize damage by wind.

Early spring, after the vines have been tied to the trellis, is also the time for the first light fertilization. Use about one-third cup of 10–10–10 for each plant, evenly spreading the nutrients in a circle around each vine.

The second season is the time to choose which training system will be used and to foster development of the trunk or trunks. No fruit should be allowed to develop during the second season. Flowers that form in the spring should be removed so that the energy can be funneled into root growth and vine development.

Terminology for Training and Pruning

Several training and pruning systems for grapes are commonly employed in the Upper Midwest. The following terms are basic for understanding them.

Trunk—The main stem of the vine arising from the ground.

Arms—The main woody branches extending from the trunk.

Shoots—New, green, leafy growth that originates from buds during the summer months.

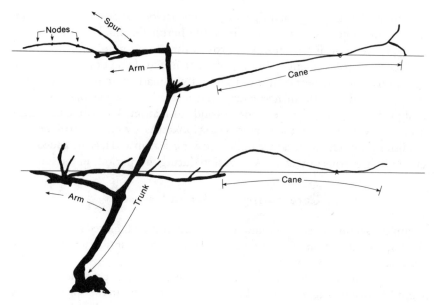

A dormant vine showing the trunk, arms, canes, spur, and nodes.

Cane — After the shoots drop their leaves in the fall, they are called canes.

Spur — A cane cut back to four or fewer buds.

Sucker — Unwanted shoots arising from buds at or below ground level.

Tendril — The curly, clasping part of shoots.

Nodes — The point on shoots or canes where leaves or buds originate.

Internode — The space between the nodes.

Regardless of which training system is selected, limit the number of shoots that develop from the main trunk. As with the first year, the terminal bud of unwanted side shoots should be removed after two or three leaves appear. Eliminate suckers that originate from the ground or from the base of the trunk.

After the first fall frost, more pruning is required: Select three or four canes and prune them back to one to two buds to form the renewal spurs. The spurs will elongate the following growing season and by fall will produce buds on the canes that will form fruit the following season.

Select two or three canes for fruit production. Prune off the ends of these canes, leaving just enough buds to match the vigor of the vine. In vigorous cultivars these may be cut back to 3 feet. At the end of the pruning operation, all that should remain above ground are the trunk, two or three canes, and the renewal spurs.

Care during the Third and Subsequent Seasons

The third year is essentially a repeat of year two, except this year some grapes can be harvested—but do not allow the vines to overproduce. I prefer to leave only one cluster for every two shoots. In year four a full crop is allowed to form.

Suckers should be removed and the plant should be pruned in both the spring and fall (except hardy cultivars like 'Beta', which are pruned in March and in late spring). The most important thing to remember is that buds formed at the end of the growing season will produce next year's grapes. Always plan to have canes with just enough buds to match the vigor of the vine and a corresponding number of renewal spurs. By keeping up this routine year after year, a good balance can be achieved for continued grape production.

Bleeding

If for some reason pruning is delayed to late spring when growth has begun, the pruned parts may exude a sap. This is commonly referred to as bleeding. It often causes great alarm, but the sap exuded is largely water, and its loss does not injure or harm the plants. Soon after the leaves appear, the bleeding stops.

Training Systems

There are several training systems, each with advantages and disadvantages. One can choose single, double, or triple trunks. Which to use depends in large part on the cultivars being grown. In all systems, a basic understanding of how pruning affects fruit production is essential.

The buds present on the canes in the fall will produce next year's grapes. A mature vine can have 600 or more buds, yet all one needs are a *few* to produce all the desirable grapes that the vine can support.

On the average, for a medium-size, healthy vine, a "few" means about 40 buds. This often means pruning away more than 90 percent of the vine. If too many buds are left, the grapes will be small, and often the overall vigor of the vine is reduced. The goal is to try to match the vigor of the vine with the number of buds. For a vine with little vigor, as few as 12 to 15 buds may be left.

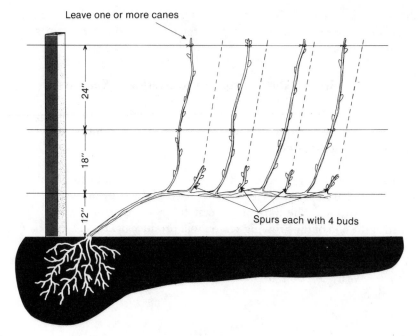

Training system for tender cultivars that need winter protection.

Notice that in the kniffin system, which is illustrated here, only four, one-year-old canes, each with about ten buds, remain after pruning. Notice also that four *spurs* are left. These spurs were formed simply by cutting one-year-old canes back to two to four buds. These spur buds will elongate and form shoots the next summer but will not produce a full grape crop until the following year. A balance between vegetative growth and fruit production can be achieved by a combination of selecting the proper number of buds on each cane and by forming renewal spurs.

Four-arm kniffin. As the diagram illustrates, the main trunk is trained to grow upright, and four arms radiate from it. The four canes that remain after pruning contain the buds that will form next summer's fruit crop. The four renewal spurs will form shoots, which will become canes the following fall. This system has been used extensively for hardy cultivars like 'Beta'. The main disadvantage is that it does not allow for maximum penetration of sunlight and, thus, fruit quality and/or yield may be affected.

Six-arm kniffin. This is a basic modification of the first system except six arms radiate from the trunk instead of four, and three wires are used instead

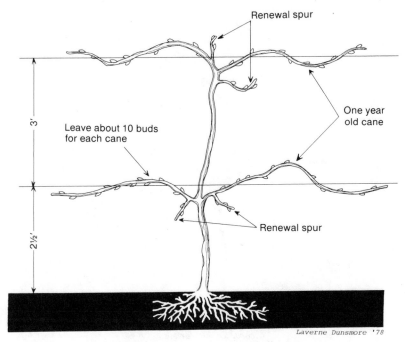

Mature vine trained to 4-cane kniffin system.

of two. This system is also suitable for hardy cultivars, but extensive shading caused by the shoots on the upper wires has limited its use.

Umbrella kniffin. In this system, the main trunk is trained to grow 4 to 10 inches below the top wire. Usually one to four shoots originate from the head of the trunk and are allowed to droop over the wires in umbrella fashion. If the trunk is trained to grow parallel to the ground for a short distance, and then allowed to go up, this system can be used for tender cultivars that need winter protection.

Fan system. A three-wire trellis is used and the trunk is trained to the lowest wire. Four or five shoots are allowed to develop in a fan shape from the trunk. The biggest disadvantage is that the canes for fruiting are often too short for maximum production. The system can be used for slower-growing, less vigorous cultivars or those with upright growth characteristics.

Geneva double curtain (GDC). The biggest advantage to this system is that it allows good light exposure. It works well for some of the more vigorous American *(labrusca)* grapes. The biggest disadvantage is the elaborate and expensive trellis system. The trellis resembles an old-fashioned clothesline with end posts and cross arms. A single wire is

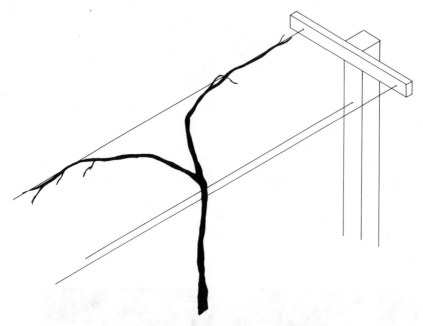

Geneva double curtain.

attached to the end posts 54 inches from the ground, and two additional wires radiate from the cross arms. The trunk of the vine is trained to the post wire, and shoots are allowed to develop on wire from the cross arms. In this system the vines are staggered so that fruit can be picked easily from both sides of the trellis.

Single cordon. This is basically a modification of the Geneva double curtain. Here the trunk is trained to a single wire 5½ to 6 feet from the soil surface, and extensions of the trunk (cordons) are allowed to grow along the wire. This method takes up considerable space and to prevent overlapping of growth, the vines should be spaced up to 14 feet apart.

Fertilizing

As far as nutrients are concerned, grapes are not a demanding crop. On reasonably fertile soil, they may require no supplemental nutrients at all. In Minnesota, in a seven-acre commercial vineyard, no nutrients were required even after five years of continued harvesting.

When nutrients are lacking, the two most likely to be in short supply are nitrogen and potassium. A nitrogen deficiency can be detected by the presence of light green leaves, reduced vine vigor, and shortened internodes.

In many Minnesota vineyards, and in other areas of the Upper Midwest, supplemental potassium is required. A potassium deficiency is indicated by the presence of yellow or scorched leaf margins and/or purplish black leaf spots. In addition, when potassium is lacking, berry size, color, quantity, and quality may be diminished, along with a reduction in overall vigor.

In severe cases of potassium deficiency, a foliar application of potassium sulfate or potassium nitrate may be necessary. Repeated applications of potassium chloride are not recommended for the vineyard because of the danger of a chloride buildup.

In soils where large amounts of potassium have been applied, and in soils with a pH below 5.0, a magnesium deficiency may develop. When this element is lacking, the symptoms show up first on older, basal leaves. The veins of the leaves remain green while the other parts turn yellow. Dolomitic limestone can correct a magnesium deficiency if the soil pH is below 5.5. Where the soil pH is higher, foliar applications of magnesium sulfate can be used. Unless the soil pH is below 5.0, liming of any kind or application of wood-ashes is not recommended.

Occasionally, other elements such as manganese, iron, zinc, and boron may be lacking.

Nutrients should be supplied in the early spring before growth begins. One bushel of well-rotted manure fortified with superphosphate for each vine can be tilled into the soil between the rows. Likewise, one-half pound of 10–10–10 per plant can be broadcast in a circle 2 feet from the plant.

Propagating

Because grapes do not breed true from seed, the plants are propagated vegetatively or by asexual means using either hardwood cuttings or layering. In this region, many of the cultivars are grown on their own roots.

In the layering process, a dormant, one-year cane that arises from the ground is selected in the early spring. From the base of the plant, a trench is dug 5 inches deep and about 12 inches long. A portion of the cane containing two to three buds is placed in the trench and covered with soil. Allow two buds of the cane to remain above ground and prune off the remaining terminal portion. The following spring before growth begins, the rooted, layered cane can be severed from the parent plant and transferred to the permanent planting site.

In commercial nurseries, grapes are more commonly propagated by hardwood cuttings selected from dormant, one-year-old wood. Normally, the canes are collected in late fall or early winter and cut to uniform size. Ideally, the canes should be about ⅜ inches in diameter and 10 to 12 inches long or with three buds. The canes are tied in bundles and stratified in a soil trench over the winter. Bundles should be placed in the trench with the basal end up. The soil is carefully replaced and mounded at the top to encourage water runoff and then mulched with straw or leaves.

In the early spring, as soon as the soil can be worked, the dormant cuttings are spaced 6 inches apart in the nursery row. When planting, make sure that the basal end is down and two buds are covered with soil. Keep the cuttings weeded and properly mulched during the growing season.

For best results, the cuttings should be partially shaded during the first month, and they must be misted or watered frequently during the entire summer to prevent drying. When fall arrives, mulch the cuttings; the following spring they can be moved to a permanent location in the vineyard.

Constructing a Trellis

Before the start of the second year, the trellis or support system should be constructed. The type of trellis depends in large part on the cultivars being grown, but for convenience, a system designed to accommodate most cultivars will be discussed.

Since grapevines are perennials that may live for several years, it is prudent to construct the trellis properly and with durable materials so that it will last. Constructing the trellis is much like building a sturdy farm fence. The end posts should be 4 to 8 inches in diameter and 9 feet long, preferably of a long-lasting wood. The life expectancies of different kinds of untreated wood vary considerably. For example, red cedar and black locust will last from 15 to 25 years; white oak, 5 to 10 years; and southern pine, red oak, cottonwood, and willow, only 2 to 7 years. Pressure-preservative-treated posts will, of course, last longer and are recommended. Posts treated with creosote should not be used because of possible injury to vines.

The end posts should be firmly braced using a combination of brace posts, thrust brace, and No. 9 galvanized wire as illustrated on page 165. Pressure-treated line posts should be 3 to 4 inches in diameter and 8 to 9 feet long. The top wire attached to these posts should be 5 to 6 feet from the soil surface. Spacing of line posts varies but good results are obtained with two vines between each post. The line posts are spaced 20 to 24 feet apart.

High tensile-strength, galvanized wire is recommended for stringing between the posts. Depending on the training system, two or three wires are used. The top strand should be No. 9 and the other(s) No. 10.

Spacing of wires also varies with the training system. Refer to the accompanying diagrams for some typical examples. Some device should be used to adjust wire tension. For the small grower, heavy-duty turnbuckles are available from hardware or farm-supply stores. To properly maintain tension, the

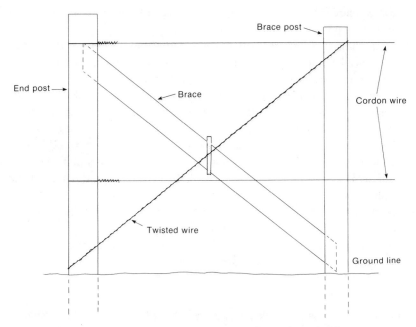

End post braced to line post; avoids use of wires beyond end post.

wires should be only loosely attached to the line posts. In fall, loosen the wires, and in spring, readjust the tension before growth begins.

There are scores of trellis systems, but space does not permit a description of each type. Some not discussed here may prove more effective in some Upper Midwest commercial operations. For more detail, see Wagner (1976), Shoemaker (1978), and Minnesota Grape Growers Association (1986).

Pests and Diseases

Birds. Throughout the Upper Midwest, birds are likely to be a serious problem for the grape grower. Various control techniques have been discussed in the chapters on tree fruits. With the exception of netting, most control methods have proved ineffective. At least one commercial grower in Minnesota has designed his own bird battler. His system consists of a specially designed tractor mount that mechanically spreads netting over the plants. The netting is expensive, but in most vineyards it is an absolute necessity.

Rodents. Some growers have reported damage from mice, especially on vines that have to be laid down and given winter protection. In most cases the damage is likely to be minimal, but if conditions warrant, trapping or use of poison baits may be necessary.

Deer. These animals are most likely to cause damage in the early spring when there is a lack of young, succulent growth for browsing. See the chapters on tree fruits for effective control measures.

Insects. Insects rarely cause problems for grapes in the Upper Midwest. Occasionally, some control may be needed for leafhoppers, grape berry moth, grape flea beetle, rose chafer, and the phylloxera aphid or louse. For additional details on grape insect pests see Stang et al. (1985).

Bacteria. Crown gall is the most serious bacterial disease affecting grapes in our area. The disease is first noticeable as a swelling on the main trunk near the soil line. Use of the Alma training method helps reduce the incidence of the disease. In addition, use care when cultivating so that the trunk is not injured or damaged. Where this disease is persistent, a multiple trunk-training system may be advised. This organism lives in the soil and cannot be controlled by spraying.

Fungal Diseases

Several fungal diseases attack grapes, and though some cultivars such as 'Beta' and 'Foch' have some resistance, most require repeated spraying with fungicides.

Black rot. This is the most prevalent and destructive fungal disease in vineyards east of the Mississippi River, but in our area the disease may cause problems only in selected areas. Early detection is essential for control, but in most cases the disease is unnoticed until the berries begin to dry and discolor when they are half-grown. Infected fallen debris such as leaves, canes, and fruit should be removed from the vineyard where practical.

Downy mildew. Initially this disease can be detected by the presence of light yellow spots on the leaves followed by the appearance of a white, moldy growth. In severe cases, shoots, tendrils, and berries are also affected. Remove fallen leaves and infected fruit from the vineyard.

Powdery mildew. Some cultivars such as 'Concord' seem quite resistant; others, such as most of the French hybrids or the American selection 'Interlaken', are susceptible. Symptoms include the appearance of a white, powdery growth on the leaves and young succulent parts of the vine. Infected berries appear rusty or scaly and often drop before they mature. Remove fallen infected leaves and fruit from the vineyard.

For more information, see Pearson and Goheen (1988). Theirs is one of the most comprehensive publications available on grape diseases.

A custom-designed tractor mount for spreading netting over grapevines.

SELECTED REFERENCES

Amerine, M. A., and V. L. Singleton. 1965. *Wine: An Introduction for Americans.* Berkeley: University of California Press.

Bailey, L. H. 1934. The Species of Grapes Peculiar to North America. *Gentes Herbarium* 3: 150–244.

Banta, E. S., G. A. Cahoon, and R. G. Hill, Jr. 1978. *Grape Growing.* Ohio State University Coop. Ext. Ser. Bull. 509.

Barrett, H. C. 1956. The French Hybrid Grapes. *Nat. Hort. Magazine* 35: 132–44.

Beach, S. A. 1898. *Self Fertility of the Grape.* Geneva, N.Y., Agr. Exper. Stat. Bull. 157: 397–441.

Brooks, R. M., and H. P. Olmo. 1972. *Register of New Fruit and Nut Varieties.* 2nd ed. Berkeley: University of California Press.

Cahoon, C. A. 1986. The Concord Grape. *Fruit Varieties Jour.* 40(4): 106–7.

Dix, I. W., and J. R. Magness. 1937. *American Grape Varieties.* USDA Circular 437.

Einset, J., and C. Pratt. 1975. Grapes. In: *Advances in Fruit Breeding.* J. Janick and J. Moore (eds.). Lafayette, Ind.: Purdue University Press.

Galet, P. 1979. *A Practical Ampelography.* Translated by Lucie Morton. Ithaca, N.Y. : Comstock Publishing.

Gloor, R. L. 1985. *A Guide to American and French Hybrid Grape Varieties.* Fredonia, N.Y.: Foster Nursery.

Gourley, J. H., and F. M. Howlett. 1941. *Modern Fruit Production.* New York: Macmillan.

Hedrick, U. P. 1908. *The Grapes of New York.* Geneva, N.Y., Agr. Exper. Stat. Report 1907.

Hedrick, U. P. 1922. *Cyclopedia of Hardy Fruits.* New York: Macmillan.

Hedrick, U. P. 1922. *Manual of American Grape Growing*. New York: Macmillan.

Hemstad, P. 1989. Grape Research in Minnesota, A Historical Perspective. *Minnesota Landscape Arboretum News* 9(3): 1, 5.

Hoover, E. 1986. *Growing Grapes for Home Use*. University of Minnesota Ext. Ser. Pub. AG-FO-1103.

Howell, G. S. 1987. *Vitis* Rootstocks. In: *Rootstocks for Fruit Crops*. R. C. Rom and R. F. Carlson (eds.). New York: Wiley-Interscience.

Johnson, H. 1971. *World Atlas of Wine*. New York: Simon and Schuster.

Jordan, T. D., R. M. Pool, T. J. Zabada, and J. P. Tomkins. 1981. *Cultural Practices for Commercial Vineyards*. Cornell University Misc. Bull. 111.

Kelly, C. B. 1944. *The Grape in Ontario*. Ontario Dept. Agr. State Branch Bull. 438.

Little, V. A. 1963. *General and Applied Entomology*. New York: Harper and Row.

Magoon, C. A., and E. Snyder.1943. *Grapes for Different Regions*. USDA Farmer's Bulletin 1936.

Marshall, J. 1978. D. MacGregor: Pioneer Grape Grower, Wine Maker. *Minnesota Horticulturist* 106(8): 238–39.

Marshall, J. 1985. A Short History of Minnesota Grape Culture. *Vinifera Wine Growers Journal* 12(3): 157–64.

Marshall, J. 1987. Burying Grapevines for Winter Protection, A Minnesota Perspective. *Vinifera Wine Growers Journal* 14(3): 188–93.

McGregor, S. E. 1976. *Insect Pollination of Cultivated Crop Plants*. USDA Agricultural Handbook No. 496.

McGrew, J. R. 1977. *Grapes Are Great But You May Have to Wait: Buying Rooted Vines Can Save a Year in Growing Fruits and Nuts*. USDA Agricultural Inform. Bull. 408.

McGrew, J. R., and G. W. Still. 1979. *Control of Grape Diseases and Insects in the Eastern United States*. USDA Farmer's Bulletin No. 1893.

Minnesota Grape Growers Association. 1986. *Growing Grapes in Minnesota*. Available from M.G.G.A., 1167 Glendon St., Maplewood, MN 55119.

Morton, L. 1985. *Winegrowing in Eastern America: An Illustrated Guide to Viticulture East of the Rockies*. Ithaca, N.Y.: Cornell University Press.

Munson, T. V. 1899. *Investigation and Improvement of American Grapes*. Texas Agr. Exper. Stat. Bull. 56: 217–85.

Pearson, R. C., and A. C. Goheen (eds.). 1988. *Compendium of Grape Diseases*. St. Paul, Minn.: American Phytopathological Society.

Pierquet, P. 1977. Some Problems Associated with Winter Protection of Grapevines. *Minnesota Horticulturist* 105(8): 210–11.

Ray, J. 1978. Showplace of Minnesota Grape Growing. *Minnesota Horticulturist* 106(8): 236–37.

Shoemaker, J. 1978. *Small Fruit Culture*. Westport, Conn.: AVI Publishing.

Snyder, E. 1937. Grape Development and Improvement. *USDA Yearbook of Agriculture* 1937: 631–64.

Stang, E. J. 1952. Grape Breeding Summary 1923–1951. *Proc. Amer. Soc. Hort. Sci.* 60: 243–46.

Stang, E. J., D. L. Mahr, and G. L.Worf. 1985. *Grapes in Wisconsin*. University of Wisconsin Coop. Ext. Ser. Pub. A–1656.

Taber, H. G., and C. Fear. 1986. *Fruit Cultivars for the Family*. Iowa State University Coop. Ext. Ser. Pub. PM 453.

Timmins, M. S., Jr. 1971. *Fences for the Farm and Rural Home*. USDA Farmer's Bulletin 2247.

Vine, R. P. 1981. *Commercial Winemaking, Processing and Controls*. Westport, Conn.: AVI Publishing.

Wagner, P. 1972. *A Winegrower's Guide*. New York: Alfred Knopf.

Weaver, R. J. 1976. *Grape Growing*. New York: Wiley.

Werner, R. 1978. Recommended Grapes for Minnesota: 1890–1977. *Minnesota Horticulturist* 106(8): 234–35.

Winkler, A. J., J. A. Cook, W. M. Kliewer, and L. A. Lider. 1974. *General Viticulture*. Berkeley: University of California Press.

Wott, J. No date. *Growing Grapes*. Purdue University Coop. Ext. Ser. Pub. HO–45.

9

Strawberries

There is probably no fruit with a more colorful and interesting history than the strawberry. The route of its origin from humble native species to the productive hybrids of today is replete with mystery, myth, and a remarkable amount of improvement in a relatively short time span.

Strawberries were known to the ancient Greeks and Romans, but the small-fruited European species did not have much appeal to the early epicureans. The Greeks had an aversion to any type of red fruit, believing it was either poisonous or shrouded with mysterious, often evil powers. Pregnant women were to avoid the fruits at all costs lest they give birth to a child with a "strawberry" birthmark (Hendrickson, 1981). During the Middle Ages, strawberries became more highly esteemed and were regarded as elixirs that could be used as cure-alls for just about everything (Hendrickson, 1981).

The origin of the term *strawberry* remains a mystery. Several writers suggest that it was derived from the straw used to cover the berries. Others believe the name was changed from *strewberry,* a reference to the berries *strewn* (scattered) among the leaves. Another idea is that dry strawberry runners resemble straw or that the yellow dots (achenes) on the fruit resemble straw.

The cultivated strawberry belongs to the rose family and is accorded the scientific name *Fragaria* x *ananassa.* The "x" denotes a hybrid origin. Both parents are native American species, but the first hybridization did not occur here.

According to historical accounts (Lee, 1964; Darrow, 1966; Scott and Lawrence, 1975), a Frenchman named Amedee François Frezier in 1714 introduced specimens of *F. chiloensis* into a garden in Brest, France, where *F.*

Photo courtesy of Minnesota Extension Service, University of Minnesota.

virginiana was being cultivated. Chance hybridization occurred, and soon the strawberry industry was borne. The role that chance played in this accidental hybridization needs to be underscored. Frezier was an army officer who had collected *F. chiloensis* in Chile, and during the long journey back to France, only five plants survived, all of which were female or pistillate. This species, though collected in Chile, is distributed all the way from South America to California and Alaska. It was fortunate that plants of *F. virginiana,* grown from seed sent from the eastern United States, were placed next to the Chilean species in this French garden.

Development of cultivars in strawberries did not begin for more than half a century after the initial chance hybridization. Amateur breeders in Europe made controlled crosses and selected several cultivars that finally made their way to the United States.

When the colonists arrived in this country, they found that American Indians used the native species *F. virginiana* both for fresh eating and in baking bread. Until about 1850, which is when commercial cultivation began, early settlers relied on native species and plants imported from Europe. Breeding of improved cultivars here was undertaken mostly by amateurs until after the turn of the century. Research by public agencies, particularly during the last 50 to 60 years, has not only made strawberry production a commercial success, but it has also helped to introduce the strawberry to the world.

In the United States, strawberries are grown commercially in 35 states and the value of production in 1989 exceeded $500 million. In the Upper Midwest, commercial pick-your-own operations are present in all five states. Wisconsin is the largest producer, where the value of the 1989 harvest was $4,026,000 (*Vegetables,* USDA Stat. Ser., January 1990).

How Many Plants?

Depending on the cultivar and the growing conditions, each strawberry plant will yield from ½ to a little over 1 quart during the growing season. Under prime conditions, 25 plants (enough for a 50-foot row) will yield from 25 to 35 quarts. About 100 plants are usually sufficient for a family of three to four.

Pollination

Individual flowers on all commercial cultivars of strawberries are bisexual with numerous stamens and pistils. All the cultivars are self-compatible; thus, only one cultivar is needed to ensure fruit production. Some self-fertilization does occur, but unless all the pistils in the flower are fertilized by pollen, an irregularly shaped berry or "nubbin" is formed.

Table 11. Upper Midwest strawberry production*

State	Acreage	Yield per acre
Iowa	600	6,000 pounds average; 10,000–12,000 good
Minnesota	1,000	4,000 pounds average; 8,000–10,000 good
North Dakota	30	7,500 pounds average
South Dakota	45	4,000–5,000 pounds average
Wisconsin	1,500	5,500–7,000 pounds average

*Data for the five states from G. Nonnecke, L. Hertz, E. Scholz, R. Peterson, and M. Dana, respectively.

Some pollen is transported to the pistils by wind and a variety of insects. Of the major pollinizing agents, honeybees are the most important; without them fruit production is sharply curtailed.

McGregor (1976), citing Connor (1970), reported that the best time for pollination seems to be one to four days after the flower opens. If cool weather persists for seven to ten days after flower-bud opening, the absence of bee pollinators may result in crop reduction or deformed fruit.

Selecting a Planting Site

The ideal site for strawberries is on land with a slight slope of 2 to 3 percent. The site should provide ample water and air movement and, in addition, offer some protection from frost. Since strawberries require extensive cultivation, erosion is likely to be a problem on steeper slopes.

Level land is acceptable if soil drainage is good, but sites should not be in low areas because of the hazard of frost damage. Northern slopes tend to delay spring blossoming, and thus offer some added protection.

In areas where damaging spring frosts are a perennial problem, sprinkler irrigation can be used to prevent damage. Begin sprinkling when the temperature drops below 32° F. The ice that forms on the buds, flowers, or fruit provides needed insulation. A rate of .10 to .15 inches of water per hour is required. To be successful, the irrigation should be continuous until temperatures are above freezing, and the ice has melted from the leaves. When wind velocities are high, sprinkling may be difficult and ineffective.

Strawberries need full sun to develop properly. Besides nutrient competition and shade, there is some danger of frost pockets forming if the plants are located too close to windbreaks. The plantings should be at least 50 feet from large trees and 25 feet from small trees and shrubs.

Soils

Strawberries will grow in a wide variety of soil types ranging from sandy to heavy loams. The plants perform very poorly on waterlogged soils or muck, and if berries are produced they are usually soft and frequently rot before maturity.

Berries perform best on sandy loams with a pH of 5.8 to 6.5 but can be grown successfully on soils that are much more alkaline. If the soil pH is below 4.5 to 5.3, liming is advised.

Soil History

Ideally, strawberries should not be grown on soil that in the previous three years was planted to potatoes, tomatoes, eggplants, peppers, raspberries, peaches, or cherries. These plants can harbor verticillium wilt, which is a serious disease of strawberries.

Likewise, an old strawberry bed should not be plowed up and used for a new site because of the possibility of multiple disease problems. Uncultivated sites or land previously in sod should also be avoided because of pests such as white grubs and weeds.

Ideally the site should have been under clean cultivation for a full year before planting strawberries. On land previously continuously cropped, application of manure will help improve production. For best results, the manure (20 tons per acre or 50 to 75 pounds per 100 square feet) should be plowed under in the fall before planting.

Selection and Care of Nursery Stock

Obtaining planting stock from a neighbor or friend is not advised because of possible disease problems. Even plants that look robust and healthy may harbor disease organisms such as viruses, which are not visible to the naked eye.

Order plants from nurseries that advertise either registered, certified, or disease-free stock. Also, on the order, request that cultivars not be substituted.

Most strawberry plants sold in the Upper Midwest have been dug in the fall and stored under constant temperature and humidity conditions during the winter months. Plants shipped from nursersies or available from garden centers are frequently in bundles wrapped in plastic bags. If conditions for planting are unfavorable when the plants arrive, the bundles should be opened and the roots moistened — but not soaked.

The plants can be stored in their original wrapping in the crisper section of the home refrigerator for several days. Make sure that the bag is tied loosely so that some air exchange is possible. Avoid purchasing plants with roots that have completely dried out, or plants packaged in plastic and stored in areas exposed to the sun.

Strawberries are commonly sold barerooted in bundles of 25 plants.

Preplanting

If manure was not plowed into the soil the fall before spring planting, a broadcast application of an inorganic fertilizer may be advisable. The kind and amount of fertilizer to apply depends on the cropping history and the fertility of the soil. For large plantings, a soil test is advised. Most home gardeners will find one pound of 10–10–10 per 100 square feet satisfactory. The fertilizer should be spread out evenly and worked into the soil before planting.

Selection of Cultivars

There are three main classes of strawberry cultivars: June bearing, everbearing, and day-neutral.

June-bearing cultivars initiate flowers under a short-day photoperiod and produce one crop each year in late spring. These are the most popular strawberries grown and are the mainstay of commercial growers in the Upper Midwest.

Everbearing and day-neutral types have nearly identical cultural requirements, but show a different response to photoperiod. Everbearers are classed

A well-managed commercial strawberry field.

as long-day plants and initiate flower buds when the daylight period exceeds 12 hours. Day-neutrals are largely unaffected by photoperiod (Durner et al., 1984).

Everbearers and day-neutrals require more work than June bearers, but they are equally, or perhaps more, productive. Both types produce a spring crop and will continue to produce throughout the summer and early fall. Day-neutrals perform best when summers are cool and when there is abundant rainfall.

Strawberries tend to be regional performers, so it is important that the cultivars selected perform well in the buyer's specific area. Besides evaluating the characteristics of the cultivars presented here, visit a local pick-your-own operation for additional information. Most commercial growers have experimented with several cultivars and can help in choosing the best ones.

In areas where late spring frosts are a problem, everbearing or day-neutral cultivars may be the best choice. Sometimes in these areas, selecting late-blooming June cultivars may be the answer. Examples include 'Badgerbelle', 'Badgerglo', 'Sparkle', and 'Micmac'.

If strawberries are desired the first season, everbearing or day-neutrals should be selected since they usually produce their best crop during the first year. For June-bearing cultivars, fruit is not harvested until the second season.

Cultivars

Refer to Tables 12 through 15 for additional information. Unless noted, all cultivars in the following list are June bearing.

Badgerbelle. Introduced in 1967 at Sturgeon Bay, Wisconsin, by F. A. Gilbert, this is a 'Robinson' x 'Jerseybelle' cross.

Badgerglo. This 1972 'Sparkle' x 'Stelemaster' selection is another introduction by F. A. Gilbert from Wisconsin.

Bounty. Parentage of this 1972 Canadian introduction is 'Jerseybelle' x 'Senga Sengana'. Berries are medium size and suitable for fresh use and freezing. The plant is susceptible to mildew and verticillium wilt but only slightly susceptible to leaf scorch.

Canoga. Donald Ourecky introduced this ('Senga Sengana' x 'Midland') x 'Holiday' cross from Geneva, New York, in 1979.

Catskill. Introduced in 1934 at Geneva, New York, the parentage is 'Marshall' x 'Howard 17.'

Crimson King. Marion Hagerstrom of Monticello, Minnesota, selected this cultivar in about 1960. According to Hagerstrom, the exact date of introduction and the parentage are uncertain. Patent rights were later sold to Stark Bros. Nursery.

Cyclone. A 1959 introduction by Ervin Denisen at Ames, Iowa. Parentage is 'Rockhill' x ('Beaver' x 'Dorsett').

Delite. From Carbondale, Illinois, this 'Albritton' x MDUS 2650 selection was introduced in 1974. The berries are large, medium soft, and fair for freezing. The plant is resistant to leaf spot, leaf scorch, and verticillium wilt.

Dunlap (Senator Dunlap). J. R. Reasoner selected this cultivar in about 1890 from unknown parentage. It was introduced in 1899 by M. Crawford of Cuyahoga Falls, Ohio. The berries are medium to large and ripen midseason. This cultivar's popularity has waned and it is rarely recommended.

Earliglow. A 1975 USDA introduction from Salisbury, Maryland, the parentage is ('Fairland' x 'Midland') x ('Redglow' x 'Surecrop'). For flavor, this is perhaps the best June-bearing cultivar in the region.

Fern. Introduced at Davis, California, in 1983, the name honors Fern Miller, a Davis community leader. The parentage is 'Tufts' x 69.62–103. The berries are medium to large with solid flesh. It is a day-neutral type.

Fort Laramie. This is a 1973 USDA introduction from Cheyenne, Wyoming. The parentage is 'Geneva' x ('Earlidawn' x 'Chief Bemidji'). The berries

Table 12. Resistance of strawberries to diseases when grown in favorable areas

Cultivar	Leaf spot	Leaf scorch	Red stele	Verticillium wilt	Virus tolerance
Badgerbelle	Resistant	Susceptible	Susceptible	Unknown	Unknown
Badgerglo	Unknown	Susceptible	Susceptible	Susceptible	Unknown
Catskill	Susceptible	Resistant	Susceptible	V. Resistant	V. Susceptible
Cyclone	Resistant	Unknown	Susceptible	Unknown	Tolerant
Earliglow	Resistant	Resistant	Resistant	Resistant	Unknown
Fort Laramie	Intermediate	Intermediate	Susceptible	Unknown	Unknown
Gem	Susceptible	Resistant	Susceptible	Unknown	Unknown
Guardian	Resistant	Resistant	Resistant	V. Resistant	Unknown
Hecker	Unknown	Unknown	Susceptible	Resistant	Tolerant
Honeoye	Resistant	Resistant	Susceptible	Resistant	Unknown
Jerseybelle	V. Susceptible	Susceptible	Susceptible	Susceptible	Susceptible
Marlate	Resistant	Resistant	Susceptible	Susceptible	Unknown
Micmac	Unknown	Resistant	Susceptible	Resistant	Unknown
Midway	V. Susceptible	Susceptible	Resistant	Intermediate	Unknown
Ogallala	Unknown	Unknown	Susceptible	Unknown	Unknown
Ozark Beauty	Resistant	Resistant	Susceptible	Susceptible	Unknown
Raritan	Susceptible	Susceptible	Susceptible	Susceptible	Unknown
Redchief	Resistant	Resistant	Resistant	Intermediate	Unknown
Redcoat	Unknown	Unknown	Susceptible	Unknown	Unknown
Robinson	Intermediate	Susceptible	Susceptible	Resistant	Tolerant
Sparkle	Susceptible	Intermediate	Resistant	Susceptible	Susceptible
Stoplight	Intermediate	Intermediate	Susceptible	Unknown	Unknown
Surecrop	Resistant	Resistant	Resistant	V. Resistant	Tolerant
Trumpeter	V. Susceptible	Unknown	Susceptible	Unknown	Tolerant
Veestar	Resistant	Susceptible	Susceptible	Resistant	Unknown

Source: Scott et al., 1983.

are large and sweet. The plant is vigorous, productive, and quite hardy. It is an everbearing cultivar that may be susceptible to mildew in some locations.

Gem ('Superfection', 'Brillant', 'Gem Everbearing', 'Giant Gem'). This mutation of 'Champion' was introduced in 1933 by Frank J. Keplinger at Farwell, Michigan. It is an everbearing cultivar.

Gorella. This import from Wageningen, Holland, was introduced in 1960. The parentage is 'Juspa' x US 3763. The berries are very large and firm with good flavor.

Guardian. This NC 1768 x 'Surecrop' cross was introduced in 1969 by the USDA at Salisbury, Maryland.

Hecker. The origin of this 1979 introduction from Davis, California, is complex and involves numbered crosses. The name commemorates Hecker Pass in California. It is a day-neutral type.

Honeoye. Donald K. Ourecky introduced this 'Vibrant' x 'Holiday' cross at Geneva, New York, in 1979. Berries are large and firm with very good

Table 13. Fruit characteristics of strawberries

Cultivar	Ripening season, days after midland	Size	Flesh firmness	Skin firmness	Dessert quality	Freezing quality
Badgerbelle	14	Large	Soft	Soft	Fair	Fair
Badgerglo	14	Large	Medium	Medium	Good	Unknown
Catskill	7	Very large	Soft	Soft	Good	Fair to good
Cyclone	3	Large	Soft	Soft	Very good	Good
Earliglow	3	Med-large	Firm	Firm	Very good	Very good
Fort Laramie	7	Medium	Medium	Medium	Good	Unknown
Gem	7	Small	Soft	Soft	Fair	Fair
Guardian	7	Very large	Firm	Firm	Good	Fair
Hecker	5	Medium	Medium	Medium	Good	Unknown
Honeoye	5	Large	Firm	Firm	Good	Good
Jerseybelle	14	Very large	Soft	Firm	Fair	Poor
Marlate	14	Med-large	Firm	Firm	Good	Unknown
Micmac	7	Large	Soft	Medium	Fair	Unknown
Midway	10	Large	Firm	Firm	Good	Very good
Ogallala	7	Medium	Soft	Soft	Good	Good
Ozark Beauty	14	Medium	Medium	Medium	Very good	Good
Raritan	7	Large	Firm	Medium	Fair	Fair
Redchief	7	Large	Firm	Firm	Good	Very good
Redcoat	10	Med-large	Medium	Medium	Good	Unknown
Robinson	10	Large	Soft	Soft	Fair	Poor
Sparkle	12	Small	Soft	Soft	Very good	Very good
Stoplight	7	Medium	Soft	Medium	Good	Very good
Surecrop	5	Large	Firm	Medium	Good	Good
Trumpeter	10	Medium	Soft	Soft	Good	Very good
Veestar	3	Medium	Soft	Soft	Very good	Good

Source: Scott et al., 1983.

freezing quality. The plant is vigorous and productive but is susceptible to verticillium wilt.

Jerseybelle. The parentage is complex and involves 'Lupton', 'Aberdeen', 'Fairfax', and 'Pathfinder'. It was introduced in 1955 at New Brunswick, New Jersey.

Kent. Nova Scotia, Canada, is the home of this ('Redgauntlet' x 'Tioga') x 'Raritan' cross introduced in 1981. The berries are large, firm, and ripen midseason. The plant is vigorous and productive but is slightly susceptible to mildew.

Marlate. I. C. Haut introduced this cultivar in 1969 at College Park, Maryland. The parentage is complex and involves 'Jerseybelle', 'Klonmore', 'Midland', and 'Tennessee Shipper'.

Micmac. This 'Tioga' x 'Guardsman' S1 cross was introduced in 1976 from Nova Scotia. The berries are large, firm, and have good flavor. The plant is vigorous and productive but is susceptible to powdery mildew.

Table 14. Characteristics of June-bearing strawberries in Minnesota*

Cultivar	Yield potential	Hardiness	Vigor	Fruit size	Attractiveness	Firmness	Texture	Flavor
Early season								
Crimson King	High	Excellent	High	Large	Very good	Fair	Very good	Fair
Earliglow	Moderate	Fair	Moderate	Medium	Excellent	Excellent	Excellent	Excellent
Veegem	Moderate	Good	Moderate	Medium	Good	Good	Good	Good
Veestar	Mod-high	Good	High	Medium	Good	Good	Good	Good
Early midseason								
Honeoye	High	Very good	High	Medium-large	Good	Very good	Good	Good
Redcoat	High	Very good	High	Medium	Good	Good	Good	Good
Scott	Moderate	Fair	Moderate	Large	Excellent	Excellent	Good	Fair
Trumpeter	Mod-high	Very good	High	Medium	Fair	Fair	Good	Good
Late midseason								
Kent	High	Very good	Mod-high	Large	Very good	Very good	Very good	Very good
Late season								
Sparkle	High	Very good	High	Medium	Fair	Good	Good	Good
Micmac	Mod-high	Good	Moderate	Medium-large	Excellent	Very good	Very good	Very good
Bounty	Mod-high	Good	Moderate	Medium	Good	Good	Very good	Good
Canoga	Moderate	Fair	Low	Large	Very good	Excellent	Good	Good

Source: Hoover et al., 1986.
*Used with permission.

Table 15. Characteristics of day-neutral and everbearing strawberry cultivars in Minnesota*

Cultivar	Yield potential	Hardiness	Vigor	Fruit size	Attractiveness	Firmness	Texture	Flavor	Comments
Aptos	Moderate	Very good	Very low	Medium	Medium	Excellent	Fair	Fair	
Brighton	Moderate	Fair	Moderate	Large	Fair	Very good	Fair	Fair	Very susceptible to fruit rots
Burlington	Not adequately tested								
Fern	Moderate-high	Good	Low	Medium	Good	Excellent	Very good	Good	
Hecker	High	Good	Moderate	Medium	Good	Very good	Good	Fair	
Sakuma	Not adequately tested								
Selva	Low-moderate	Poor	High	Very large	Excellent	Excellent	Fair	Poor	Sensitive to alkaline soils
Tribute	High	Very good	Moderate	Medium-large	Good	Very good	Very good	Good	Resistant to red stele root rot
Tristar	Moderate	Very good	Moderate	Medium	Very good	Very good	Very good	Very good	Resistant to red stele root rot
†Ft. Laramie	High	Excellent	High	Large	Good	Poor	Fair	Fair	Very susceptible to powdery mildew
†Ogallala	Moderate-high	Excellent	High	Small	Fair	Poor	Good	Good	

Source: Hoover et al., 1986.
*Used with permission.
†Everbearing.

Midway. Salisbury, Maryland, is the home of this 'Dixieland' x 'Temple' cross introduced in 1960.

Northland. A. N. Wilcox developed this 'Burgundy' x 'Premier' cross, which was introduced at Excelsior, Minnesota, in 1982. The berries are medium to large, soft, and mild flavored. The plant is vigorous, hardy, and somewhat susceptible to leaf spot. This cultivar is more productive than 'Redcoat' in North Dakota and western Minnesota.

Ogallala. This is regarded as one of the best everbearing cultivars for the Upper Midwest. It is a complex hybrid involving several cultivars and *Fragaria ovalis.* It was introduced from North Platte, Nebraska, and Cheyenne, Wyoming, in 1958.

Ourown. A 'Gem' x 'Temple' cross, introduced in 1975 from Waushara County, Wisconsin. The berries are medium to large and have good dessert and excellent freezing quality. The plant is everbearing, vigorous, and hardy.

Ozark Beauty. J. B. Winn introduced this 'Red Rich' x 'Twentieth Century' cross from Westfork, Arkansas, in 1955. The cultivar is everbearing.

Raritan. Fredrick Hough introduced this 'Redglow' x 'Jerseybelle' cross in 1968 at New Brunswick, New Jersey.

Redchief. Introduced in 1968 by the USDA at Salisbury, Maryland, this is a cross of N.C. 1768 x 'Surecrop.' It is a popular commercial cultivar in southern Minnesota and Iowa.

Redcoat. This 'Sparkle' x 'Valentine' selection was introduced in 1957 at Ottawa, Ontario. It is adapted to a variety of soil types and even does well on calcareous soils. 'Redcoat' is the most popular cultivar grown in North Dakota and is the mainstay of commercial growers.

Robinson ('Kardinal King,' 'Neet,' 'Scarlet Beauty'). John C. Haley introduced this 'Howard 17' x 'Washington' selection at Sister Lakes, Michigan, about 1940.

Scott. D. H. Scott and A. D. Draper introduced this 'Sunrise' x 'Tioga' hybrid from the Maryland Wye Institute in 1979. The berries are large, firm, mild flavored, and good for dessert and freezing. The plant is resistant to most of the major strawberry diseases.

Sparkle ('Paymaster'). J. Clark introduced this 'Fairfax' x 'Aberdeen' cross from New Brunswick, New Jersey, in 1942.

Stoplight. E. L. Denisen of Iowa State University introduced this selection in 1971. The parentage is complex and involves ('Florida Ninety' x 'Cyclone') x a second-generation self of 'Dunlap.'

Sunrise. Introduced at Salisbury, Maryland, in 1964, this is a US 4152 x 'Stelemaster' cross. The berries are medium size and are recommended primarily for fresh use. The plant is very vigorous and resistant to red stele, verticillium wilt, leaf scorch, and mildew but is very susceptible to leaf spot.

Surecrop. 'Fairland' x Maryland-US-1972 is the parentage of this USDA selection introduced in 1956 from Salisbury, Maryland.

Tribute. This is another D. H. Scott and A. D. Draper selection from Beltsville, Maryland. It was introduced in 1981 from complex parentage using numbered crosses. The berries are medium to small, firm, and somewhat tart. The plant is day-neutral and resistant to several races of red stele and powdery mildew. It is somewhat resistant to verticillium wilt and leaf scorch.

Tristar. Like 'Tribute' this is another 1981 Scott and Draper complex hybrid from Beltsville, Maryland. This is also a day-neutral cultivar with small to medium sweet berries. The plant has disease resistance similar to 'Tribute'.

Trumpeter. A. N. Wilcox introduced this 'Burgundy' x 'Howard 17' (selfed seedling) selection at Excelsior, Minnesota, in 1960.

Veegem. This 'Valentine' x 'Fulton' cross is a 1980 Canadian introduction by C. L. Ricketson. It was originally released to replace 'Redcoat.' The plant is moderately productive and the firm berries are slightly larger than 'Redcoat.' 'Veegem' is moderately resistant to leaf scorch and powdery mildew. It has shown slight susceptibility to verticillium wilt. This cultivar has outstanding quality for freezing.

Veeglow. This is the second 1980 introduction by C. L. Ricketson. Like 'Veegem,' it was introduced as an alternative for 'Redcoat.' The parentage is 'Redglow' x 'Vibrant.' The plant is about as productive as 'Redcoat' and has slightly larger fruit with similar firmness. 'Veeglow' is moderately resistant to leaf scorch, but is susceptible to powdery mildew. It is only slightly susceptible to verticillium wilt.

Veestar. C. L. Ricketson introduced this 'Valentine' x 'Sparkle' hybrid from Ontario in 1967. The berries are medium size, firm, and slightly acid with excellent flavor. The plant is moderately productive and susceptible to leaf scorch. It is somewhat resistant to verticillium wilt. This cultivar is probably the second choice of commercial growers in North Dakota. It is slightly less productive than 'Redcoat.'

Vesper. J. N. Moore and L. F. Hough introduced this 'Utah Shipper' x 'Jerseybelle' hybrid in 1962 at New Brunswick, New Jersey. The berries are very large, soft, and are primarily used fresh for dessert. The plant is very productive but is not resistant to several of the major diseases.

Planting

Strawberries grown in the Upper Midwest usually give the best results if they are planted in the early spring as soon as the soil can be worked. When planting, the soil should be well tilled and free of clods. Evenly spread the

**Fruit zones—
strawberries**

Cultivar	Iowa	Minn.	N. Dak.	S. Dak.	Wis.
Badgerbelle		X			X
Badgerglo					X
Bounty		X	T		X
Canoga		X			X
Catskill			X		X
Crimson King	X	X			
Cyclone	X	X		X	X
Delite	X				
Dunlap				X	X
Earliglow	X	X			X
Fern	T	T	T	T	T
Fort Laramie	X	X	T	X	X
Gem		X	X	X	X
Gorella			T		T
Guardian	X				X
Hecker	T	T	T	T	
Honeoye	X	X	T	X	X
Jerseybelle		X			X
Kent	X	X	T	X	X
Marlate	X				
Micmac	X	X			X

Cultivars may not perform well in all areas of the state. Check with local growers for additional information.
X = recommended for planting; T = recommended for trial.

**Fruit zones—
strawberries, continued**

Cultivar	Iowa	Minn.	N. Dak.	S. Dak.	Wis.
Midway	X		X		X
Northland		X	X	X	
Ogallala	X	X	X	X	X
Ourown					T
Ozark Beauty				T	X
Raritan					X
Redchief	X	X			X
Redcoat	X	X	X	X	X
Robinson					X
Scott					X
Sparkle	X	X	X	X	X
Stoplight	X	X	X		X
Sunrise	X				X
Surecrop	X		X		X
Tribute	X	T	T	T	T
Tristar	X	T	T	T	X
Trumpeter	X	X	X	X	X
Veegem		X	T		
Veeglow			T		
Veestar	X	X	T	T	T
Vesper				T	X

Cultivars may not perform well in all areas of the state. Check with local growers for additional information.
X = recommended for planting; T = recommended for trial.

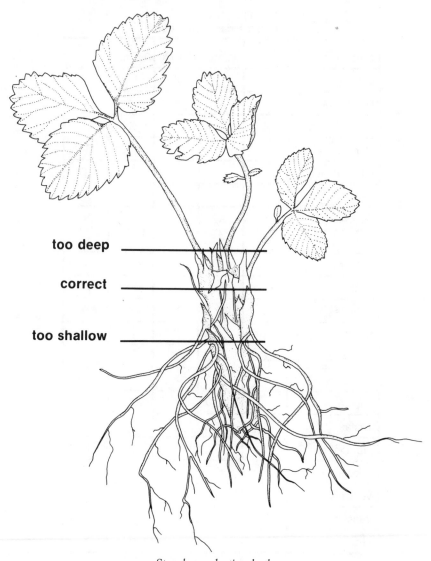

too deep

correct

too shallow

Strawberry planting depths.

roots and position the plant so that the crown (where the leaves arise) is just above the soil surface. Firm the soil around the roots to eliminate air spaces, and after planting give each plant one cup of water or one cup of starter solution. To make a starter solution, add two to three tablespoons of a complete fertilizer such as 10–10–10 or 12–12–12 to one gallon of water. Since the fer-

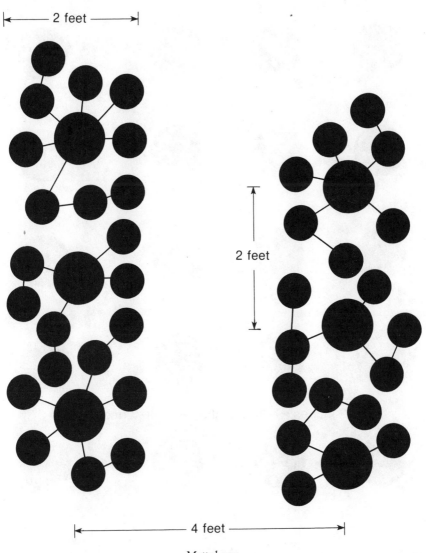

Matted row.

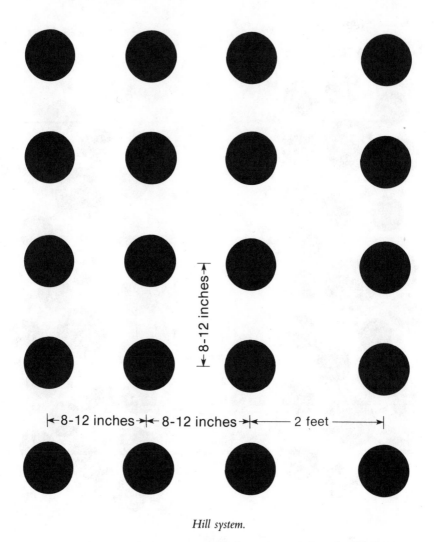

Hill system.

tilizer may be slow to dissolve, it should be mixed several hours before planting.

The Planting Plan

Three planting plans are commonly used for strawberries in the Upper Midwest.

The *matted-row system* is the one most often used on June-bearing cultivars. In this system, plants are often set 18 to 24 inches apart with 4 feet between

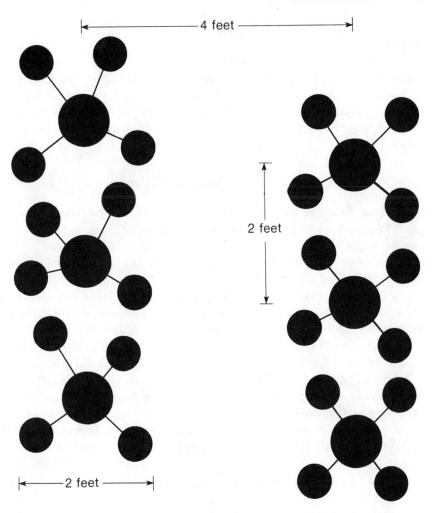

Spaced row.

rows. The plants are allowed to form runners until a matted row about 2 feet wide is formed. Excess runners are removed by cultivation so that a walkway for cultivation and harvesting is present between each matted row.

The *spaced-row system* is more difficult to establish, but there are likely to be fewer disease problems, and yield and fruit quality are usually better than in the matted row. In this system, the rows are spaced 4 feet apart, and plants within the rows 24 inches apart, just as in the matted-row system. The only difference is that runner plants are spaced by hand so that they are arranged 6 to 9 inches apart. Excess runners are removed by cultivation. In this system, there are fewer plants and less competition. As a result, a better crop is usually produced.

The *hill system* is recommended for everbearing and day-neutral cultivars. Plants are set 8 to 12 inches apart in rows 8 to 12 inches apart. The rows are established in blocks of threes with a 2-foot walk space between each block. In this system all runners that develop are removed by cultivation for the first six to eight weeks. This encourages greater productivity of the mother crown.

Culture of June-Bearing Cultivars

All blossoms should be pinched out during the first year on June-bearing cultivars. Removal of blossoms allows more energy to be channeled into runners and vegetative growth.

If manure or inorganic fertilizer was incorporated into the soil before planting, additional nutrients probably will not be needed during the early summer weeks. If, however, the plants appear weak, lack vigor, or have light green (yellow) leaves, some additional fertilizer may be needed after the first four weeks of growth. At this time apply one pound of 10–10–10 per 25 feet of row. Take care to avoid getting fertilizer on the leaves. If this should occur, brush it off immediately. If the plants fail to respond, a soil test is required.

Except in rare cases on very sandy soils, fertilizers containing nitrogen should not be used on strawberries until after the June harvest, and after renovation is completed. Nitrogen applied before the harvest may stimulate excess vegetative growth and make the berries soft. Soft berries are difficult to harvest, and they may also be more susceptible to fruit rot problems.

Renovation of the Planting

More than one writer has stated that the worst weed that develops in the strawberry bed is the strawberry plant itself. Renovation of the bed or removal of these excess "weeds" will greatly improve the quality of the harvest each year.

The best time for renovation is immediately after the harvest. Some growers prefer to mow off the leaves with a rotary mower about an inch above the crown. For small home plantings the bed can be lightly raked, and the debris removed from the area. In theory, this practice should stimulate new growth and help reduce leaf-spot diseases, but if it is done improperly the plants may suffer. For example, if the plants are mowed too low or if raking is severe, injury to the crown may occur.

The practice of burning over the planting area after harvest has been abandoned by most growers in the Upper Midwest. With this method plants may be damaged, and there is always the risk of an uncontrolled fire.

Whether or not the leaves are mowed off, the row width should be narrowed to about 10 to 12 inches. This can be accomplished by hand hoeing, but rototilling is faster and easier. Ideally, after the rows are narrowed the remaining plants should be thinned so that they are 8 to 10 inches apart. Only healthy and vigorous plants should remain. The life of the planting can usually be extended if annual renovation is practiced.

Fertilizing

The most important time to fertilize June-bearing cultivars is after the harvest, or before the onset of fall flower-bud formation. Most growers prefer to fertilize immediately after renovation. About 5 pounds of 10–10–10 or 12–12–12 per 100 feet of row is commonly used. In gardens where a soil test confirms adequate potassium and phosporus levels, 1 pound of 33–0–0 per 100 feet of row may be used. Another fertilizer application may be needed about the second week in August if the plants exhibit nitrogen deficiency symptoms. This is most likely to occur on irrigated, sandy soils.

Life of the Planting

There are those rare cases where growers report a good harvest for 5 to 6 years or more, but for most growers, good-quality berries can be expected for only about three harvests. In June-bearing cultivars, the best crop will be produced the first year after planting; after that there will be a steady decline in both quality and quantity of production. The best hope for extending the life of the planting is annual renovation and good cultural practices.

Culture of Everbearing and Day-Neutral Cultivars during the Planting Year

Blossoms on everbearing and day-neutral cultivars should be removed until the plants have five new leaves (about July 1). After that, flowers that form will produce the fall harvest, which usually begins in August. Any runners that form should also be removed during the first few weeks after planting. The goal is to funnel energy into crown and blossom production.

After planting, keep the plants hand weeded for about four to five weeks, then mulch with straw, corncobs, or sawdust. Mulching not only conserves water but also helps keep the plants cool, a condition that is essential for good production in these cultivars. Fertilize the plants every four to five weeks using ¼ pound of 10–10–10 per 100 feet of row or ¼ teaspoon per hill.

Second Growing Season

Culture in subsequent seasons is essentially a repeat of the first year except for the following differences:

> Do not remove blossoms.
>
> Remove the mulch when growth begins in the spring and begin the fertilization schedule recommended for the first year.
>
> Replace or replenish the mulch to conserve soil moisture and to control weeds.

Everbearing and day-neutral strawberries usually produce their best crop the first year, and continued cultivation after two or three harvests is usually not practical. In plantings that appear healthy and disease free, some growers allow a few runners to develop so that new plants can be selected for replanting. Commercially, day-neutral cultivars are usually grown for only one season.

Water Requirements

Strawberries have a shallow root system. Hull et al. (1977) reported that 75 percent of the roots are in the top 3 inches of soil and 90 percent are in the top 6 inches. With this shallow root system, strawberries need an average of 1 inch of water per week during the growing season.

Drought periods immediately after planting are particularly detrimental and often result in death of the plant. One Minnesota grower in 1976 lost several thousand new plants to drought. The next year he installed an irrigation system.

Drip or trickle irrigation systems can be used, but they are ineffective for frost protection. Most commercial growers use sprinkler or overhead irrigation systems. This type of irrigation system is also useful to help cool day-neutral cultivars when temperatures exceed 82 to 85° F. For the home gardener with just a few plants, the garden hose with a sprinkler attachment gives satisfactory results.

The importance of water to strawberry culture has been underscored by Scholz and Askew (1986). They report that lack of water is probably responsible for more low yields and failures than any other factor.

Winter Mulch

Strawberries need to be mulched each fall for protection against cold temperatures, which can injure the crown, roots, and buds, and from soil heaving.

The plants will need protection before temperatures fall to 20° F.; moreover, at temperatures below 15° F., the fruit buds are injured.

Applying the mulch too early in the fall before growth ceases may cause smothering of some plants. The exact time to apply the mulch will vary from year to year and from one area to another. It is usually best to wait until after the first hard frost and then monitor local weather conditions.

Mulch Material

As with the summer mulch, the material selected should be reasonably free of weed seeds. Clean wheat straw is one of the best materials available. Oat straw, shredded cornstalks, Sudan grass, and marsh hay are also acceptable. Materials like sawdust or leaves, which have a tendency to pack tightly, should not be used since they may smother the plants. Some commercial growers are experimenting with clear plastic and polyethylene or polypropylene fabrics. Clear plastic is proving to be less acceptable than the fabrics because of excessive heating on warm spring days.

When organic mulches such as straw are used, they should be spread evenly, 3 to 4 inches deep, over the entire planting.

Removal of Winter Mulch

In the spring, the mulch should be left on as long as possible. Lift up the mulch periodically and check the condition of the plants. As long as the majority of the leaves on each plant remain green, leave the mulch on. One or two yellow leaves in the center of each plant is no cause for alarm.

Keeping the mulch on as long as possible may delay blooming until danger of frost is past, and it will also help prevent soil heaving. Remove only enough of the mulch to allow the plants to come through. The excess material can be placed between rows.

Growing Strawberries in Raised Beds

Where space is limited or the soil is too wet or heavy to successfully grow strawberries, some Upper Midwestern growers have discovered raised beds. The beds may be single, multileveled, square, round, or pyramid-shaped.

Since over 90 percent of the strawberry roots are in the top 6 inches of soil, the beds should be about 6 inches high. With this arrangement it is possible to grow the plants even on highly saturated, muck soils.

For the home gardener with limited space, the square pyramid is easy to construct and is productive. One common design presented by Hill et al. (1977) has a bottom level 6 feet square, middle 4 feet, and top 2 feet. At ground level, a 9-inch spacing allows 28 plants. On the middle level, with

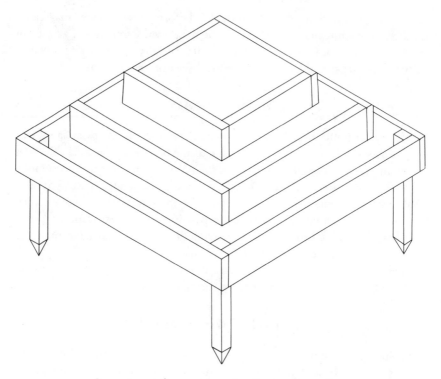

Square terrace for growing everbearing strawberry plants.

9-inch spacing, there are 16 plants; on the top level, an 8-inch spacing allows 9 plants.

Raised beds dry out more quickly and require more frequent irrigation. In addition, the mulch material for winter protection will need to be thicker, and it is much more difficult to keep it in position since it may be displaced by wind.

Additional details on the construction of raised beds and novelty items such as strawberry barrels are discussed by Wott and Hayden (n.d.), Fear et al. (1987), and Shoemaker (1978).

Chemical Weed Control

Use of herbicides to control weeds in home strawberry plantings is not recommended. Most of the chemicals available are costly and require specialized training and equipment. They are, in short, rarely justified. Improper choice or application of chemicals can severely damage plants and affect fruit quality. Proper site selection and soil management before planting can eliminate many weed problems.

Harvesting and Storing

Berries should be picked in the early morning when it is cool; if possible, avoid picking when the plants are wet. The fruit should be harvested when it is fully colored; those with white areas are not fully ripe.

At harvest, pinch off a small section of stem, leaving the green whorl of leaves (calyx) attached to the berry. Usually the fruit is harvested every other day. After harvesting, keep the berries out of the sun and refrigerate them as soon as possible.

Diseases

For the grower who begins with good, healthy planting stock, strawberry diseases are usually not a serious problem in most areas of the Upper Midwest. To maintain healthy plants, the grower must, of course, follow good cultural practices such as winter protection, clean tillage, removal of trash, regular fertilization, and providing extra water when needed. In short, good cultural practices can substitute for expensive chemical sprays.

Leaf Diseases

Fungi cause most of the diseases that affect strawberry leaves. The severity of the problem is often correlated with weather conditions. Usually problems arise when there is an abundance of moisture and the growing season is cool.

The common fungal diseases often produce the same kind of damage and are difficult to distinguish. For example, the symptoms of leaf spot, leaf blight, and leaf scorch are very similar. In all three diseases, spots ⅛ to ¼ inch in diameter appear on the leaves. The spots may be round or irregular but usually appear purple in the center or throughout, or have purple borders.

Renovation and thinning help reduce the incidence of these diseases. In severe cases, all three can be controlled by using fungicide sprays.

Powdery mildew rarely causes problems except in some places that receive little sunlight or poor air movement. In severe cases of infection, leaf margins roll inward and the thin, white, cabinetlike mold is evident on the lower leaf surface. Overhead irrigation should not be used when this disease is present. In severe cases sulfur is sometimes used to control the disease, but it may injure leaves and flower stalks.

Root Diseases

There are several soil-borne fungi that can cause root disorders in strawberries. As with the leaf diseases, problems are likely to be more severe when there is more than average rainfall and the growing season is cool.

Most of the root disease damage is to the vascular system (water- and food-conducting system) so that typical symptoms are first noticeable in above-ground parts. The plants may appear stunted, having yellowing leaves that in time may dry up and wilt.

Root diseases like black rot or red stele are usually more of a problem on heavy or poorly drained soil, so choosing the proper planting site is one of the best preventive measures. With other diseases like verticillium wilt, prevention is best achieved by avoiding soils previously planted to crops such as potatoes, peppers, tomatoes, eggplant, gladiolus, chrysanthemums, or other fruits and vegetables known to be susceptible to this fungus. Shoemaker (1978) reported that once verticillium wilt becomes established in soils, it may remain alive for 25 years.

Fruit Diseases

Gray mold *(Botrytis)* and leather rot *(Phytophthora)* are two fungal diseases that occasionally appear in some plantings. Other fungal diseases are usually of little consequence in the Upper Midwest.

Gray mold affects both green and mature fruit. At maturity the berry develops a brown spot that spreads, making the fruit unusable. The disease organism often enters the plant after it has been injured by frost. Commonly, the infection occurs where the berries touch the soil. Prevention of crowding and maintaining adequate nutrient levels are recommended preventive methods.

Mulching to prevent the berries from touching the soil is also effective. Fungicidal control will help, but it is costly, and in most cases, the home gardener will find it uneconomical. To prevent the spread of the disease, stay out of the planting when it is wet.

Preventive measures for leather rot are the same as for gray mold. Green fruit infected with this disease has brown spots or spots outlined by brown edging. At maturity, in severe cases the fruit becomes tough, leathery, and often has a bitter taste.

Viruses

The best preventive measure is to purchase certified, virus-free stock. The symptoms of virus diseases are varied and in many cases impossible to confirm without laboratory diagnosis.

"Running out" of strawberries, or when they become unproductive, is a typical viral symptom along with leaf spotting, leaf yellowing or withering, stunting, and a general decline in vigor. There are no sprays to control viral diseases, so it is essential to start with healthy plants and to avoid planting on soils previously planted to strawberries or near wild strawberries.

Other Pests

Slugs. These gray brown mollusks leave a slime trail, which is easily detected. The pests eat holes in the leaves and fruit. Baits containing metaldehyde are often used, but these are not recommended because of the potential of accidental poisoning to pets and children. A shallow saucer of beer or pickle juice is an effective, acceptable substitute.

Mites. Cyclamen mite (very rarely) and spider mite (occasionally) cause problems by sucking nutrients from the leaves. Cyclamen mites damage young unfolded leaves, and often the stems fail to elongate, producing a rosette of leaves. In addition, berries may be deformed. Spider mites feed on the undersides of the leaves, often causing a rusty brown color. When infestation is severe, the plants may be stunted with a reduced yield. For chemical control, only miticides (not insecticides) are effective.

White grub. The larvae of these June beetles are common where crop rotation is not practiced and on newly plowed sod. Infected plants may appear stunted or wilted, or have reduced vigor. Larvae feed on the roots and affect the vascular system. Chemical control after infection is usually not practical.

Tarnished plant bug. The adult is a brownish gray insect ⅙ to ¼ inch long, marked with yellowish and black dashes. The juveniles and adults feed on buds and flowers, and may cause the berries to be deformed or nubbinlike. This insect is easily controlled by chemical sprays.

Strawberry weevil. This snout beetle girdles the flower stems, shutting off the supply of nutrients to the blossom. Properly timed sprays are effective.

Sap beetle. These insects are about ¼ inch long with orange or yellow markings. They feed on ripe or damaged fruit. Picking ripe fruit on a regular basis helps reduce the damage.

Strawberry leaf roller. To be effective, chemical control of this pest must be achieved before the leaves are folded and "cemented" together by the action of the insect. The immature form of the insect in the folded leaf is about ½ inch long and gray green or bronze.

Birds. Use of netting in some areas may be necessary to prevent damage to fruit by birds.

For control of other pests such as spittlebugs, aphids, cutworms, or nematodes, consult your county agent or the cooperative extension service in your state. When proper precautions are taken before planting and good cultural practices are followed, these pests rarely cause serious problems.

SELECTED REFERENCES

Anderson, W. 1969. *The Strawberry, a Word Bibliography*. Meluchen, N.J.: Scarecrow Press.

Anonymous. 1978. *Strawberry Diseases*. USDA Farmer's Bulletin 2140.

Askew, R. G., and N. S. Holland. 1984. *Strawberries*. North Dakota State University Coop. Ext. Ser. Cir. H–16 (rev.).

Brooks, R. M., and H. P. Olmo. 1972. *Register of New Fruit and Nut Varieties*. 2nd ed. Berkeley: University of California Press.

Childers, N. F. (ed.). 1980. *The Strawberry, Cultivars to Marketing*. Gainesville, Fla.: Horticultural Publications.

Collins, W. B. 1966. Effects of Winter Mulches on Strawberry Plants. *Proc. Amer. Soc. Hort. Sci.* 88: 331–35.

Connor, L. J. 1970. Studies of Strawberry Pollination in Michigan. In: *Indispensible Pollinators*. Arkansas Agr. Ext. Ser. Misc. Pub. 127.

Converse, R. H. (ed.). 1987. *Virus Diseases of Small Fruits*. USDA Agricultural Handbook No. 631.

Darrow, G. M. 1937. Strawberry Improvement. *USDA Yearbook of Agriculture* 1937: 445–95.

Darrow, G. M. 1966. *The Strawberry History, Breeding and Physiology*. New York: Holt, Rinehart, and Winston.

Denisen, E. L. 1987. *NCR-22 Report on Small Fruit*. Iowa State University Department of Horticulture.

Denisen, E. L., P. C. Crandall, and C. C. Doll. 1953. Influence of Summer Mulching and Runner Removal on Everbearing Strawberries. *Proc. Amer. Soc. Hort. Sci.* 62: 235–45.

Dennis, F. G., Jr., J. Lipecki, and C. Kiang. 1970. Effect of Photoperiod and Other Factors on Flowering and Runner Development of Three Strawberry Cultivars. *Jour. Amer. Soc. Hort. Sci.* 95: 750–54.

Durner, E. A., J. A. Barten, D. G. Himelrick, and E. B. Polling. 1984. Photoperiod and Temperature Effects on Flower and Runner Development in Day-Neutral, June bearing, and Everbearing Strawberries. *Jour. Amer. Soc. Hort. Sci.* 109: 396–400.

Fear, C., and H. G. Taber. 1986. *Iowa Commercial Fruit Production*. Iowa State University Coop. Ext. Ser. Pub. PM–672d.

Fear, C., H. G. Taber, M. Gleason, and D. Lewis. 1987. *Growing Strawberries at Home*. Iowa State University Coop. Ext. Ser. Pub. PM–717 (rev.).

Fletcher, S. W. 1917. *The Strawberry in North America, History, Origin, Botany, and Breeding*. New York: Macmillan.

Galletta, G. J. 1980. Strawberry Production in the Eastern United States. In: *The Strawberry, Cultivars to Marketing*. N. F. Childers (ed.). Gainesville, Fla.: Horticultural Publications.

Galletta, G. J., and R. S. Bringhurst. 1990. Strawberry Management. In: *Small Fruit Crop Management*. G. J. Galletta and D. G. Himelrick (eds.). Englewood Cliffs, N.J.: Prentice-Hall.

Hayden, R. A. 1977. *Fertilizer for Strawberries*. Purdue University Coop. Ext. Ser. Pub. HO–64.

Hayden, R. A. 1978. *Growing Strawberries in Indiana*. Purdue University Coop. Ext. Ser. Pub. HO–46.

Hedrick, U. P. 1925. *The Small Fruits of New York*. New York State Agr. Exper. Stat. Report 33.

Hendrickson, R. 1981. *The Berry Book*. Garden City, N.Y.: Doubleday.

Hertz, L. B. 1977. *The Use of Bees in Strawberry Production*. University of Minnesota Fruit Growers Letter, April.

Hertz, L. B. 1980. *Strawberries*. University of Minnesota Ext. Ser. Hort. Fact Sheet No. 19.

Hertz, L. B. 1987. *Fruit for the Home*. University of Minnesota Ext. Ser. Pub. AG–BU–0470.

Hill, R. G., Jr., and E. K. Alban. 1963. Strawberry Stands and Yields as Related to Weed Control Methods. *Proc. Amer. Soc. Hort. Sci.* 82: 892–98.

Hill, R. G., Jr., J. D. Utzinger, and E. J. Stang. 1977. Strawberries Like Full Sun and a Good Deal of Attention. In: *Growing Fruits and Nuts*. USDA Agricultural Inform. Bull. 408.

Hoover, E., C. Rosen, and J. Luby. 1986. *Commercial Strawberry Production in Minnesota*. University of Minnesota Ext. Ser. Pub. AG–FO–2836.

Hull, J., Jr., J. Moulton, and J. Flore. 1977. *Commercial Strawberry Culture in Michigan*. Michigan State University Coop. Ext. Ser. Bull. E–682.

Jahn, O. L., and M. N. Dana. 1966. Fruiting and Growth of the Strawberry Plant. *Proc. Amer. Soc. Hort. Sci.* 88: 352–59.

Johnson, H. G. 1977. *Strawberry Diseases*. University of Minnesota Ext. Ser. Plant Path. Fact Sheet No. 2.

Klingbeil, G. C. 1974. *June-bearing Strawberry Cultivar Suggestions*. University of Wisconsin Coop. Ext. Ser. Fact Sheet A–2059.

Klingbeil, G. C., C. F. Koval, and E. K. Wade. 1979. *Strawberries for the Home Garden*. University of Wisconsin Coop. Ext. Ser. Pub. A–1597.

Koval, C., and E. Wade. 1979. *Strawberry Pest Control for Home Gardeners*. University of Wisconsin Coop. Ext. Ser. Pub. A–2127.

Lee, V. 1964. Antoine Nicholas Duchesne-First Strawberry Hybridist. *Amer. Hort. Mag.* 43: 80–88.

Lounsberry, C. C. 1930. Visits of Honey Bees. In: *Honey Plants of Iowa*. L. H. Pammel and C. M. King (eds.). Iowa Geological Survey Pub. 7.

Luby, J. J. 1986. Day-Neutral Strawberry Cultivars and Production Systems. *Michigan State Hort. Soc. Annual Report* 116: 144–50.

Luby, J. J. 1986. Performance of Strawberry Cultivars in Minnesota. *Michigan State Hort. Soc. Annual Report* 116: 137–43.

Luby, J. J., E. Hoover, S. Munson, D. Bedford, D. Wildung, and W. Gray. 1984. Performance of Strawberry Cultivars in Minnesota: 1983. *Advances in Strawberry Production* 3: 11–14.

Luby, J. J., S. T. Munson, and E. E. Hoover. 1987. Sensory Evaluation of Fresh and Frozen Fruit from Day-Neutral Strawberry Cultivars. *Advances in Strawberry Production* 6: 11–13.

Maas, J. L. (ed.). 1984. *Compendium of Strawberry Diseases*. St. Paul, Minn.: American Phytopathological Society.

Mahr, D. L., E. J. Stang, M. N. Dana, and S. N. Jeffers. 1987. *Strawberry and Raspberry Pest Control for Wisconsin*. University of Wisconsin Coop. Ext. Ser. Pub. A–1934.

McGregor, S. E. 1976. *Insect Pollination of Cultivated Crop Plants*. USDA Agricultural Handbook No. 496.

Moore, J. N. 1969. Insect Pollination of Strawberries. *Jour. Amer. Soc. Hort. Sci.* 94: 362–64.

Morrison, F. D. 1986. *Strawberries*. Kansas State University Coop. Ext. Ser. Pub. MF–598.

Nonnecke, G. R., S. M. Streicher, and J. C. Herman. 1987. *Alternative Ag. Enterprises—Strawberries*. Iowa State University Coop. Ext. Ser. Pub. PM–1295a.

Ourecky, D. K. 1976. Frost Tolerance in Strawberry Cultivars. *HortScience* 11: 413–14.

Ourecky, D. K. 1976. *The Strawberry Growers Handbook*. Willoughby, Ohio: Meister Publications.

Peterson, R. M., and D. M. Martin. 1987. *Strawberries*. South Dakota State University Coop. Ext. Ser. Pub. FS–841.

Plakidas, A. G. 1964. *Strawberry Diseases*. Baton Rouge: Louisiana State University Press.

Ricketson, C. L. 1976. *The Strawberry in Ontario*. Ontario Ministry of Agriculture and Food.

Scheel, D. C. 1982. The Effect of Clear Polyethylene Winter Mulch on the Growth and Yield of Strawberries. *Advances in Strawberry Production* 1: 29–30.

Scholz, E., and R. G. Askew. 1986. *Strawberry Production and Marketing in the Northern Great Plains.* North Dakota State University Coop. Ext. Ser. Pub. EB–42.

Scott, D. H. 1962. Breeding and Improvement of the Strawberry in the United States of America — A Review. *Hort. Res.* 2: 35–55.

Scott, D. H., G. M. Darrow, and F. J. Lawrence. 1983. *Strawberry Varieties in the United States.* USDA Farmer's Bulletin 1043.

Scott, D. H., and F. J. Lawrence. 1975. Strawberries. In: *Advances in Fruit Breeding.* J. Janick and J. N. Moore (eds.). Lafayette, Ind.: Purdue University Press.

Shoemaker, J. S. 1978. *Small Fruit Culture.* Westport, Conn.: AVI Publishing.

Tomkins, J. P., and D. K. Ourecky. 1978. *Growing Strawberries in New York State.* Cornell University Coop. Ext. Ser. Inform. Bull. 15.

Valleau, W. D. 1918. How the Strawberry Sets Its Fruit. *Minnesota Horticulturist* 46: 449–54.

Wott, J., and R. A. Hayden. No date. *Strawberry Barrels.* Purdue University Coop. Ext. Ser. Pub. HO–68.

Zych, C. C. 1966. Fruit Maturation Times of Strawberry. *Fruit Varieties and Horticulture Digest* 20: 51–53.

Zych, C. C., and D. Powell. 1968. *Commercial Production of Strawberries.* University of Illinois Cir. 983.

10

Brambles

The brambles, which in the Upper Midwest consist mainly of raspberries and blackberries, are all members of the rosaceous genus *Rubus*. On a worldwide scale, *Rubus* is a very large and, to say the least, confusing genus. Several hundred species have been described, but because of the failure of the early taxonomists to thoroughly understand the genetics and breeding behavior that exist in the genus, many of these species today have been reduced to synonomy or exist only as "paper species."

Red and Yellow Raspberries

Although the nomenclature of the species of *Rubus* involved in the origin of the cultivated red raspberry is still somewhat confusing, most authors use *R. idaeus* variety *strigosus* for the American red raspberry and *R. idaeus* variety *vulgatus* for the European red raspberry. Both varieties have been considered separate and distinct species by some investigators, but they hybridize readily with little or no evidence of sterility. The great Swedish botanist, Carolus Linnaeus, gave the European red raspberry the species name *idaeus* undoubtedly because writers in the early Christian Era believed it came from Mount Ida (Ourecky, 1975). However, Jennings (1988) has pointed out that modern botanists have failed to find raspberries growing there, and some have suggested that the Ide Mountains in Turkey may be the correct place of origin.

Regardless of whether the red raspberries are considered distinct varieties or species, both types grown here have yielded several cultivars, and they have been repeatedly hybridized to produce today's modern cultivars. According to Haskell (1954), the first record of raspberry cultivation dates to Turner in 1548 in England and then was largely ignored for over a hundred years. By 1826, he reports, there were 23 "sorts" and 25 synonyms, but these were not generally distinguished by English gardeners.

The first record of commercial cultivation of raspberries in the United States dates to William Prince of Flushing Landing, New York, in 1771 (Ourecky, 1975). Initially, both American and European cultivars were grown and were later hybridized to produce hardier, disease-resistant selections. By 1925, over 415 red cultivars were available (Hedrick, 1925).

Occasionally, largely for their novelty, yellow or amber raspberries are grown. These plants have all the characteristics except fruit color of the red cultivars, and in reality are genetic segregates of the reds. These are of no commercial consequence, and for the most part, their cultivation is confined to a few home gardens.

Today British Columbia is the world's leading producer of red raspberries. In the United States, commercial production occurs mainly in northern California, the western portions of Oregon and Washington, and to a limited extent in the northeastern U. S. (Crandall and Daubeny, 1990). In the Upper Midwest, Minnesota, Iowa, and Wisconsin are the leading producers.

Black Raspberries

The black raspberries, sometimes called blackcaps, have been selected from the native American species *R. occidentalis*, which is distributed near woodland borders from Ontario to the Carolinas. According to Ricketson et al. (1970), black raspberries appeared under cultivation as early as 1832, but Darrow (1967) reports they did not become commercially important until 1870.

The black raspberries are not widely grown in the Upper Midwest, largely because they generally are not as hardy as some of the red cultivars, and also because of their susceptibility to disease. Galletta and Violette (1989) report that black-raspberry production mainly for fresh-fruit consumption is increasing in the East. Black raspberries for commercial processing are grown principally in Oregon (Crandall and Daubeny, 1990).

Purple Raspberries

Purple raspberries are first-generation hybrids of blacks and reds. They are sometimes accorded the name *R. neglectus*, but this is not universally recognized.

The fruit on purple raspberries, except for color, resembles the red raspberry in overall appearance. The plants lack the hardiness of the red cultivars, and they have never been grown extensively in the Upper Midwest. Purple raspberries, according to Darrow (1967), gained some commercial importance after the introduction of the cultivar 'Columbian' in 1891. Today, commercial production is limited and occurs mainly in the northeastern U. S.

Blackberries

Blackberries are even more in a state of taxonomic confusion than the raspberries. There is a myriad of named species, many of which are of doubtful validity. In addition, there are countless hybrids. For an update of the species names used in blackberry breeding, see Jennings (1988), Galletta and Violette (1989), and Crandall and Daubeny (1990).

Both European and American blackberry species have been used in breeding work and some very important cultivars ('Boysenberry', 'Loganberry', 'Sunberry', 'Tayberry', 'Tumbleberry', and 'Youngberry') have been selected from crosses between blackberries and raspberries. For the United States, Shoemaker (1978) recognized the following kinds of blackberries:

Erect or semi-erect. These are the principal kinds of blackberry grown in the Upper Midwest. 'Darrow' is the hardiest and the most commonly grown.

Western trailing. These are grown principally in the Pacific Coast states. The most important western trailing forms are the 'Thornless Evergreen' blackberry, 'Marion' blackberry, 'Boysenberry', 'Youngberry', and 'Loganberry'. There have been many attempts to grow the western trailing types (especially the 'Boysenberry') on a trial basis in home gardens in the Upper Midwest, but with little success. All the forms are very tender and must be completely covered with mulch for winter protection.

Southeastern trailing blackberries or dewberries. According to Shoemaker (1978), these are injured easily by low temperatures and will not succeed in the North.

Darrow (1937) states that blackberry cultivation began with selections from wild species growing mainly in North America shortly after the beginning of the 19th century. The first public blackberry-breeding program did not begin until 1909 (Texas), and this was followed by other research initiated in New York, North Carolina, and by the U.S. Department of Agriculture. In 1978 Moore (1979) reported there were only seven state and USDA breeding programs.

Erect and trailing blackberries have never achieved much popularity in the Upper Midwest because the few cultivars that are available lack cold hardiness. The best chances for success appear to be in southern Wisconsin and southern Iowa, but in some years, low-temperature injury can occur in these areas as well.

Commercial production of blackberries is limited mainly to two regions of the U. S. About 95 percent of production occurs in the Pacific coastal states of Oregon, Washington, and California. The other minor-producing area, which accounts for about 3 percent of the harvest, is in Texas, Oklahoma, and Arkansas (Skirvin and Hellman, 1984).

Other Brambles

In addition to the major cultivars of raspberries and blackberries, a few other species of *Rubus* are occasionally grown in the Upper Midwest for their fruit, attractive flowers, or for landscape purposes. For gardening use of the following species see Snyder (1980): *Rubus allegheniensis*, highbush blackberry; *R. deliciosus*, boulder raspberry; *R. odoratus*, purple flowering raspberry; *R. parviflorus*, thimbleberry; and *R. parvifolius*, Japanese raspberry.

Pollination

All the bramble cultivars listed here are potentially self-fruitful; thus only one cultivar needs to be planted to ensure production of fruit.

It is generally agreed that although self-pollination may occur in most of the cultivars, the transfer of pollen from anther to stigma will be greatly facilitated by the presence of insect pollinators. With all the brambles, honeybees are the best pollinating agents. When pollinating agents are absent, both the number and size of the berries are greatly reduced. For commercial plantings, one strong colony of bees per acre is recommended.

How Many Plants?

Well-managed blackberries may yield 1½ to 2 quarts per plant, and the expected yield from vigorous raspberry cultivars is 1 to 1½ quarts per plant. Raspberries are frequently sold in bundles of 25, which is a good start for a family of four. Since blackberries must be regarded as suitable for trial planting, only 12 plants are suggested.

Selection and Care of Nursery Stock

Obtaining stock from a friend or neighbor's garden is not recommended because of possible disease problems. It is safer to buy certified or inspected, one-year-old stock labeled as No. 1 from reliable nurseries. Dormant barefoot stock where the buds have not started to swell or leaf out is best.

Bundles of raspberries with well-developed root systems.

After obtaining the stock, protect the roots from drying out, and if planting must be delayed, "heel in" the plants in a shallow trench in the garden,
making sure that the roots are thoroughly covered. If cold-storage facilities
are available, keep the plants at 35° F. Do not delay planting any longer than
necessary.

Brambles, like strawberries, blueberries, and other small fruit, are also
available as tissue-cultured plants. (TC) Brambles propagated by TC are becoming increasingly popular with commercial growers, and Handley (1989)
reports they now account for about 15 percent of bramble production. In
comparison to plants produced through traditional methods of propagation,
TC plants are more expensive, but they grow faster and produce a higher
yield earlier in the life of the planting—plus they are more likely to be disease
free. For a discussion of the advantages and disadvantages of using TC, see
the publication by North Star Gardens in the reference section and the chapter on blueberries.

Life of the Planting

A well-cared-for raspberry planting can be expected to last from 6 to 10
years, and a few have exceeded 20 years. Because of the unfavorable growing

Mulched bundles of barerooted raspberries.

conditions in the Upper Midwest, most plantings of blackberries rarely last longer than 6 years, and often their life is considerably shorter.

Red Raspberry Cultivars

(Unless noted, all produce a single crop in early summer.)

Amity. An everbearing cultivar introduced from Corvallis, Oregon, in 1984. The parentage is ('Fallred' x OR–US 1347) x (PI 338908 x 'Heritage'). Canes reach a height of 5 to 5½ feet and are nearly smooth. Berries are medium-large, quite firm, and have a tendency to adhere to the receptacle. Plants are somewhat more productive and a week earlier than 'Heritage'.

Boyne. Introduced in 1960 from Morden, Manitoba, Canada, the parentage is 'Chief' x 'Indian Summer'. This cultivar is extremely hardy and has largely replaced 'Latham' because of its superior disease resistance. Canes are 5 to 5½ feet tall and can be grown without support. Berries are medium size and sweet, but are soft and do not store or ship well.

Fallred. This is an everbearing cultivar introduced from Durham, New Hampshire, in 1964. The parentage is N.H. 7 x N.Y. 287. The plant suckers freely and the canes are vigorous but have a tendency to break

'Boyne' is extremely hardy and is resistant to many diseases.

easily. Probably best grown with support. Berries are medium size with good flavor, but they are soft.

Heritage. This is another everbearing cultivar introduced in 1969 from Geneva, New York. The parentage is ('Milton' x 'Cuthbert') x 'Durham'. Canes are sturdy, vigorous, and 5 to 6 feet tall. Berries are firm and medium size. For most areas this is considered the best everbearing cultivar.

Itasca. E. T. Anderson introduced this 'Newburgh' x self cross in 1965 at Excelsior, Minnesota. Canes are vigorous, smooth, and nearly spinefree. Berries are soft, medium-large, and resemble 'Latham'. Plants are susceptible to anthracnose. This cultivar is best adapted to cool, humid areas of the Upper Midwest.

Killarney. 'Chief' x 'Indian Summer' is the parentage of this 1961 introduction from Morden, Manitoba. Canes are sturdy, 5 to 5½ feet tall. Berries are medium size, firm, and good quality. 'Killarney' is recommended for home use or fresh-market sales. Ripening time is about a week after 'Boyne'.

Latham. This cultivar was introduced in 1920 at Excelsior, Minnesota, from a cross of 'King' x 'Louden'. Canes are very vigorous but must be topped or supported. Berries are large and moderately firm, with fair to good quality, but have a tendency to crumble. This was the standard in the Upper Midwest for over 50 years, but disease problems (mainly viral) have caused its popularity to wane.

Liberty. Ervin L. Denisen introduced this 'Sunrise' S2 x 'Newburgh' cross from Iowa State University in 1976. This cultivar does not sucker freely and rows are easy to maintain. Berries are early maturing, medium size, and excellent for dessert and freezing. The plant is very productive and requires topping or trellising.

Newburgh. Richard Wellington introduced this 'Newman' x 'Herbert' cross in 1929 at Geneva, New York. Berries, which mature midseason, are large, firm, and good to fair for dessert and freezing. The plant may be susceptible to leaf spot.

Nordic. This 1987 introduction from Excelsior, Minnesota, is a cross of 'Boyne' x 'Fallred'. Berry size and quality are similar to 'Boyne'. For freezing it was judged superior to 'Boyne', and may also have more disease resistance. Canes are very hardy and productive.

Redwing. Another 1987 introduction from Excelsior, Minnesota, this is an everbearing cultivar obtained by crossing 'Heritage' x 'Fallred'. It was released to replace 'Heritage' where earlier fall fruiting is desired. Fruit yield, size, and color are similar to 'Heritage,' but maturity time is 10 to 14 days earlier.

Reveille. I. C. Haut introduced this ('Indian Summer' x 'Sunrise') x 'September' cross from College Park, Maryland, in 1966. Berries are large with excellent red color, but are too soft for commercial use. This cultivar has an excellent reputation for being able to withstand fluctuating winter temperatures. At North Star Gardens in Minnesota, this was the only cultivar exhibiting no winter damage after temperatures dropped from the 60s to $-7°$ F. in four days during November 1986.

Sentinel. Introduced from College Park, Maryland, by I. C. Haut in 1966, this is a 'Sunrise' x 'Milton' cross. The medium berries are firm and good quality. The plants produce many suckers and reportedly exhibit some resistance to fluctuating winter temperatures.

Sentry. This cultivar is another I. C. Haut selection from College Park, introduced in 1966. The parentage is 'Sunrise' x 'Taylor'. Berries are medium to large and are of excellent quality for dessert and freezing. This cultivar is very tolerant of fluctuating winter temperatures (more so than 'Boyne'). Canes are tall, very hardy, and productive.

September. This 'Marcy' x 'Ranere' selection is an everbearer introduced by George L. Slate from Geneva, New York, in 1947. Berries are very large and are excellent for dessert and freezing. Canes are vigorous and should be trellised for the heavy fall crop.

Taylor. Richard Wellington introduced this 'Newman' x 'Lloyd George' cross from Geneva, New York, in 1935. Berries are large, firm, and can

Fruit zones—
red raspberries

Cultivar	Iowa			Minn.				S. Dak.				N. Dak.			Wis.			
	4b	5a	5b	1	2	3	4	1	2	3	4	A	B	C	1	2	3	4
Amity				T	T	T									X	X	T	T
Boyne	X	X	X	X	X	X	X	X	X	X	T	X	X	X	X	X	X	X
Fallred		X	X	X	X	X	T	X	X	X	T				X	X	X	T
Heritage	X	X	X	X	X	X	T					T	T	T	X	X	X	X
Itasca					X	X												
Killarney												X	X	X				
Latham	X	X	X	X	X	X	X	X	X	X	T				X	X	X	X
Liberty	T	X	X	X	X	X						T	T	T	T	T	T	T
Newburgh	X	X	X	X	X	X	X								T	T	T	T
Nordic	X	X	X	X	X	X	X	T	T			T	T	T	T	T	T	T
Redwing	X	X	X	X	X	X	X	T	T			T	T	T	T	T	T	T
Reveille	T	T	T	T	T	T	T					T	T	T	X	X	X	X
Sentinel				X	X	X						T	T	T	T	T	T	
Sentry															X	X	X	X
September		X	X					X							X	X		
Taylor															X			X

X = recommended for planting; T = recommended for trial.
See zone map on page 20.

withstand handling without crumbling. Canes are tall and require topping or support. The plants are more susceptible than 'Newburgh' to mosaic virus.

Yellow Raspberry Cultivars

Amber. This summer-bearing cultivar was introduced by George L. Slate from Geneva, New York, in 1950. The parentage is 'Taylor' x 'Cuthbert'. The large berries mature very late and are rated very good for dessert and good for freezing. 'Amber' is very susceptible to leaf-curl virus.

Fallgold. E. M. Meader introduced this everbearer from Durham, New

**Fruit zones—
yellow raspberries**

Cultivar	Iowa			Minn.				S. Dak.				N. Dak.			Wis.			
	4b	5a	5b	1	2	3	4	1	2	3	4	A	B	C	1	2	3	4
Amber		X	X	X	X	X	T								X	X	X	T
Fallgold	T	X	X	X	X	X	T	T	T			T	T	T	X	X	X	T

X = recommended for planting; T = recommended for trial.
See zone map on page 20.

Hampshire, in 1967. The parentage is NH 56–1 x ('Taylor' x *R. pungens oldhami*) F_2. Berries are supersweet, soft, and ripen with 'Heritage'. Although not as productive as 'Heritage', it is very hardy. At farmers' markets, this novelty yellow cultivar usually brings a higher price than red raspberries.

Black Raspberry Cultivars

Allen. George L. Slate introduced this 'Bristol' x 'Cumberland' cross in 1957 at Geneva, New York. Berries are large, firm, and many ripen at one time midseason.

Blackhawk. This 'Quillen' x 'Black Pearl' cross was introduced from Ames, Iowa, in 1955. The large, black berries ripen late and are very good for dessert and good for freezing. At Iowa State University, this was the highest-yielding of all black cultivars tested. Plants are vigorous and show resistance to anthracnose.

Bristol. Richard Wellington introduced this 'Watson Prolific' x 'Honeysweet' cross from Geneva, New York, in 1934. Berries are medium-large and firm, and ripen midseason. The plant lacks the hardiness of 'Blackhawk' and is susceptible to anthracnose.

Cumberland. For many years this was the most widely grown black raspberry in the eastern U. S., but its popularity has declined because of disease problems. It was introduced in 1896 by David Miller of Camp Hill, Pennsylvania, as a supposed seedling of 'Gregg', but according to Hedrick (1925), this origin is doubtful. Berries are large and firm with very good flavor. The plant is susceptible to anthracnose, virus diseases, and orange rust.

Logan ('New Logan'). Considerable confusion exists concerning the origin

Fruit zones—
black raspberries

Cultivar	Iowa			Minn.				S. Dak.				N. Dak.			Wis.			
	4b	5a	5b	1	2	3	4	1	2	3	4	A	B	C	1	2	3	4
Allen		X	X												X	X	T	T
Blackhawk	T	X	X	X	X			X	X	T		X	X	X	X	X	T	T
Bristol		X	X	X	X										X	X		
Cumberland												T	T	T	X	X	T	T
Logan		X	X															
John Robertson								X	X	T	T	T	T	T				

X = recommended for planting; T = recommended for trial.
See zone map on page 20.

and date of introduction of this cultivar. It apparently originated in Illinois, but attempts to trace its history have been unsuccessful. The berries mature about a week before 'Cumberland' and are good for dessert and fair for freezing. The plants are susceptible to anthracnose and crown gall but are apparently more resistant to viral diseases than 'Cumberland'.

John Robertson. From unknown parentage, this cultivar was selected by pioneer horticulturist John Robertson from Hot Springs, South Dakota. It was introduced about 1935 by South Dakota State University. This selection does quite well in the Black Hills and in the southeastern portion of South Dakota. Berries are medium size and of very good quality.

Purple Raspberry Cultivars

Amethyst. E. L. Denisen introduced this 'Robertson' x 'Cuthbert' cross from Ames, Iowa, in 1968. The medium berries mature midseason and are good for dessert and freezing. Plants are very productive and tolerant of anthracnose.

Brandywine. From a technical standpoint, this is not a true purple raspberry, since it was produced by crossing New York 631 (a purple raspberry) x 'Hilton' (a red). It was selected by Donald K. Ourecky of the New York Agricultural Experiment Station and introduced in 1977. Berries

**Fruit zones—
purple raspberries**

Cultivar	Iowa			Minn.				S. Dak.				N. Dak.			Wis.			
	4b	5a	5b	1	2	3	4	1	2	3	4	A	B	C	1	2	3	4
Amethyst	X	X	X	X	X	X	X					T	T	T	X	X		
Brandywine		X	X	X	X	X	T	T	T			X	T	T	X	X	X	X
Clyde								X	X									
Royalty		X	X	X	T			T	T			T			X	X	X	T
Sodus	T	X	X									T			X	X	T	

X = recommended for planting; T = recommended for trial.
See zone map on page 20.

are very large, reddish purple, firm, and tart. Canes are quite thorny and vigorous, and may reach a height of 8 to 10 feet. Plants are extremely productive but are not as hardy as 'Amethyst'.

Clyde. Introduced in 1961 from Geneva, New York, this is a cross of 'Bristol' x N.Y. 17861 ('Newburgh' x 'Indian Summer'). Berries are large, firm, and tart. Canes are vigorous but require support to keep the fruit off the ground. 'Clyde' is tolerant of anthracnose. This cultivar is very rare today and may not be available commercially.

Royalty. Geneva, New York, is the home of this 1982 cross of ('Cumberland' x 'Newburgh') x ('Newburgh' x 'Indian Summer'). Berries mature late and are very large and sweet. The plants have more disease resistance than 'Brandywine' but are not as productive.

Sodus. This 'Dundee' x 'Newburgh' cross was introduced by George L. Slate at Geneva, New York, in 1935. The large, firm, tart berries mature late and are good for dessert and freezing. Plants are vigorous, productive, and quite resistant to drought.

Blackberry Cultivars

Darrow. George L. Slate selected this ('Eldorado' x 'Brewer') x 'Hedrick' cross introduced from Geneva, New York, in 1958. Berries, which mature over a long fruiting season, are glossy black, large, firm, and mildly subacid. Canes are vigorous and very productive. Some clones of this cultivar sold commercially have proved to be partially or completely sterile because of an apparent genetic factor. Nurseries can avoid this

**Fruit zones—
blackberries**

Cultivar	Iowa			Minn.				S. Dak.				N. Dak.			Wis.			
	4b	5a	5b	1	2	3	4	1	2	3	4	A	B	C	1	2	3	4
Darrow		T	T	T	T											T	T	T	
Thornfree		T	T	T	T											T	T		

T = recommended for trial.
See zone map on page 20.

problem by taking propagating stock from plants that are proven fruit
producers (Converse, 1986).

Thornfree. This is a USDA selection introduced from Beltsville, Maryland, in
1966. Parentage is ('Brainerd' x 'Merton Thornless') x ('Merton Thornless' x 'Eldorado'). Berries are large, firm, and tart, with very good
flavor. Canes are thornless and semi-upright with medium vigor.
'Thornfree' is not as winter hardy as 'Darrow'.

'Chester Thornless' in 1985 and 'Hull Thornless' in 1981 are the two
newest thornless blackberries introduced from Illinois. They are probably
hardier than 'Thornfree', but have not been adequately tested in the Upper
Midwest. 'Illini' is a new, thorny blackberry released from Illinois in 1989,
but it too remains untested. Handley (1989) suggests 'Illini' for trial where
'Darrow' can be grown successfully.

Selecting the Planting Site

As with strawberries, the site selected should be chosen with disease protection in mind. Raspberries are susceptible to a variety of virus diseases, thus
if possible, the new planting should be separated by a minimum distance of
300 feet from other types of brambles, both cultivated and wild. Red and yellow cultivars can be grown together, but ideally the other brambles should
be kept separate.

Like strawberries, the brambles are also susceptible to verticillium wilt,
and thus should not be grown on soils previously planted to tomatoes, eggplant, potatoes, gladiolus, mums — or any other fruit, vegetable, or flower
crop susceptible to the disease.

The brambles can be grown on level land, provided there is good soil
drainage and air movement. A slight slope with a northern exposure is best.
This type of site allows some frost protection as well as air movement and

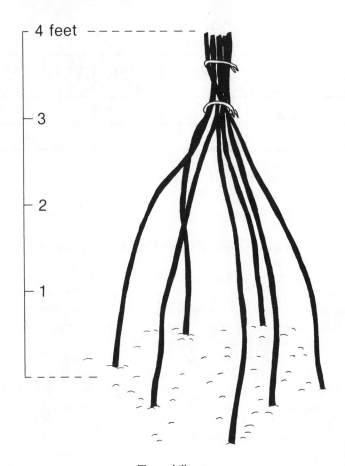

Teepee-hill system.

soil drainage. In addition, soils on northern slopes generally hold moisture better, which is a critical factor when growing brambles.

The site should be in full sun and offer some degree of wind protection. Brambles planted in open, windswept areas are frequently damaged or killed by the drying effects of winter winds. In addition, wind may dessicate fruit spurs and flowers at and shortly after blossoming. If an open area is the only site available, added extra winter protection is necessary. Also avoid root competition by locating the planting at least 50 feet away from trees, shrubs, windbreaks, or other fruits. Pesticide spray drift from fruit trees during the raspberry harvest may contaminate the berries and make them unusable.

The brambles perform best on deep, fertile soils with plentiful organic matter, although they will grow on almost any type of soil except those that

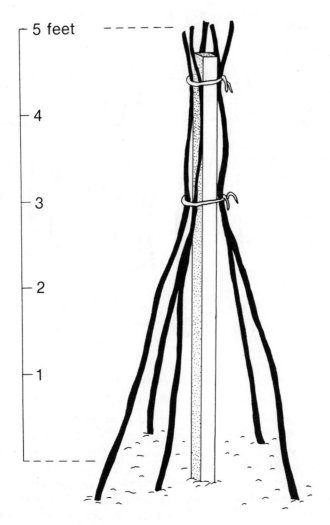

Staked-hill system.

are waterlogged. Raspberries should not be planted on sandy soils unless irrigation equipment is available. They are not fussy about soil pH but will perform best at a pH range of 5.8 to 6.5.

Preparing the Soil

If possible, the soil for brambles should be plowed the fall before spring planting. Because brambles need soils with good moisture-retentive proper-

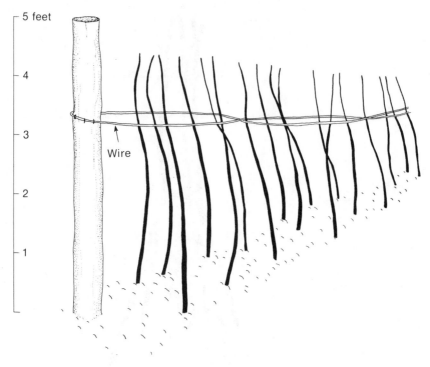

Wire trellis-hedgerow system.

ties, it is highly recommended that liberal amounts of well-rotted manure be applied before fall plowing. In home plantings, four bushels per 50 square feet should be sufficient. For large areas, up to 20 tons of horse or cow manure per acre is recommended.

The site can be previously grown in a farm crop such as corn, but a green manure crop such as alfalfa or clover is preferred. Areas previously in sod are acceptable, but unless the area is plowed in the fall, grass is likely to be a major weed problem, requiring extensive cultivation.

Land previously treated with herbicides should be approached with caution since carry-over problems may result. For a list of compatible herbicides, check with your cooperative extension service.

When and How to Plant

In all areas of the Upper Midwest, only spring planting is advised. The plants should be set as soon as the soil can be worked. Delaying planting until late in the spring often results in considerable loss of plants.

There are two common planting plans for the brambles. In the *hill system*

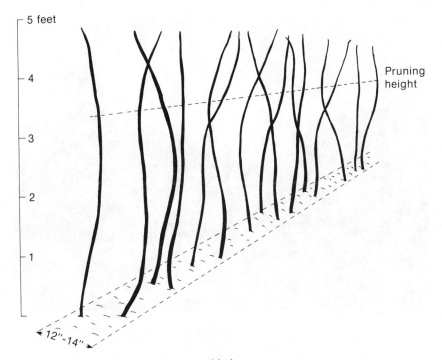

Unsupported-hedgerow system.

the plants are widely spaced in the row. Wide spacing permits cultivation both across and between rows. This system seems to work best for brambles that do not sucker or sucker very little, such as the black and purple raspberries. Suggested spacing for these cultivars is 3 to 3½ feet between plants and 7 to 8 feet between rows. If large, tractor-type cultivation is anticipated, the rows should be 10 to 12 feet apart, depending on the equipment used.

The *hedgerow system* is usually used for red and yellow raspberries and blackberries. These cultivars sucker extensively, and as growth proceeds, a solid row or hedge is formed. This system is more space-saving than the hill system, but cultivation is confined to one direction.

With the hedgerow system, red raspberries are usually set 2 feet apart in rows 6 to 8 feet apart. Suggested spacing for blackberries is 3 to 4 feet between plants and 8 to 10 feet between rows.

On soils where liberal amounts of manure were applied the previous fall, additional nutrients are not usually needed at planting time. If manure was not applied, application of complete fertilizer such as 10–10–10 is recommended. On most soils, 10 pounds per 100 feet of row or ½ cup per hill

Unsupported hedgerows of 'Boyne' raspberries.

should be sufficient. Work the fertilizer into the soil thoroughly before planting.

The real secret to getting the plants to take off quickly and to practically eliminate loss is to soak the roots in water for three to four hours before planting. The holes for planting should be one-third deeper and wider than the root spread.

Black and purple raspberries should be set about one inch deeper than they were originally growing in the nursery. Use some careful measurements here since these plants are frequently smothered if they are planted too deep.

Depth of planting of red and yellow raspberries and blackberries is not so critical. Usually about two inches deeper than they were originally growing is about right. Immediately after planting, water each plant with one to two quarts of water or use a starter solution. For details on how to prepare a starter solution, see the chapter on strawberries.

Pruning at Planting Time

Shoemaker (1978) reported that when the plants are pruned to ground level, a poor stand often results, especially when planting is delayed until late spring. He reports that vigorous canes are usually pruned to 12 to 18 inches

Raspberries grown with the staked-hill system. Photo courtesy of L. Dunsmore.

and less vigorous ones to 6 to 12 inches. For the Upper Midwest, Hertz (1988) suggests cutting the tops back to within 6 to 8 inches of the ground.

For black and purple raspberries, it is recommended that all canes or handles should be cut off at ground level immediately after planting. This is a precautionary measure to prevent the spread of the fungal disease known as anthracnose.

For blackberries, the Northeastern Regional Agricultural Research Service recommends that the tops be cut back to 6 inches at planting time. To prevent the spread of disease, all the parts pruned off at planting time should be removed from the site and destroyed.

Cultivating and Mulching

Keep the new planting free of weeds by frequent cultivation. Weeds may harbor diseases, and, of course, they compete with the raspberries for nutrients and water. Cultivation is also necessary to keep the planting from spreading over too large an area and to prevent the establishment of unwanted plants.

Cultivation may be by hand hoeing or by mechanical means, but regardless of the method used, cultivate only 2 to 3 inches deep to avoid injury to shallow roots. Herbicides are commonly used by commercial operations, but they are not recommended for the home gardener. These chemicals are costly and may damage the planting unless the grower has considerable background knowledge on their proper use. Herbicides do not eliminate cultivation; they merely supplement it.

Discontinue cultivation soon after harvest or about the end of July to avoid stimulating new growth, which may be damaged during the winter months. Brambles, like the other fruit cultivars, need a "hardening-up" period before winter arrives.

Much of the cultivation can be eliminated by mulching. Mulching not only helps eliminate weeds, but it also keeps the roots cooler and helps conserve water. Mulched raspberries generally are more productive and have larger berries.

The mulch should not be applied until after the planting has been established in early summer. Straw is probably the most commonly used mulch material, and to be effective in keeping the weeds down, it should be 6 to 8 inches deep. Five to six inches of crushed corncobs, 8 to 10 inches of leaves, or 3 to 4 inches of sawdust are also commonly used as mulch. When available in large amounts, compost is the preferred material.

Mulch does have the distinct disadvantage of being a potential fire hazard, and it may serve as an attractant for rodents. In spite of these potential problems, it is still recommended.

Irrigating

The brambles require 1 to 1½ inches of water per week. As with strawberries, the most practical type of irrigation is the overhead-sprinkler system since it also affords a means of frost protection.

Supplemental irrigation during drought periods is most critical from bloom until after the harvest is completed. If adequate water supplies are not present during this time, the berries may be small and the fruiting canes that will produce next year's crop may not develop properly.

Most brambles receive their water supply from the top 2 feet of soil, so when watering, it is advisable to soak the soil thoroughly so that the moisture can penetrate to this depth. A good soaking once a week during drought periods is much more advantageous than more frequent, shallow waterings.

After harvest, excessive irrigation may stimulate new growth, which will not properly harden before winter. It is probably best not to irrigate during this time unless a prolonged drought period threatens to check growth.

In very late fall, just before the ground freezes, it is also advisable to soak the soil one more time if it is very dry. Providing additional moisture will help prevent winter dehydration of the canes and facilitate bending of the canes for the brambles that need winter protection.

Fertilizing

Stable manures applied on an annual basis are best for maintaining soil fertility when brambles are grown. They are best applied in late fall after growth has ceased, but they can also be applied in the early spring before growth begins. Apply horse or cow manure at a rate of 300 to 400 pounds per 1,000 square feet or 100 to 150 pounds of poultry manure per 1,000 square feet.

When manure is not available, inorganic fertilizers may be used, but they are best applied in the early spring before growth begins. These supply needed nutrients, but they do not contribute to the humus content of the soil. When brambles are grown using the hedgerow system, uniformly spread 5 to 6 pounds of 10-10-10 per 100 feet of row. The fertilizer should be confined to the narrow growing area, which is normally about two feet wide. Avoid getting the fertilizer on the crowns since this may injure them.

For black and purple raspberries, which are normally grown in the hill system, apply ½ cup of 10-10-10 in a 6- to 8-inch band around each clump.

Applying fertilizer during the growing season is not recommended because it may result in soft berries or stimulate late-summer growth that may not harden properly.

Understanding the Growth and Fruiting Habits of the Brambles

The crown and roots of the brambles are described as perennials because, basically, they live for several years. The above-ground parts are biennial, living just two years.

When a bramble is planted, one to three new canes, which are called primocanes, arise from the base or crown of the plant. In addition to these, the red and yellow raspberries and the blackberries also produce primocanes from the roots. Primocanes arising from the roots often appear at some distance from the original plants since the roots tend to grow outward, in horizontal fashion.

On everbearing types (also called fall-fruiting or primocane-fruiting types), fruit is produced in the fall of the first growing season on the tips of the primocanes. These same canes will produce a second but usually less satisfactory crop during the second growing season. Most growers have found that they get the best results if they dispense with the second crop. For this reason, in the early spring following the fall harvest, all canes are cut back to 1 to 2 inches from the ground.

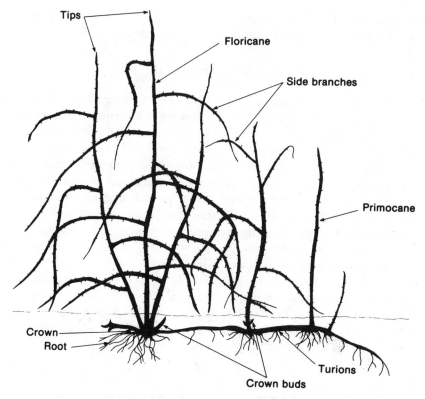

First- and second-year raspberry canes.

On all other brambles, only leaves and flower buds are formed on the primocanes during the first growing season. During the second growing season, the canes (now called floricanes) flower and fruit, then die. After fruiting, the floricanes are of no value, and they constitute not only an energy drain on the planting, but also a potential source of disease. For these reasons, they should be cut back to the ground immediately after harvest, removed from the planting, and destroyed.

Pruning, Training, and Thinning Red and Yellow Raspberries

After planting, the new primocanes should be contained in a narrow, 1- to 2-foot-wide row (18 inches appears to be ideal). Excess canes that develop outside the row are removed by hand hoeing, mechanical cultivation, or by mowing.

A trellis or support system is optional for the brambles, but it does help in preventing wind damage and may make harvesting easier. Natural dwarfs like 'Boyne' do not require a support system, but many of the other cultivars produce long primocanes that will either need to be topped or supported.

There is a myriad of support or trellis systems, but those of a permanent nature are in the long run more economical and time saving. Only two permanent trellis sytems will be discussed.

In the first, wooden posts are used (refer to the chapter on grapes for information on durability and methods of post preservation). The posts should be 3 to 5 inches in diameter and about 8 feet long. When setting the posts, 2½ to 3 feet should be in the ground. The posts should be spaced 20 feet apart. Near the top of each, bolt or nail an 18- to 20-inch crosspiece. Approximately 24 to 30 inches from the top, a second crosspiece should be placed in position. On the ends of each crosspiece attach No. 12 galvanized wire and run it the length of the row. The canes are then trained to grow within the 4-wire support system.

The second system involves only a slight modification of the first. Here a double row of steel fenceposts are used. Each set of posts should be spaced about 12 to 14 inches apart. Again, a 4-wire system is used with spacing similar to that described for the wooden-crossarm system.

With both trellis systems, a wire clip is frequently attached to the wires to prevent spreading.

During the first growing season, no pruning of yellow or red raspberries is advised except to remove damaged or diseased primocanes.

Thinning

In the early spring following the first growing season, the weak canes (floricanes) should be removed. After thinning, the remaining canes should be spaced about 6 to 8 inches apart.

First Pruning

At the start of the second growing season (just as the tips of new leaves are appearing), the tips of the floricanes should be cut back to 5 to 6 feet from ground level. Canes shorter than 5 feet do not require pruning unless the tips have died back during the winter. Where dieback has occurred, prune back to healthy tissue.

If a second crop is desired on *everbearing* cultivars, no pruning is required except to remove the tips that fruited the previous summer. If only one harvest is desired (strongly recommended), all canes should be cut back to ground level.

Second Pruning

Immediately after harvest during the second growing season, remove all canes that have borne fruit. After pruning, only the new primocanes should remain.

Red raspberry plant before thinning and pruning. The same plant after thinning and pruning.

Subsequent Pruning

During the third and subsequent growing seasons, pruning and thinning are essentially a repeat of the first years of growth. Each year the plants need to be thinned and topped in the early spring. After harvest, the canes that bore fruit should be removed.

Pruning, Training, and Thinning Purple and Black Raspberries

Black and purple raspberries usually do not require a support or trellis system. The canes that arise are formed from the crown. Black raspberries do not sucker, but occasionally some cultivars of purple raspberries do.

First Pruning

During the first growing season, when the canes of *black* raspberries reach 24 inches high, the top 3 to 4 inches should be pinched or pruned off. Repeat this procedure when *purple* raspberries reach 30 to 36 inches high. Because all canes will probably not reach the proper height at the same time, it will be necessary to go over the planting several times.

Thinning

During the early spring following the first growing season, prune out the weak canes. Generally canes ½ inch or larger in diameter should be selected to remain. This usually means 3 to 5 canes per hill.

Pruning and thinning raspberries after the summer harvest. Photo courtesy of L. Dunsmore.

Second Pruning

Right after thinning, cut back the laterals (side branches) to 6 to 18 inches long, depending on their health and vigor. During the second growing season, remember to top the new primocanes when they reach the desired height, as was described for the first growing season.

Third Pruning

Immediately after harvest, remove all canes that bore fruit.

Subsequent Pruning and Thinning

On an annual basis, thin the plants in the early spring and cut back the laterals. During the early summer, top the new primocanes to the desired height. After harvest, remove the canes that produced fruit.

Pruning, Training, and Thinning Erect Blackberries

Blackberries usually do not require a support system, though some growers prefer one. Commonly, wooden posts similar to those described for red raspberries are positioned 15 to 20 feet apart in rows. Usually a single wire is attached to the posts 30 inches above the ground. Canes that develop are tied to the posts with string.

After planting, the new primocanes are contained in the narrow hedgerow, as was described for red and yellow raspberries.

During the planting year no pruning or training is required. First-year growth is usually less than 2 feet and is well branched.

Topping

During the second and third growing seasons, new primocanes will grow quite tall and will require topping to promote lateral or side branches. When the primocanes reach 36 inches, about 2 to 3 inches of the tip is removed. After the third year, to increase fruit production, primocanes should be topped when they reach a height of 4 to 4½ feet.

Lateral- or Side-Branch Pruning

To maintain a manageable row, lateral branches from the primocanes are usually cut back in the spring before growth begins to a length of 12 to 18 inches.

Thinning

To prevent blackberries from becoming a thicket, weak and crowded canes should be removed. After pruning in the spring, the remaining canes should be spaced 4 to 8 inches apart.

Removing Dead Canes

Commercial growers in Arkansas and in the Southwest rarely remove dead canes after harvest. Often the canes are left in the field for several years without any noticeable disease problems (Lipe and Martin, 1984). Whether this practice should be followed in the North is questionable. For now, promptly removing fruit-bearing canes immediately after harvest seems to be the safest course to follow. Removal of old canes will make the planting more attractive, and it may prevent disease.

Propagating

Home propagation of the brambles is not usually advised; however, if the plants are healthy, many growers find this is a convenient and economical way to obtain stock.

Red and Yellow Raspberries

In the early spring, select one-year suckers. Sever these from the parent plant and move to the permanent planting site. New primocanes from root suckers can also be transplanted, but generally the one-year-old canes give the best results. Two- to three-inch sections of roots can also be used for propagation. Place the root sections horizontally on a seed bed and cover with 2 inches of soil. The following spring, the new plants that arise from the cuts can be transplanted to the permanent growing site.

Blackberries

These plants can be propagated in the same way as red and yellow raspberries. Root cuttings usually give the best results. Here the cuttings are planted in the location where they will fruit.

Purple and Black Raspberries

In late summer (usually August) bury the tips of the canes 2 to 4 inches deep. The next spring sever the tip plants, leaving 4 to 8 inches of old cane attached, and move to the permanent planting location.

Winter Protection

Whether special winter protection is needed will depend on the cultivar being grown and the location.

Red and Yellow Raspberries

Except in open, windswept areas and in the more northerly areas where temperatures drop below $-35°$ F., most of the cultivars recommended do not need any special winter protection.

In areas where protection is needed, the canes in very late fall (just as the ground freezes) are carefully bent over and the tips are covered with a shovelful of soil.

Blackberries

Hardy blackberry cultivars are injured when the air temperature drops below $-20°$ F., and some cultivars (especially the thornless ones) may be injured when the temperature falls close to zero. In most areas of the Upper Midwest where blackberries are attempted, winter protection is advised. For best results, the canes should be bent over and the tips covered with soil. In addition, in some areas the plants should be covered with 3 to 4 inches of mulch such as straw.

Commercial pick-your-own raspberry field. Photo courtesy of L. Dunsmore.

Black and Purple Raspberries

In many areas of the Upper Midwest, these cultivars will require winter protection. In general, the hardy cultivars may withstand − 25° F.

In windswept areas and in the more northerly areas, the canes should be bent over, and the tips covered with soil. Since these plants are grown in hills, bending of the canes can be facilitated by using a potato fork to loosen the soil around each plant. A straw mulch is also advised.

Harvesting

To minimize the spread of disease, avoid harvesting brambles when they are wet. The best time to harvest is in the morning when the dew is gone and the berries are cool.

Pick raspberries when they develop full color and the fleshy edible portion readily separates from the center part or receptacle of the fruit. With blackberries, use color and taste as the criteria for when to harvest. With these plants the core stays with the fleshy part when the berries are picked.

The most desirable container for brambles is the pint. For pick-your-own operations, do not allow customers to put berries into larger containers. Smashed berries and dripping juice do not impress the picker or the grower.

Raspberry cane infected with anthracnose.

For off-farm sales, pick the fruit just before it is to be delivered. Even under ideal storage conditions of 32° F. and 95 percent relative humidity, the berries can be stored for only a short time. Overripe, improperly stored fruit may start to mold and deteriorate in a matter of hours after picking.

Diseases

Many of the disease problems discussed here can be minimized by selecting disease-free planting stock and by following good cultural practices such as proper thinning, pruning, cultivating, and fertilizing.

Fungal diseases can usually be kept at a minimum if the plants are sprayed each spring with liquid lime sulfur. The time for spraying is just as the leaves start to unfold or when they are about ¼ inch long. Lime sulfur is the most important preventive spray for brambles, and for many growers it is the only pesticide used. Berries from plants treated with lime sulfur can be marketed as organically grown.

Leaf and Cane Diseases

Anthracnose or cane spot. This is most severe on black raspberries, but the other brambles are also susceptible. The most obvious symptom is the presence of gray to white spots, often with red or purple borders, that are up to ¼ inch in diameter. In severe cases, the spots are also present on leaves and flower stems. Control the disease by removing pruned parts from the planting and by spraying with lime sulfur.

Leaf spot. Small spots up to ⅛ inch in diameter appear on leaves and shoots. The red cultivars seem to be most susceptible. Control measures are similar to those for anthracnose.

Spur blight. This is another fungus that is most common on red cultivars. Symptoms include the presence of bluish brown or purplish brown spots from ½ inch to several inches long on the primocanes. Berries formed on the canes the second year are small, aborted, and dry. Dormant sprays and sanitation are the control measures.

Verticillium wilt. Symptoms arising from infection of this soil-borne fungus vary widely, but usually a dark blue color is evident on the stem. Often a broad, blue stripe or streak radiates from the base of the cane; in severe cases the entire cane may have a bluish hue. The leaves on affected plants turn yellow, wilt, and eventually dry up. There are no sprays to control verticillium wilt. Only preventive measures are effective: avoid planting on land previously grown to flowers, fruit, and vegetables that are susceptible to the disease.

Powdery mildew. Symptoms on the leaves are similar to those described for strawberries. This disease is usually more prevalent in seasons with abundant rain and high humidity. A fungicide spray program can control the disease.

Orange and yellow rust. These fungal diseases produce yellow or orange rust spots that usually appear on the undersides of the leaves. There are no effective sprays. Obtaining rust-free planting stock and following good cultural practices are the best preventive measures. Plants infected with orange rust usually have to be dug out and eliminated.

Diseases Affecting the Entire Plant

The brambles are susceptible to a variety of viral diseases. The three most common are mosaic, leaf curl, and streak. Symptoms vary, but mosaic-infected plants may show a reduction in leaf size, coupled with a green or yellow mottling of the leaves. With leaf curl, the plants are stunted and the leaves appear crinkled by downward and outward curling. Plants infected with streak show many symptoms typical of verticillium wilt.

Another virus that has become very common in the Upper Midwest is the raspberry bushy dwarf virus (RBDV). Symptoms vary but may include stunting, yellowing leaves, and crumbly berries. This virus spreads by pollen carried by bees; thus, it is extremely important to remove infected plants.

There are no sprays to control viruses so it is important to start with disease-free planting stock. The diseases are spread by pollen and insect vectors, and though controlling the vectors is sometimes recommended, this is rarely practical. Once infection occurs, the diseased plants should be removed and destroyed.

Diseases Affecting Roots

Crown gall is a bacterial disease that shows up as a warty gall on roots or at the base of the canes. There are no effective sprays. Infection of this soil-borne bacterium often occurs when the plant is damaged during cultivation. Infected plants should be destroyed.

Insects and Mites

Application of insecticides and miticides on a regular basis is not recommended; however, occasionally some of the pests listed here may reach population levels that require attention.

Raspberry fruitworm-byturus. The white larval form of this tiny beetle is found inside the berries, where it feeds. The adults are small and reddish or yellowish brown, and they feed on buds, flowers, and leaves.

Raspberry saw fly. The larvae of this insect are up to ¾ inch long, pale green, and have many white, spiny projections. The larval forms feed on leaves, but unless several leaves are skeletonized, no control is usually required.

Raspberry cane borer. These black and yellow, striped beetles make a double row of puncture marks when laying their eggs near the stem tip. The emerging larvae then tunnel inside the stems. The first symptom of infection is wilting of the stem tip. Prune the canes into healthy tissue below the infection.

Raspberry cane maggot. New primocanes often wilt at the tips when tiny (up to ¼ inch) white maggots bore into the canes. Cut wilted or damaged areas back to healthy tissue.

Rednecked cane borer. Infected canes often have cigar-shaped enlargements or swellings an inch or more long. Prune out damaged sections.

Raspberry crown borer. The larval form of this moth bores into the crowns and lower portions of canes, where they feed. Severely infected plants should be removed. Some insecticides are effective when applied during the dormant period.

Other insects and mites. A variety of other pests such as sap beetles, aphids, mites, leafhoppers, and scale insects may occasionally cause damage to brambles. Control measures and descriptions for most of these appear in the pest sections for the other fruits. For pesticide recommendations, consult the county extension service.

SELECTED REFERENCES

Anonymous. 1963. *Raspberry Anthracnose.* Purdue University Coop. Ext. Ser. Mimeo BP 4–1.

Anonymous. 1978. *Controlling Diseases of Raspberries and Blackberries.* USDA Farmer's Bulletin 2208.

Anonymous. 1979. *Growing Blackberries.* USDA Farmer's Bulletin 2160.

Anonymous. 1979. *Growing Raspberries.* USDA Farmer's Bulletin 2165.

Askew, R. G., and N. S. Holland. 1984. *Raspberries for North Dakota.* North Dakota State University Coop. Ext. Ser. Cir. N–38 (rev.).

Bailey, L. H. 1932. The Blackberries of North America. *Gentes Herbarium* 2: 270–423.

Boynton, D., and M. Wilde. 1959. Development of Black Raspberry Fruit. *Proc. Amer. Soc. Hort. Sci.* 73: 158–63.

Brooks, R. M., and H. P. Olmo. 1972. *Register of New Fruit and Nut Varieties.* 2nd ed. Berkeley: University of California Press.

Caldwell, J. D. 1984. Blackberry Propagation. *HortScience* 19(2): 193–94.

Converse, R. H. 1966. *Diseases of Raspberries and Erect and Trailing Blackberries.* USDA Agricultural Handbook 310.

Converse, R. H. 1984. Blackberry Viruses in the United States. *HortScience* 19(2): 185–87.

Converse, R. H. 1986. Sterility Disorder of 'Darrow' Blackberry. *HortScience* 21(6): 1441–43.

Crandall, P. C., and H. A. Daubeny. 1990. Raspberry Management. In: *Small Fruit Crop Management.* G. J. Galletta and D. G. Himelrick (eds.). Englewood Cliffs, N.J.: Prentice-Hall.

Darrow, G. M. 1937. Blackberry and Raspberry Improvement. *USDA Yearbook of Agriculture* 1937: 496–533.

Darrow, G. M. 1942. *Blackberry Growing.* USDA Farmer's Bulletin 1399.

Darrow, G. M. 1967. The Cultivated Raspberry and Blackberry in North America—Breeding and Improvement. *Amer. Hort. Mag.* 46(4): 203–18.

Darrow, G. M., and G. F. Waldo. 1948. *Growing Erect and Trailing Blackberries.* USDA Farmer's Bulletin 1995.

DeBoer, D. W., R. M. Peterson, and N. D. Evers. 1983. Trickle and Sprinkler Irrigation of Red Raspberries. *HortScience* 18(6): 930–31.

DeGomez, T. E., L. W. Martin, and P. J. Breen. 1986. Effect of Nitrogen and Pruning on Primocane Fruiting Red Raspberry 'Amity'. *HortScience* 21(3): 441–42.

Denisen, E. L. 1976. Small Fruits in Iowa. *HortScience* 11(4): 342.

Denisen, E. L. 1983. Breeding Raspberries for Tolerance to Adverse Climate Conditions. *Acta Hort.* 140: 143–46.

Galletta, G., and C. Violette. 1989. The Bramble. In: *Bramble Production Guide.* M. Pritt and D. Handley (eds.). Northeast Regional Agr. Engineering Ser. Pub. NRAES–35.

Handley, D. 1989. Plant Selection. In: *Bramble Production Guide.* M. Pritt and D. Handley (eds.). Northeast Regional Agr. Engineering Ser. Pub. NRAES–35.

Haskell, G. 1954. The History and Genetics of the Raspberry. *Discovery* 15: 241–46.

Hedrick, U. P. 1925. *The Small Fruits of New York.* Albany, N.Y.: J.B. Lyon.

Hendrickson, R. 1981. *The Berry Book.* Garden City, N.Y.: Doubleday.

Hertz, L. B. 1978. *Raspberry Varieties Important in Minnesota.* University of Minnesota Fruit Growers Letter, January 1978.

Hertz, L. B. 1987. *Fruit for the Home.* University of Minnesota Ext. Ser. Pub. AG–BU–0470.

Hertz, L. B. 1988. *Raspberries.* University of Minnesota Ext. Pub. AG–FS–1108.

Hill, R. G., Jr., J. D. Utzinger, and R. C. Funt. 1979. *Growing Bramble Fruit.* Ohio State University Coop. Ext. Ser. Bull. 411.

Jennings, D. L. 1988. *Raspberries and Blackberries: Their Breeding, Diseases and Growth.* San Diego: Academic Press.

Johnson, H. G. 1980. *Raspberry Diseases.* University of Minnesota Ext. Ser. Plant Path. Fact Sheet No. 8.

Keep, E. 1961. Autumn Fruiting in Raspberries. *Jour. Hort. Sci.* 36: 174–85.

Lawrence, F. J. 1986. A Review of Interspecific Hybridization in *Rubus. HortScience* 21(1): 58–61.

Lipe, J. A., and L. W. Martin. 1984. Culture and Management of Blackberries in the United States. *HortScience* 19(2): 190–93.

Luby, J. 1986. Raspberry Cultivar Performance in Minnesota. *Michigan State Hort. Soc. Annual Report* 116: 170–75.

Mahr, D. L., E. J. Stang, M. N. Dana, and S. N. Jeffers. 1987. *Strawberry and Raspberry Pest Control for Wisconsin.* University of Wisconsin Coop. Ext. Ser. Pub. A-1934.

McGregor, S. E. 1976. *Insect Pollination of Cultivated Crop Plants.* USDA Agricultural Handbook 496.

Moore, J. N. 1979. Small Fruit Breeding—A Rich Heritage, A Challenging Future. *HortScience* 14: 333–41.

Moore, J. N. 1980. Blackberry Production and Cultivar Situation in North America. *Fruit Varieties Jour.* 34: 36–42.

Moore, J. N. 1984. Blackberry Breeding. *HortScience* 19(2): 183–85.

Morris, J. F. 1970. *Growing Blackberries.* Texas Agr. Ext. Ser. Pub. B-990.

Morrison, F. D. 1984. *Raspberries and Blackberries.* Kansas State University Coop. Ext. Ser. Pub. MF-720.

North Star Gardens. 1988. *Raspberries—Grower Guide and Catalog.* 19060 Manning Trail N., Marine on St. Croix, MN 55047-9723.

Ourecky, D. K. 1975. Brambles. In: *Advances in Fruit Breeding.* J. Janick and J. N. Moore (eds.). Lafayette, Ind.: Purdue University Press.

Ourecky, D. K. and G. L. Slate. 1969. *Heritage, A New Fall Bearing Red Raspberry.* Geneva, N.Y., Agr. Exper. Stat. Res. Cir. 19.

Peterson, R. M., and D. Martin. 1977. *Growing Raspberries in South Dakota.* South Dakota State University Coop. Ext. Ser. Pub. FS-345 (rev.).

Ricketson, C., L. A. Hikichi, and C. B. Kelly. 1970. *Raspberries and Blackberries in Ontario.* Ontario Department of Agriculture Pub. 473.

Sheets, W. A., R. M. Bullock, and R. Garren, Jr. 1972. Effect of Plant Density, Training, and Pruning on Blackberry Yield. *Jour. Amer. Soc. Hort. Sci.* 97: 262–64.

Shoemaker, J. S. 1978. *Small Fruit Culture.* Westport, Conn.: AVI Publishing.

Skirvin, R. M., and E. W. Hellman. 1984. Blackberry Products and Production Regions. *HortScience* 19(2): 195–97.

Snyder, L. C. 1980. *Trees and Shrubs for Northern Gardens.* Minneapolis: University of Minnesota Press.

Stang, E. J., D. M. Boone, and D. L. Mahr. 1980. *Growing Raspberries in Wisconsin.* University of Wisconsin Coop. Ext. Ser. Pub. A1610.

Taber, H. G., and C. Fear. 1986. *Fruit Cultivars for the Family.* Iowa State University Coop. Ext. Ser. Hort. Pub. PM 453.

Taber, H. G., D. R. Lewis, and L. E. Sweets. 1985. *Growing Raspberries at Home.* Iowa State University Coop. Ext. Ser. Hort. Guide F-13-83.

Tomkins, J. 1977. Cane and Bush Fruits Are the Berries; Often It's Grow Them or Go Without. In: *Growing Fruits and Nuts.* USDA Agricultural Inform. Bull. 408.

Van Adrichem, M. C. 1970. Assessment of Winter Hardiness in Red Raspberries. *Canada Journal Plant Science* 50: 181–87.

Waldo, G. F. 1934. Fruit Bud Formation in Brambles. *Proc. Amer. Soc. Hort. Sci.* 30: 263–67.

Wott, J. A. No date. *Raspberries.* Purdue University Coop. Ext. Ser. Pub. HO-44.

11

Currants and Gooseberries

For many years, currants and gooseberries were placed in separate genera, but today most authors have united the species into a single genus, *Ribes*. This member of the family Saxifragaceae contains about 150 species distributed mainly in the temperate regions of the Northern Hemisphere as well as North Africa and the Andes (Keep, 1975).

In addition to the garden types, there are a few species used in the Upper Midwest for hedges and shrub ornamentals. Fruit, when produced on these landscape plants, is edible, but it is not widely used. For details on the landscape value of *Ribes alpinum* (alpine currant); *R. cynosbati* (prickly gooseberry); and *R. odoratum* (clove currant, buffalo currant), see Snyder (1980). 'Jostaberry', a new edible fruit created by hybridizing currants and gooseberries, is discussed in chapter 13.

Currants and gooseberries are extremely hardy, and their culture extends nearly to the Arctic Circle. These plants are well adapted for culture in almost all areas of the Upper Midwest.

Theories abound concerning the origin of the name *gooseberry*, but it remains a mystery. It seems logical to try to connect the *goose* to the *berry*, but as Hendrickson (1981) has pointed out, geese do not eat gooseberries nor are the berries served with roast goose. He recants the theory that the green of the berry may in some way be associated with terms like *greenhorn fool, silly goose*, or *fool*.

To most Americans, gooseberries remain an undiscovered delicacy even though they have been cultivated here since 1812. According to Moore (1979), a considerable commercial gooseberry industry existed at the beginning of the 20th century, but shortly thereafter, it began to decline. Today, culture of both gooseberries and currants is confined largely to home gardens.

The most important American species involved in gooseberry breeding has been *R. hirtellum*. This species is native to parts of Canada and ranges as far south as Virginia. Another species, *R. missouriense*, is distributed from Tennessee northwest to South Dakota. Most cultivars grown today have been selected from the American species or from hybrids between them and the European gooseberry, *R. uva-crispa*.

Like many other fruit types, the number of available cultivars has declined drastically. In 1925, Hedrick listed 225 gooseberry and 185 currant cultivars. Moore (1979), citing Coville (1937), reported that by 1937, research by public agencies had produced 6 currant and 18 gooseberry cultivars, but that most were released during a time period when interest in these crops was rapidly declining. From 1937 to 1979, only 9 additional currants and 2 gooseberry cultivars had been released by experiment stations in North America (Moore, 1979).

According to Keep (1975), the first record of gooseberry cultivation in Britain dates to 1276–92. Gooseberry and currant culture has been much more popular in Europe than in the United States. It was English gardeners especially who rapidly developed a fondness for gooseberries, and Gourley and Howlett (1941) note that by 1831 at least 722 cultivars were known.

The reasons why these plants never became popular here are unknown, but disease problems undoubtedly played a prominent role. Attempts to grow the somewhat larger-fruited English gooseberry here were plagued by mildew problems, and in addition, cultivation of many species of *Ribes* was discouraged or forbidden after the discovery that these plants served as the alternate host for white pine-blister rust. The disease-causing organism, *Cronartium ribicola*, was apparently introduced into North America on pine seedlings from Europe about 1892 (Leppik, 1970). This rust fungus causes little damage to *Ribes* except in cases of severe infection; then, it may cause premature leaf drop. The real damage may occur on the white or 5-needled pine, *Pinus strobus*. Severity of infection varies widely. The disease cannot spread from one pine to another; rather, it "ping pongs" back and forth between *Ribes* and pine. The European black currant is extremely susceptible to this blister rust, and for this reason it is rarely grown in the Upper Midwest. There are, however, some hybrid black-currant cultivars available that are immune (see the cultivar section). Other currant cultivars vary in their susceptibility, but the popular 'Red Lake' is apparently quite susceptible. 'Viking' is the only cultivar recommended for the Upper Midwest which exhibits some resistance.

Gooseberries, like currants, also vary in their susceptibility, but there are no recommended resistant cultivars. Some progress in abating the disease has been achieved through the breeding of rust-resistant cultivars, but these will not be available to the home gardener for some time (Ritter, 1982). Judging from the standpoint of available cultivars and the historical records, it would appear that currants have been even less popular than gooseberries. According to Bunyard (1917), red currants were unknown to the ancient Greeks and Romans. Apparently, they were first mentioned by German writers in the 15th century. Hedrick (1925) believed the plants were first cultivated in the Netherlands and around the Baltic Sea. However, Keep (1975) has pointed out that both Bunyard (1917) and Thayer (1923) tap France and adjoining countries as the first cultivation center because the first domesticated red currants are indigenous there.

White currants, which are merely color forms of the reds, along with the European black currant, *R. nigrum*, are also natives to the Old World. Red currant cultivars available today contain one or a combination of three species: *R. rubrum*, *R. petraeum*, and *R. sativum* (Keep, 1975). Most American cultivars are assigned to *R. sativum*. They were first introduced here in 1620 (Gourley and Howlett, 1941).

Several American black-currant cultivars have been derived from the native American species *R. odoratum* and *R. americanum*, but they have never been grown commercially. Since their first introduction in 1832 (Hedrick, 1925), these plants have either been grown as ornamentals or confined to a few home fruit gardens.

Hendrickson (1981) reports that currants originally got their name from a variety of raisin obtained from seedless grapes being grown in Corinth, Greece. *Corinth* was first corrupted to *Corauntz*, and finally to *currant*.

Pollination

Most gooseberries and red currant cultivars are self-compatible, but Harmat et al. (1990) report that the degree of self-fertility depends on the year and the location. For this reason, they recommend for commercial growers that 1 to 2 percent of the planting be planted to a pollenizer cultivar. Most black currants are self-sterile, thus two or more different cultivars should be planted for cross-pollination. Bees are the major pollinators.

How Many Plants?

A yield of about three to four quarts of fruit per plant is considered excellent for both gooseberries and currants. Well-maintained plantings should last 10 to 15 years or longer. Fruit from these plants is used for jam, jelly, pie, and wine.

Selecting Nursery Stock

Barerooted, healthy, one- to two-year-old nursery stock is recommended for both currants and gooseberries. Potted material offers no advantage over bareroot stock, and plants older than two years are not worth the increased cost. Tissue-cultured (TC) plants are also available and are recommended for commercial plantings.

Gooseberry Cultivars

Colossal. Frank M. Schwab selected this open-pollinated seedling from an unknown European-type gooseberry in Mankato, Minnesota. It was introduced in 1974 by Herschel R. Boll of Champaign, Illinois. This gooseberry produces the largest fruit (up to 1 ½ inches in diameter) of any cultivar discussed here. European-type gooseberries for the Upper Midwest have a poor performance record because of disease problems, but several growers in the Mankato area report this cultivar to be vigorous, hardy, and tolerant of disease.

Downing. This seedling of *R. hirtellum* x *R. uva-crispa* is thought to have originated in Newburgh, New York, about 1855. The plants are quite hardy and productive. The berries at maturity are small and pale green. This cultivar is rarely grown today and may not be available commercially.

Poorman. This is another hybrid of *R. hirtellum* x *R. uva-crispa*, which originated from Brigham City, Utah, in about 1888. The hardy plants are less productive than 'Downing' and with fewer spines, but the fruit is larger. The berries at maturity are red. Recently this cultivar has waned in popularity.

Pixwell. 'Oregon Champion' x *R. missouriense* is the parentage of this 1932 introduction from North Dakota. This hardy cultivar has few thorns and the medium-size, pink fruit is borne in long clusters, making picking easy.

Welcome. The University of Minnesota Horticultural Research Center introduced this open-pollinated seedling of 'Poorman' in 1957. The plant is very hardy and has few spines. Berries are light dull red at maturity and are somewhat larger than 'Pixwell'.

Currants

In addition to the red and white currants, black currants are occasionally seen in Upper Midwest gardens.

The American black currant, *R. americanum*, exists mostly as a wild plant in moist woods and swamps. There are a few named cultivars, but none can

Developed by the University of Minnesota,
'Welcome' is one of the best gooseberry cultivars for the Upper Midwest.

Fruit zones— gooseberries

Cultivar	Iowa			Minn.				S. Dak.				N. Dak.			Wis.			
	4b	5a	5b	1	2	3	4	1	2	3	4	A	B	C	1	2	3	4
Colossal				T	T													
Downing															X	X	X	X
Poorman				X	X	X						T	T	T	X	X	X	X
Pixwell	X	X	X	X	X	X	X	X	X	X	X	X	X	X	X	X	X	X
Welcome	X	X	X	X	X	X	X	X	X	X	X	X	X	X	X	X	X	X

X = recommended for planting; T = recommended for trial.
See zone map on page 20.

be recommended for the Upper Midwest. This species performs best in the colder regions of North Dakota, northern Minnesota, and in parts of northern Wisconsin.

The European black currant, *R. nigrum*, cannot be recommended for planting in most areas because of its susceptibility to white pine-blister rust. There are, however, three cultivars that are immune to white pine-blister rust that seem worthy of trial planting in all areas of the Upper Midwest. They were developed in Ottawa, Ontario, and have the hybrid of *R. nigrum* ('Kerry') and *R. ussuriense* in their parentage. Two of the cultivars, 'Crusader' and 'Coronet', were released in 1948 and 'Consort' in 1952.

Red and White Cultivars

Cascade. This open-pollinated seedling of 'Diploma' was introduced by the University of Minnesota Horticultural Research Center in 1942. The red fruits are very large and ripen a week earlier than 'Red Lake'.

Cherry. According to Hedrick (1925), this cultivar originated in Italy and was introduced into France about 1840. It was later introduced into Flushing, New York, in 1846 by Dr. William Valk. The red fruit clusters are small and difficult to pick.

Perfection. C. G. Hooker introduced this 'Fay' x 'White Grape' cross from Rochester, New York, in 1887. This old-time cultivar is very similar to 'Wilder'. The berries are red and mature early to midseason. The plant is quite hardy, but the canes have a tendency to break easily.

Red Lake. This is the most popular red-currant cultivar grown in America and probably the best for the Upper Midwest. It was introduced by the University of Minnesota Horticultural Research Center from unknown parentage in 1933. The fruits are dark red and very large. The plant is moderately vigorous and very productive.

Viking. The date of origin of this *R. petraeum* x *R. rubrum* cross imported from Europe is unknown. The berries are red and mature late. This cultivar is seldom planted except where white pine-blister rust is a problem. Keep (1975) reports that it is not totally immune, and that young leaves may be infected, but the fungal hyphae soon die. 'Viking' may be difficult to locate.

White Grape. This is an old-European, white-fruited cultivar that has been cultivated in this country for over 150 years. It is seldom planted except in Wisconsin.

Wilder. According to Hedrick (1925), this seedling of 'Versailles' originated in Indiana in about 1877 and was introduced in 1897. The berries are red and large. Today, it is rarely grown except occasionally in Wisconsin, South Dakota, and Iowa.

'Red Lake' currant in flower.

Fruit on 'Red Lake' currant. Photo courtesy of L. Hertz.

Fruit zones—
currants

Cultivar	Iowa			Minn.				S. Dak.				N. Dak.			Wis.			
	4b	5a	5b	1	2	3	4	1	2	3	4	A	B	C	1	2	3	4
Cascade												X	X	X				
Cherry	X	X	X															
Perfection	X	X	X															
Red Lake	X	X	X	X	X	X	X	X	X	X	X	X	X	X	X	X	X	X
Viking				X	X	X	X											
White Grape												X	X	X	X	X	X	X
Wilder	X	X	X					X	X	X	X				X	X	X	X

X = recommended for planting.
See zone map on page 20.

Location of the Planting Site

Currants and gooseberries will grow in a variety of soil types, but they perform poorly on very sandy and waterlogged soils. They grow best on cool, moist soils that have a high percentage of organic matter. Low areas should be avoided because cold temperatures may injure the flowers, which appear very early in the spring. A northern or northeastern exposure with a slight slope is best. The ideal pH range is 5.5 to 7.0, but the plants will grow in soils less acidic or more alkaline.

Currants and gooseberries will grow in partial shade, but they perform best in full sun. Plants in full sun should be mulched to keep the roots cool. The site must have good air movement to prevent frost damage and to minimize disease problems.

Before planting rust-susceptible gooseberry or currant cultivars, it is advisable to check with neighbors regarding plantings of white pine. These cultivars should not be located within 1,500 feet of any white-pine nursery or within 900 feet of a designated control area for white pine-blister rust.

The accompanying map redrawn from Ritter (1982) gives the blister-rust hazard zones for Minnesota. In zones 1 and 2, where infection is usually not severe, he suggests planting white pine for landscaping in groups of two or three. The danger of losing all the pines in the group is remote. To prevent rust infection, Ritter advises (1) planting in favorable areas; (2) removal of the lower whorl of branches when the pines are about two feet tall (for commer-

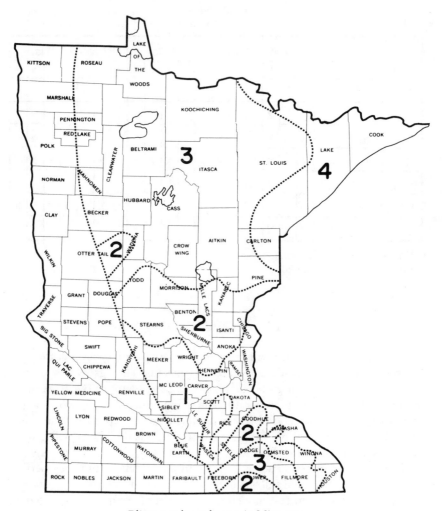

Blister-rust hazard zones in Minnesota.

cial forest plantations, prune branches frequently until a minimum of nine feet of clean trunk is achieved); (3) removal of grass and other vegetation around the base of the trees; and (4) removal of wild *Ribes* near white pines. In zones 3 and 4, where blister-rust infection can be severe, the advisability of planting most *Ribes* cultivars near white pine is questionable.

To obtain information on blister-rust hazard zones for other states, check with the county extension office or the state department of agriculture.

Planting and Spacing

Before planting, spade or till in liberal amounts of organic matter such as well-rotted manure, compost, or peat—preferably in the fall before spring planting. The area should also be cultivated frequently to eliminate quackgrass and other troublesome perennial weeds.

In the Upper Midwest, early spring, before the plants start to leaf out, is the best time to plant. Before planting, soak the roots in water for three to four hours.

Currants and gooseberries should be spaced 3 to 5 feet apart in rows 6 to 10 feet apart.

Dig a hole one-third wider and deeper than the root spread. Set the plants about an inch deeper than they grew in the nursery. When filling the planting hole, frequently press the soil to eliminate air pockets. After planting is completed, select only four to five of the biggest canes to remain and prune these back to one-third their original length. Finally, give each plant two to three gallons of water.

Mulching

Mulching is beneficial for plants grown in partial shade and is required for plants placed in full sun. The mulch not only suppresses weeds but also helps to conserve moisture and keep the soil cool. To be effective, the mulch should be a minimum of 4 to 6 inches deep. Good mulch materials are ground corncobs, compost, straw, old hay, granulated peat, sawdust, and well-rotted manure. The mulch should be replenished annually, and if materials with high carbon-to-nitrogen ratios such as sawdust are used, supplemental nitrogen will be required.

Fertilizing

Well-rotted manure is ideal for both currants and gooseberries. One bushel per plant is the recommended amount, and it should be applied in late fall or early spring before growth begins. When manure is not used, apply one cup per plant of 10–10–10 fertilizer in the spring. The fertilizer should be spread out evenly under the branches and extend a foot from the drip line.

Pruning

Currants and gooseberries should be pruned in early March, or before growth begins in the spring. These plants fruit on one-, two-, and three-

Bush before pruning   **Bush after pruning**

Pruning currants and gooseberries.

year-old canes. The idea behind pruning is to remove canes older than three years and to thin out excessive new canes.

Ideally a mature plant after pruning in the spring should have 9 to 12 remaining, upright canes. This can be achieved by beginning pruning in the fourth year to remove the oldest cane. For every older cane removed, let one or more new canes develop until a balance of 9 to 12 canes is achieved.

Propagating

Since currants and gooseberries do not breed true from seed, they should be propagated vegetatively.

There are a variety of propagation methods. Many require special equipment and/or asceptic conditions, but the simplest techniques are practically foolproof and demand only labor and patience. Mound (stool) and trench layering are two of the easiest methods for propagating *Ribes*. The techniques discussed here are slightly modified from Hartmann and Kester (1975).

In the mound method, mature plants are cut to an inch above the ground in the early spring. When the new, emerging shoots are 3 to 5 inches tall, soil is mounded around their bases to a depth of 2 to 4 inches. As the shoots increase in size, more soil is added to a depth of 6 to 8 inches. The following spring the mounded shoots with their attached roots can be severed from the parent plant and placed in a permanent location.

The trench method is used when only a few plants are desired. With this technique, a shallow trench 2 inches deep is dug and a cane from the parent plant is bent over into the trench and covered with about an inch of soil. A number of wickets made from stiff wire should be used to keep the cane flat on the bottom of the trench. As new shoots emerge, soil is mounded around their bases as in the mound method. The final soil depth should be 6 to 8 inches. The following spring the plants can be severed and placed in a permanent location.

Dormant cuttings also root readily when planted in good garden soil and kept moist. Harvest one-year-old cuttings 6 inches long in November and store in a refrigerator or bury them outdoors until planting in a nursery row in April or early May.

Harvesting

Taste and development of the mature color are the best guides for when to harvest gooseberries and currants. In contrast to most types of fruit, these berries can usually be left on the plant for a week or more after they mature. Gooseberries grown in full sun are an exception. To prevent sunscald these should be harvested as they mature, and after picking they should be kept out of the sun. Currants to be used for jelly should be harvested just before maturity to ensure high levels of pectin. Both types of berries will store under refrigeration for several weeks.

Diseases and Pests

Currants and gooseberries usually do not require a regular spray schedule to control the few fungal diseases and other pests. Good cultural practices such as mulching, fertilizing, and proper pruning go a long way in preventing problems.

Diseases

Leaf Spot. These diseases first show up as small, circular, brown spots on leaves. The spots enlarge, forming a gray center with a brown border. On close examination, small black flecks, which represent the fruiting body of the fungus, can be seen within the spots. When infection is severe, the leaves may turn yellow and drop prematurely. Raking and removal of infected leaves is an essential step in preventing reinfection in subsequent years.

Anthracnose. Small brown spots may appear on leaves, canes, and fruit anytime during the growing season. As the spots enlarge they may become angular with a purplish margin. Severe infection may cause early leaf drop. Rake and destroy infected leaves.

Powdery mildew. This fungal disease is most common on gooseberries, but it can also affect currants. The disease is manifested by the appearance of a gray white, moldy growth that may completely cover the leaves.

Botrytis. Dieback of the shoot tips and a gray mold rot of the berries are symptoms of this fungal disease. Infection seems most severe in areas with poor air circulation and during wet, humid summers.

White pine-blister rust. This disease causes little damage to either gooseberries or currants. Symptoms include rust spots on the undersurface of the leaf.

Cluster cup rust. Sedges are the alternate host of this disease. Infected leaves may appear swollen and have reddish orange spots. Damage is usually minimal.

Currant mosaic. This disease causes the leaves to become chlorotic (yellowing) with light and dark patches. In time, white areas may appear on the leaves.

Insects

Imported currant worm. The immature forms of this sawfly feed on the leaves and may completely defoliate the plant. The feeding worm is about ¾ inch long and blush green with many black spots.

Currant aphid. Leaves on infected plants often develop raised, reddish, or discolored wrinkled areas between the veins, and they often curl downward. This is caused when the aphid sucks juice from the undersurface of the leaf. This insect attacks foliage as soon as the first leaves unfold in the spring.

Currant borer. Immature forms of a family of clear-winged moths damage the canes. Pale yellow, wormlike larvae feed on the pith inside the canes, causing them to weaken and die. If a cane is cut lengthwise, evidence of the feeding tunnels will be apparent. Infected canes should be pruned out at ground level and destroyed.

Currant stem girdlers. Wilting of new shoots in the late spring is a symptom of this type of sawfly infection. Like currant borers, the larvae tunnel through the pith inside the cane. These pests also feed on willows and poplars, and infection may be more severe near these plants. Prune and destroy infected canes.

Gooseberry fruitworm. This greenish, dark-striped worm feeds on the developing fruit of both currants and gooseberries. The adult is a moth.

Currant fruit fly. The adult deposits eggs inside the developing fruit and these hatch into numerous, small white maggots that feed on the surrounding tissue. Infected berries may discolor and drop prematurely. Berries should be raked and destroyed soon after they drop because the maggots leave the berries and enter the soil, where they pupate and spend the winter.

San Jose scale. More than 60 kinds of fruit and ornamental trees are attacked by this pest (Johnson and Lyon, 1976). The insect produces a protective, flat, gray covering about 1 to 2 millimeters in diameter. Under the covering, the insect spends most of its life sucking juice from the plants. The canes are favored target areas and in time may be weakened or killed.

Fourlined plant bug. This insect feeds on a variety of cultivated plants; it is attractive and easy to recognize. The adult is about 7 millimeters long and the body is yellowish green with four prominent stripes on the back. The insect damages the plant by sucking juice from the leaves and young stems.

Dormant oil applied just before the buds swell is very effective in controlling aphids, scale, and some other insect pests. Lime sulfur used at the green-tip bud-break stage, and again two to three weeks after flowering, is helpful in controlling some of the fungal diseases. For information on other fungicides and insecticides, contact a local entomologist or the county extension agent.

SELECTED REFERENCES

Brooks, R. M., and H. P. Olmo. 1972. *Register of New Fruit and Nut Varieties.* 2nd ed. Berkeley: University of California Press.

Bunyard, E. A. 1917. The History and Development of the Red Currant. *Jour. Royal Hort. Society* 42: 260–70.

Coville, F. V. 1937. Improvement of Currants and Gooseberries. *USDA Yearbook of Agriculture* 1937: 534–44.

Filler, D. M. 1976. Gooseberries and Currants. *Minnesota Horticulturist* 104(3): 68–69.

Gourley, J. H., and F. M. Howlett. 1941. *Modern Fruit Production.* New York: Macmillan.

Harmat, L., A. Porpaczy, D. G. Himelrick, and G. J. Galletta. 1990. Currant and Gooseberry Management. In *Small Fruit Management.* G. J. Galletta and D. G. Himelrick (eds.). Englewood Cliffs, N. J.: Prentice–Hall.

Hedrick, U. P. 1925. *The Small Fruits of New York.* New York State Agr. Exper. Stat. Report 33: 243–54.

Hendrickson, R. 1981. *The Berry Book.* Garden City, N.Y.: Doubleday.

Hertz, L. 1980. *Currants and Gooseberries for the Home Fruit Garden.* University of Minnesota Ext. Ser. Hort. Fact Sheet 39.

Hill, L. 1977. *Fruits and Berries for the Home Garden.* Charlotte, Vt.: Garden Way Publishing.

Holland N. S., and R. Askew. 1977. *Currants, Gooseberries, Grapes.* North Dakota State University Coop. Ext. Ser. Cir. H–350.

Johnson, W. T., and H. H. Lyon. 1976. *Insects that Feed on Trees and Shrubs.* Ithaca, N.Y.: Cornell University Press.

Keep, E. 1975. Currants and Gooseberries. In: *Advances in Fruit Breeding.* J. Janick and J. N. Moore (eds.). Lafayette, Ind.: Purdue University Press.

Leppik, E. E. 1970. Gene Centers of Plants as Sources of Disease Resistance. *Ann. Rev. Phytopath.* 8: 323–44.

Moore, J. N. 1979. Small Fruit Breeding—A Rich Heritage, A Challenging Future. *HortScience* 14: 333–41.

Morrison, F. D. 1984. *Currants, Gooseberries, Elderberries, Blueberries.* Kansas State University Coop. Ext. Ser. Pub. MF–719.

Rake, B. A. 1958. History of Gooseberries in England. *Fruit Yearbook* 10: 84–87.

Ritter, L. B. 1982. White Pine for the Urban Landscape. *Minnesota Horticulturist* 110(4): 100–101.

Shoemaker, J. S. 1978. *Small Fruit Culture.* Westport, Conn.: AVI Publishing.

Snyder, L. C. 1980. *Trees and Shrubs for Northern Gardens.* Minneapolis: University of Minnesota Press.

Stang, E. J., J. Houland, D. L. Mahr, and D. M. Boone. 1982. *Growing Currants, Gooseberries and Elderberries in Wisconsin.* University of Wisconsin Coop. Ext. Ser. Pub. A1960.

Thayer, P. 1923. The Red and White Currants. *Ohio Agr. Exper. Stat. Bull.* 371: 309–94.

Blueberries

The blueberry, along with the bilberry, cranberry, and huckleberry, belongs to the genus *Vaccinium*, which is a member of the family Ericaceae. About 150 species in this genus are native to the Northern Hemisphere. Most are found in North America and eastern Asia (Bailey et al., 1976). Another genus in the family, *Gaylussacia*, which contains the true huckleberries, is often confused with blueberries. True blueberries have 50 to 75 tiny seeds that are barely noticeable, but the huckleberries in *Gaylussacia* have 10 large, bonelike seeds.

Blueberries are relative newcomers to American gardens, since virtually all available cultivars were developed during this century. Before 1916, when the first cultivars were developed, blueberries were harvested from wild plants (Galletta, 1975). By 1986, Eck (1988) reported that there were over 18,088 hectares (44,677 acres) of cultivated blueberries in North America.

Until very recently, blueberries for the home garden in most areas of the Upper Midwest were considered a novelty, and virtually no commercial plantings existed. Exacting soil requirements and the lack of suitable cultivars for the often-harsh climate have been the major limiting factors. Acid-soil requirements have not changed, but recently released, hardy, productive cultivars have sparked new interest for the home gardener. Blueberries are also now being grown as a trial crop by some Minnesota and Wisconsin farmers.

Three major groups of blueberries are harvested in the United States: low-bush, highbush, and rabbiteye.

Lowbush Blueberries

Some cultivars of lowbush blueberries have been released recently, but the commercial harvest is still almost exclusively from wild plants often aided in their production. In many areas it is common to burn over part of the harvest area. Burning helps control unwanted vegetation, and it also aids in pruning.

Lowbush blueberries are usually 6 to 18 inches high and are a complex of several species. The two most common species are *V. angustifolium*, low sweet blueberry, and *V. myrtilloides*, velvet leaf blueberry. Besides in Minnesota and Wisconsin, lowbush blueberries are also harvested principally in Maine, New Hampshire, Michigan, Massachusetts, New York, and West Virginia (Shoemaker, 1978).

Highbush Blueberries

Credit for taming the wild blueberry into a domesticated plant suitable for commercial cultivation must go to Dr. F. W. Coville and Elizabeth White. Coville began his work in 1906 and soon enlisted the aid of White, a blueberry enthusiast from Whitesbog, New Jersey. White provided the land for Coville's research, and she assisted in securing superior wild plants for use in breeding. This association continued for many years, and by the time of Coville's death in 1937, 68,000 hybrid seedlings and 15 named cultivars had been produced. After his death, 15 additional cultivars selected from seed and seedlings in Coville's collection were released (Galletta, 1975).

The blueberry breeding after Coville was continued at the USDA by Dr. George M. Darrow. He expanded the program to include both private and state agencies so that blueberries could be tested at a number of locations. By 1979, Moore reported that 11 states were involved in blueberry breeding programs.

Highbush blueberries, which range in height from 3 to 9 feet or more, have been selected from intraspecific hybrids involving mainly *V. corymbosum*. These highbush blueberries have never been of much importance in the Upper Midwest, primarily because they require a long growing season and the plants lack winter hardiness. To overcome these problems, breeders have focused on crossing hardy lowbush species such as *V. angustifolium* with the more productive, highbush types to select cultivars suitable for northern gardens. These new hybrids are the hope for the fledgling commercial industry in the Upper Midwest and the best choice for home gardeners.

The principal states involved in highbush production are Michigan, New Jersey, North Carolina, and to a lesser extent, New York, Washington, Oregon, Arkansas, Oklahoma, and Missouri (Eck, 1988).

*Larger, potted blueberries usually fruit earlier
and are easier to transplant than smaller, barerooted plants.*

Rabbiteye Blueberries

Rabbiteye blueberries, named because of the resemblance of the developing fruit's pink color to the eyes of some rabbits, are grown principally in Georgia, Florida, Mississippi, and Texas. The major species involved in breeding work has been *V. ashei*. These blueberries, which may reach a height of 33 feet, are extremely cold sensitive.

Pollination

Blueberry plants are usually self-compatible, but when two or more cultivars are present, cross-pollination produces fruit that ripens earlier and is larger. Different cultivars should not be planted more than 4 rows apart. Bees are the major pollinators.

Selecting Nursery Stock

Blueberries are most commonly sold as one-, two-, or three-year-old potted or barerooted plants. I prefer the larger, older plants because they will come

'Northblue' blueberry is one of three superior cultivars released by the University of Minnesota.

into production much earlier and they have a better-developed root system, which makes transplanting less risky. Barerooted plants can be satisfactory, but the fine, fibrous roots can be injured easily if they are not kept moist and covered before planting.

The Best Cultivars

The three best cultivars available for most blueberry-growing areas of the Upper Midwest are 'Northblue', 'Northsky', and 'Northcountry'. All three were developed by the University of Minnesota Horticultural Research Center and are hybrids of lowbush and highbush types. 'Northblue' and 'Northsky' were introduced in 1983; 'Northcountry' was introduced in 1986. Table 16, using data from Hoover et al. (1984), Luby et al. (1986), and Hoover (1988 personal communication), compares the cultivars.

Other Cultivars

Berkeley. This 'Stanley' x ('Jersey' x 'Pioneer') cross was introduced in 1949 from Weymouth, New Jersey. The light blue fruit is very large, stores

Table 16. A comparison of three blueberry cultivars

	Northblue	Northsky	Northcountry
Fruit yield	3–9 lb./bush	1–3 lb./bush	2–7 lb./bush
Fruit characteristics	Dark blue, firm; good fresh flavor; processed flavor superior to many highbush cultivars	Sky blue, sweet; good fresh flavor; processed flavor superior to many highbush cultivars; fruit size smaller than 'Northblue'	Sky blue, sweet; good fresh flavor; processed flavor superior to many highbush cultivars; fruit size similar to 'Northsky'
Plant height	20–30 in. tall	10–18 in. tall	15–25 in. tall, spreading
Use	Foundation shrub, home garden	Foundation shrub, home garden	Foundation shrub, home garden

Sources: Hoover et al. (1984); Luby et al. (1986); Hoover (personal communication).

well, and resists cracking. The ripening time is midseason. Plants are medium size with medium vigor.

Bluecrop. ('Jersey' x 'Pioneer') x ('Stanley' x 'June') is the parentage of this 1952 introduction from Weymouth, New Jersey. The light blue, medium-size fruit is firm and resistant to cracking. Maturity time is midseason. The plants are upright, spreading, vigorous, and productive.

Bluehaven. Stanley Johnston and J. E. Moulton introduced this 'Berkeley' x 19-H cross from South Haven, Michigan, in 1952. The light blue, large fruit is firm with excellent fresh flavor. Maturity time is midseason. The plants are upright and productive.

Blueray. This is another ('Jersey' x 'Pioneer') x ('Stanley' x 'June') cross introduced from Weymouth, New Jersey, in 1955. The light blue fruit is very large, firm, and resistant to cracking. The plants are upright, spreading, and productive. Ripening time is midseason.

Bluetta. New Brunswick, New Jersey, is the home of this (North Sedwick lowbush x 'Coville') x 'Earliblue' hybrid introduced in 1968. The light blue, firm, medium-size fruit ripens early. The plant is short, compact, and spreading, and is a consistent producer. 'Bluetta' is considered one of the more winter-hardy highbush blueberries.

Coville. Introduced in 1949, this is another ('Jersey' x 'Pioneer') x 'Stanley' selection from the USDA station at Weymouth, New Jersey. The large fruit is light blue, firm, and tart until fully ripe. The plants produce mature fruit in late midseason. Productivity with this cultivar has not been consistent, and Shoemaker (1978) reports it is largely self-incompatible. Without cross-pollination from another cultivar, fruit set may be poor.

Earliblue. 'Stanley' x 'Weymouth' is the parentage of this 1952 introduction from Weymouth, New Jersey. Like 'Weymouth', it matures very early. The large fruit is light blue, firm, and resists cracking. The plant is upright, vigorous, and productive.

Elliot. The USDA in Beltsville, Maryland, is responsible for this 'Burlington' x US1 cross introduced in 1973. The medium-size, light blue berries are firm with a good, mild flavor. Ripening time is very late in the season. The plants are upright, vigorous, and productive.

Jersey. F. V. Coville introduced this 'Rubel' x 'Grover' cross from Whitesbog, New Jersey, in 1928. The medium-size, blue fruits are firm and store well. Like 'Elliot', this cultivar also matures late. The bush is erect, spreading, and vigorous, and can be very productive. Shoemaker (1978) reports that the flowers on 'Jersey' are less attractive to bees and have less pollen than other cultivars. In the absence of adequate numbers of pollinators, the fruit may be small, seedless, and late maturing.

Northland. Stanley Johnston and J. E. Moulton introduced this 'Berkeley' x 19-H selection from South Haven, Michigan, in 1967. The firm fruit is medium blue in color and medium in size. The plants produce mature fruit early in the season, and they are much more hardy than many of the other highbush types.

Patriot. Named in recognition of the U.S. Bicentennial, this ('Dixi' x Michigan lowbush) x 'Earliblue' cross from Beltsville, Maryland, was introduced in 1976. The large blue fruits, which mature early in the season, are firm and store well. The plant is upright, relatively open, and is much more hardy than many of the other cultivars grown in the East.

Pemberton. 'Katharine' x 'Rubel' is the parentage of this 1941 introduction from Whitesbog, New Jersey. This late-maturing selection has medium to large, dark blue fruits that are firm with fair to good quality. Fruit cracking may be a problem during wet conditions. The plant is erect, vigorous, and productive.

Rancocas. This ('Brooks' x 'Russell') x 'Rubel' cross was introduced from Whitebog, New Jersey, by F. V. Coville in 1926. The fruits are small, light blue, and often crack badly after a rain. The plant has medium vigor, is erect, productive, and quite winter hardy. The name commemorates Rancocas Creek in New Hampshire.

Rubel. This wild selection of *V. australe* made by Elizabeth White of Whitesbog, New Jersey, was among the first cultivars introduced by F. V. Coville in 1916. The small to medium, late-maturing fruit is firm and considered excellent for processing. The plants are upright, vigorous, and productive.

**Fruit zones—
blueberries**

Cultivar	Iowa			Minn.				S. Dak.				N. Dak.			Wis.			
	4b	5a	5b	1	2	3	4	1	2	3	4	A	B	C	1	2	3	4
Berkeley			T															
Bluecrop		T	T	T	T										T	T	T	T
Bluehaven															T	T	T	T
Blueray		T	T	T	T										T	T	T	T
Bluetta		T	T	T	T										T	T	T	T
Coville		T	T															
Earliblue															T	T		
Elliot		T	T															
Jersey		T	T															
Northblue	T	T	T	X	X	X	T								X	X	X	X
Northcountry	T	T	T	X	X	X	T								X	X	X	X
Northland	T	T	T	T	T										X	X	T	T
Northsky	T	T	T	X	X	X	T								X	X	X	X
Patriot		T	T	T	T										T	T	T	T
Pemberton															T	T		
Rancocas				T	T										T	T		
Rubel															T	T	T	

X = recommended for planting; T = recommended for trial.
See zone map on page 20.

The Planting Site and Soil

A gentle, sunny slope with a northern exposure is ideal for blueberries, but level ground is acceptable if it is well drained. Low areas subject to late-spring frosts should also be avoided. Plant away from trees and shrubs since blueberries are very poor competitors for water, sun, and nutrients.

Soil requirements for blueberries are very exacting for maximum productivity. The roots are fibrous but very fine, and they lack the vigor to penetrate heavy clay soils. Over 90 percent of the roots are usually in the top 6 inches of soil. Blueberries perform best in a soil with good drainage that has a high

Table 17. Sulfur application rates to change soil pH to 4.5

| Initial pH | Application rate (pounds per 1,000 square feet) | |
	Sandy soil	Loam soil
7.0	19	58
6.5	15	46
6.0	12	35
5.5	8	24
5.0	4	12

Source: Hoover et al. (1984).

percentage of organic matter. Sandy loam soils are best. On very coarse, sandy soils, addition of organic matter is essential.

pH

For maximum productivity, the soil pH should be 4.5 to 5.5. For large plantings, a soil analysis should be made before planting.

Home gardeners with just a few plants can lower the pH by adding acid or sphagnum peat. Iron sulfate can also be used, and it is available with directions for use at large garden centers or nurseries. Aluminum sulfate, often recommended for azaleas and rhododendrons, *should not* be used because the aluminum portion may be toxic to blueberry roots.

Commercial growers usually use sulfur to lower the pH since it is less expensive. The sulfur should be applied in the fall before spring planting. Table 17, from Hoover et al. (1984), gives the sulfur application rates to change soil pH to 4.5.

Planting

In the Upper Midwest, blueberries should be planted in the early spring as soon as the soil can be worked. Barerooted plants should be soaked in water for three to four hours before planting.

The home gardener should space blueberries 3 to 4 feet apart in rows 6 feet apart. To accommodate tillage, spraying, and harvesting equipment, commercial growers usually space the rows 8 to 10 feet apart.

The planting hole should be 2 feet deep and 2 feet wide. On well-drained soils, one to two bushels of acid peat added to the soil mix gives good results. Gardeners with heavy clay soil should consider a planting mix of equal parts of sand, peat, and topsoil. Plants should be set about 2 inches deeper than they grew in the nursery.

Little or no pruning is required at planting time except for possible removal of damaged roots and weak, spindly stems. Developing flower buds should be pinched out during the first two years of growth. Begin harvesting fruit the third year after planting.

The Barrel Method

Fifty-gallon metal barrels cut in half with holes drilled in the bottom have been used by some gardeners. The barrels are sunk into the soil and filled with peat, sand, and topsoil. One plant is placed in each barrel.

Mulching

Blueberries will benefit from mulching probably more than any other fruit crop discussed in this book. Since most of the roots are in a zone 2 to 6 inches beneath the soil surface, they can easily be injured by deep cultivation. This root zone, of course, will also dry out quickly during drought periods. A good mulch helps conserve moisture, insulates the roots from high temperatures, and cuts down on the need for cultivation. The mulch should be 4 to 6 inches deep and extend from the base of the plants about 6 to 8 inches beyond the drip line. Peat, compost, and well-rotted manure are preferred mulches, but if these are not available, shredded leaves, wood chips, straw, corncobs, or sawdust can be used. These latter mulches all have a rather high carbon-to-nitrogen ratio and will require supplemental nitrogen to aid in the decomposition process.

Water Requirements

During the growing season, blueberries require a minimum of an inch of water per week. Even with a mulch, frequent shallow irrigation will be required during drought periods. Home gardeners with just a few plants can use a sprinkling can to add one-half to one gallon of water per plant each week. Commercial growers commonly use overhead-irrigation systems. Water is probably best applied during the early morning hours. During the ripening period, water should be kept off the fruit since it may cause cracking or splitting.

Blueberries that do not receive enough water often lack vigor, occasionally develop reddened leaves that drop early, and produce a reduced yield of inferior quality.

Pruning

Blueberries normally reach full production size five to six years after planting. During this development phase, extensive pruning is not required. Pruning should be done in March or before the buds begin to swell in the spring. As mentioned, flower buds should be removed during the first two years along with weak, spindly canes. Up to the full production stage, concentrate on removing twiggy growth clusters near the base of the plant, diseased or damaged canes, and weak lateral growth. When the plants approach maturity, canes older than five years should be removed. How much additional pruning is required will depend on growing conditions and cultivar selection.

Left unpruned, many cultivars have a tendency to overproduce many small berries of less-than-desirable quality. Heavy pruning, in contrast, may reduce the number of developing berries, but the fruit may be larger and more desirable. Unfortunately, for the gardener, since no pruning guidelines will cover all situations, some experimentation is necessary. On plants that overbear, try heading back some of the canes to four to five buds or removing a few of the weaker laterals. On upright plants with dense centers, remove some of the canes and laterals to let in more light. Also, remember that weak, spindly plants often perk up and exhibit more vigor after pruning. On these plants, experiment with tip pruning of the canes and removal of the weakest shoots.

When pruning, Shoemaker (1978) suggests several additional facts to remember.

> Fruit buds produced during the summer will yield next year's harvest.
>
> There is a tendency for most blueberry cultivars to overproduce.
>
> Center thinning may be required on upright cultivars.
>
> Low-branch pruning is required on spreading cultivars.
>
> Extensive pruning results in earlier ripening and larger berries.
>
> Plant vigor is correlated with quality of fruit produced.
>
> Without pruning, plants may produce many berries of inferior quality.

Fertilizing

Blueberries do not require extensive fertilization, but since the plants do require an acid environment, the amount and type of fertilizer used should be carefully regulated.

On soils where other fruits and vegetables have been successfully grown in the past and where the pH has been lowered to the proper range, the fertilizer can probably be limited initially to ammonium sulfate (20-0-0). This acid fertilizer will help maintain the proper pH and supply necessary nitrogen.

In the early spring before growth begins, add ¼ cup of ammonium sulfate per plant. Spread the fertilizer evenly in a circle that extends 6 to 8 inches from the crown to the drip line. As the plants mature, gradually increase the amount applied to a maximum of ½ pound per plant. When not enough nitrogen is available, the plants will exhibit stunted growth and yellowing of older leaves, which may ultimately turn red and die.

When the soil pH rises above the preferred range, iron may become unavailable for uptake. The major symptoms of iron deficiency are yellowing between leaf veins, stunted basal leaves, and yellowing of new shoots. At this stage the soil pH should be adjusted, but spraying the leaves with ferrous sulfate or iron chelate will provide only a temporary solution to the problem. Iron chelate can also be added to the soil. Add 1 ounce for each new plant. Mature plants will require 4 ounces.

In some cases, supplemental potassium, phosphorus, and magnesium may be needed. To avoid toxicity and to maintain soil pH, these nutrients should be applied as potassium sulfate, superphosphate, and magnesium sulfate (Epsom salts). How much to apply should be determined by a soil test.

Much has been written about the detrimental effects of manure on blueberries, but organic gardeners have been using it for years with great success. The amount to apply is one to two bushels of horse, sheep, or cattle manure per plant per year.

Propagating

For the home gardener, blueberries are probably most easily propagated using the mound method described for *Ribes*. The plants can also be grown from hardwood and softwood cuttings, but these methods usually require a considerable amount of time and expertise to maintain the proper rooting environment. For details on these methods, see Shoemaker (1978) and Hartmann and Kester (1975).

During the last few years an increasing number of blueberry plants have been produced through tissue culture. This propagation method can produce large numbers of disease-free plants quickly in a relatively small area. In 1989, one Minnesota company—Minn. Vitro, Inc. Plant Propagation and Tissue Labs—produced 637,000 plants (24,517 blueberries) in a 500-square-foot lab and office space. After initial production in tissue-culture labs, the plants are transferred to greenhouses and to the field for additional growth before they are sold.

Harvesting, Storage, and Use

During the ripening process, blueberries change color from green to red to blue. For maximum flavor, the fruits should be harvested 3 to 6 days after they turn completely blue. The berries ripen unevenly in a cluster; select only the ripe fruit for picking. When harvesting, handle the berries gently so that the whitish outer covering of the fruit is not rubbed off. This "bloom" helps extend the storage life of the fruit. The fruit is usually picked two or three times each week, and it should be cooled immediately and stored between 32 and 40° F.

Blueberries can be eaten fresh or used for preserves, jelly, pies, cakes, sauces, and juice. When fermented, the juice can also be made into wine and liquors.

Diseases and Pests

Since blueberries have never been grown extensively in the Upper Midwest, little is known about disease and pest problems here. The most extensive treatment of the subject is by Hoover et al. (1984). The brief discussion presented here is essentially a modified synopsis of that work. For the remainder of this chapter, pests and diseases known to occur in Minnesota and possibly in other Upper Midwestern states are marked with an asterisk (*).

In the past, home gardeners with only a few plants have usually encountered few pest or disease problems, and a regular spray program has not been necessary. As the plants become more common and the commercial industry expands, this may change. For now it would appear that good cultural practices such as proper pruning, fertilization, mulching, and irrigating are the most important measures for preventing disease. Good sanitation procedures such as removing diseased branches, fallen fruit, and leaves will also help.

*Birds

Birds are troublesome pests wherever blueberries are grown. To protect the fruit, netting may be the most practical solution.

Fungal Diseases

Mummyberry. Shoot dieback and berries that turn beige brown are the symptoms of this disease. To lessen the chances of reinfection, rake and destroy fallen berries.

Stem cankers. Small red spots appear on the canes, first near the soil. As the spots enlarge, the canes are girdled and die. To prevent spread of the disease, remove and destroy infected canes.

Phomopsis twig blight. Wilting and dieback of infected twigs are typical symptoms, but leaf spots and crown infections may also occur.

Powdery mildew. See *Ribes* diseases.

Anthracnose. The fruits are infected with orange-colored spore clusters. The fungus overwinters on infected canes and twigs.

Botrytis blight. Gray brown mold in fruit, twigs, blossoms, and leaves is a typical symptom. The disease is most prevalent during prolonged periods of cool, damp weather. Proper pruning, avoiding overfertilization, and preventing frost injury to the flowers are good preventive measures.

Viruses

Blueberry stunt virus. Shortened internodes and proliferation of clustered young shoots are typical symptoms. The leaves of infected plants are often small and curled and have chlorotic (yellow) leaf margins. The disease is spread by leafhoppers. Remove and destroy infected plants.

Ringspot virus. Red spots first appear on the upper surfaces of older leaves. Control insect vectors and rogue out infected plants.

Blueberry shoestring virus. New shoots may have reddish streaks of varying lengths; these streaks may also appear on the leaf midrib. Ripe berries frequently remain pink instead of turning blue. This disease is thought to be transmitted by aphids. Eliminate and destroy infected plants.

Insects

Blueberry blossom weevil. Swelling flower and leaf buds are favorite target areas. The flower buds may fail to open, and very frequently turn purple. Leaf buds that open often produce small, malformed leaves. Remove trash and practice clean cultivation.

Blueberry leafminer. This pest forms a triangular tent within which it feeds on the leaves. No control is necessary unless populations are large.

Blueberry maggots. The adult insect, which resembles a small housefly, lays eggs beneath the skin of the fruit, and the maggot that hatches devours the contents. This is the most serious insect pest of blueberries. Clean picking of fruit when it is ripe is a good cultural control.

Blueberry stem borer. These insects bore into the stem, causing tip wilting. Prune out canes below the area of infection.

Cherry fruitworm. Red larvae feed on the developing fruit. Clean cultivation and removal of dead twigs are the cultural-control methods.

Cranberry fruitworm. Developing larvae web the berries together and feed on the fruit. Clean cultivation is the best cultural control.

Cranberry rootworms and grubs. These pests seem to be a problem only where fields have not been fallowed for a year before planting. Repeated cultivation during the fallow period to destroy roots usually eliminates the pest. Sawdust used for mulching sometimes harbors white grubs.

Plum curculio. Clean cultivation is the best cultural control for this snout beetle, which feeds on leaves, blossoms, and berries.

SELECTED REFERENCES

Bailey, L. H., E.Z. Bailey, and staff of the Liberty Hyde Bailey Hortorium. 1976. *Hortus Third.* New York: Macmillan.

Ballinger, W. E., and L. J. Kushman. 1970. Relationship of Stage of Ripeness to Composition and Keeping Quality of Highbush Blueberries. *Jour. Amer. Soc. Hort. Sci.* 95: 239–42.

Brooks, R. M., and H. P. Olmo. 1972. *Register of New Fruit and Nut Varieties.* 2nd ed. Berkeley: University of California Press.

Camp, W. H. 1945. The North American Blueberries with Notes on Other Groups of Vaccinaceae. *Brittonia* 5:203–75.

Childers, N. F. 1983. *Modern Fruit Science.* Gainesville, Fla.: Horticultural Publications.

Coville, F. V. 1937. Improving the Wild Blueberry. *USDA Yearbook of Agriculture* 1937: 559–74.

Darrow, G. M. 1960. Blueberry Breeding: Past, Present, Future. *Amer. Hort. Mag.* 39(1): 14–33.

Darrow, G. M., and J. N. Moore. 1962. *Blueberry Growing.* USDA Farmer's Bulletin 1951 (rev.).

Eck, P. 1966. Botany. In: *Blueberry Culture.* P. Eck and N. F. Childers (eds.). New Brunswick, N.J.: Rutgers University Press. Pp. 14–44.

Eck, P. 1988. *Blueberry Science.* New Brunswick, N.J.: Rutgers University Press.

Eck, P., R. E. Gough, I. V. Hall, and J. M. Spears. 1990. Blueberry Management. In: *Small Fruit Crop Management.* G. J. Galletta and D. G. Himelrick (eds.). Englewood Cliffs, N. J.: Prentice-Hall.

Galletta, G. J. 1975. Blueberries and Cranberries. In: *Advances in Fruit Breeding.* J. Janick and J. N. Moore. (eds.). Lafayette, Ind.: Purdue University Press.

Gough, R. E. 1983. Time of Pruning and Bloom Date in Cultivated Highbush Blueberry. *HortScience* 18(6): 934–35.

Gough, R. E. 1984. Split-root Fertilizer Application to Highbush Blueberry Plants. *HortScience* 19(3): 415–16.

Hertz, L. B. 1978. *Blueberries.* University of Minnesota Ext. Ser. Hort. Fact Sheet 41 (rev.).

Hoover, E. 1988. Personal communication.

Hoover, E., C. Rosen, D. Wildung, J. Luby, L. Hertz, J. Heaps, and W. Stienstra. 1984. *Blueberry Production in Minnesota.* University of Minnesota Ext. Ser. Pub. AG-FO-2241.

Klingbeil, G. C. 1974. *Growing Blueberries in Wisconsin.* University of Wisconsin Coop. Ext. Ser. Fact Sheet A2194.

Luby, J. J., and C. E. Finn. 1986. Quantitative Inheritance of Plant Growth Habit in Blueberry Progenies. *Jour. Amer. Soc. Hort. Sci.* 111(4): 609–11.

Luby, J. J., D. K Wildung, C. Stushnoff, S. T. Munson, P. E. Read, and E. E. Hoover. 1986. 'Northblue', 'Northsky' and 'Northcountry' Blueberries. *HortScience* 21(5): 1240–42.

Lyrene, P. M., and J. R. Ballington, Jr. 1986. Wide Hybridization in *Vaccinium. HortScience* 21(1): 52–57.

Moore, J. N. 1979. Small Fruit Breeding—Rich Heritage, A Challenging Future. *HortScience* 14(3): 333–41.

Moore, J. N., and D. H. Scott. 1966. Breeding Value of Various Blueberry Varieties and Selections for Northeastern United States. *Proc. Amer. Soc. Hort. Sci.* 88: 331–37.

Shoemaker, J. S. 1978. *Small Fruit Culture.* Westport, Conn.: AVI Publishing.

Stiles, W. C., and J. S. Bailey. 1966. Blueberries in the Home Garden. In: *Blueberry Culture.* P. Eck and N. F. Childers. (eds.) New Brunswick, N.J.: Rutgers University Press.

Taber, H. G., and C. Fear. 1986. *Fruit Cultivars for the Family.* Iowa State University Coop. Ext. Ser. Pub. PM–453.

Wildung, D. K., and K. Sargent. 1986. *Establishment Studies with Minnesota Blueberries.* University of Minnesota Ext. Ser. Pub. AG–FO–2902.

Wildung, D.K., and K. Sargent. 1986. *Blueberry Establishment Calendar.* University of Minnesota Ext. Ser. Pub. AG–FO–2903.

Chapter

13

Other Fruits

Choosing which fruits to include in this chapter was difficult; certainly many more could have been added. Those selected are generally not widely grown by home gardeners. This may be because of the exacting soil and cultural requirements of plants like the cranberry. Or perhaps it is because the taste quality of the buffalo berry may not always appeal to the palate. I suspect that another reason, possibly the most important, is that many of these plants are poorly known. Elderberries and *Amelanchier* (Juneberry) are a case in point, yet both are easy to grow, are extremely hardy, and yield fruit with multiple uses. In contrast, the kiwifruit has wide appeal, but unfortunately, many cultivars remain untested and are so new that we have not quite figured out how best to grow them.

Actinidia — Kiwifruit

Just a few years ago the word *kiwi* was reserved largely for ornithologists with a fascination for the national bird of New Zealand. Today, for supermarket shoppers from coast to coast, kiwi is also known as a delicious fruit. Originally known only to the "yuppie" crowd or those who sought the exotic, the kiwi has now become commonplace. Without a doubt, it is the candidate for "new fruit of the decade."

To cash in on the new popularity of the kiwi, some nurseries now offer new and hardy plants for the home garden. These plants, at the present time, represent a challenge for gardeners in the Upper Midwest, but before spending $29.95 for two plants, a few facts should be known.

History of the Kiwifruit

The commercial kiwifruit now in supermarkets belongs to the genus *Actinidia*, a member of the family Actinidiaceae. This species and about 50 others in the genus are all indigenous to Asia. The commercial kiwi, originally known as Chinese gooseberry or Yangtoo vine, occurs naturally along forest margins in the Yangtze Valley.

Scheer and Juergenson (1976) reported that the species was noticed by an Englishman in China in 1847, but there was apparently no attempt to export the plant until around 1900. In the early part of this century, kiwi seeds were introduced into New Zealand and the United States. At first the plants were considered somewhat of a horticultural novelty being grown primarily for their foliage and flowers.

At the end of World War II, New Zealand began growing large acreages of kiwi for the fruit harvest. Soon, supply exceeded local demand, and there was a vigorous marketing campaign to increase exports.

The first order of business was to change the name. Chinese gooseberry did not have much appeal, but the pet name "kiwi," adopted by New Zealand gardeners, seemed like a winner. Commercial production of kiwifruit also occurs in the U.S. California is the leading producer, and in 1989 growers there harvested a record 36.3 thousand tons, 11 percent above 1988 (*Noncitrus Fruits and Nuts,* January 1990).

"Hardy" Kiwis for the Upper Midwest?

Some nursery catalogs offer "new, hardy kiwis" that will "grow most anywhere!" Supposedly, some of the plants will survive at − 25° F. and others at even lower temperatures. Is there something missing in these ads?

First, the commercial kiwifruit bears the scientific name *Actinidia deliciosa* (changed from *A. chinensis* in 1986) and is classified as subtropical. The growing season for this species is about 210 days and the temperature range is 0 to 115° F.

Second, if the fine print is read carefully, one will notice that the true kiwi is probably not being offered at all. Most of these nurseries have selected another member of this genus and tacked on the name *kiwi*.

The species most commonly being promoted is *A. arguta*, which Upper Midwest gardeners have known for years as Bower *Actinidia*. This species is considered for trial mainly in South Dakota, the southern half of Minnesota and Wisconsin, and in northern Iowa. It seems to perform best in a well-drained, clay loam in full sun. This species does produce an edible fruit, but it is about the size of a cherry. It is grown primarily as a foliage plant and for its bell-shaped flowers. *A. arguta* is hardy to about − 25° F., but the flowers are injured when the temperature drops below freezing.

Actinidia arguta *is one of the more hardy kiwifruit species for trial in the Upper Midwest.*

Another companion species, *A. kolomitka,* may be suitable for trial in the Upper Midwest. This is supposedly the hardiest of the species. Unfortunately, it is reportedly the most difficult to grow, and it, too, produces a small fruit. This species apparently does very poorly in full sun; thus, some experimentation with various grades of shade-cloth may be necessary to successfully grow the species here.

All the *Actinidia* species listed here are vines, and they must be grown on some sort of trellis and treated much like a grape. The plants are largely dioecious, which means that for fruit production, both male and female plants must be present.

During the last few years, scores of *Actinidia* cultivars have appeared on the market. Some of the selections from *A. arguta, A. kolomitka,* and hybrids of these two species seem worthy of trial in the Upper Midwest, but only limited research has been conducted on their performance here. These plants are so new that it is not possible to give many meaningful tips on their culture in the Upper Midwest.

Most of my information concerning *Actinidia* culture comes from the *Actinidia Enthusiasts Newsletter.* This newsletter, published yearly since 1984, contains information on propagating, breeding, growing, processing, and marketing the fruits of *A. deliciosa,* as well as the so-called hardy kiwifruits from around the world. Gardeners who are serious about attempting kiwifruit culture will find this publication very useful.

In 1988, over 100,000 kiwi vines were sold in the U.S., and the price ranged from as low as $3 to more than $20 per plant. Cheaper is not always better, nor is a high price a guarantee of a vigorous specimen. Numerous testimonials appearing in the *Actinidia Enthusiasts Newsletter* attest to the range in quality from the hundreds of nurseries that sell these plants.

When buying nursery stock, look for age and size specifications, not price alone. If the plants are grown from tissue culture, have they been transplanted once or several times to larger pots? Are the plants grown from cuttings one, two, or three years old? What is the caliper size of the stem? In general, older, larger plants should cost more, and in theory, they should have a better chance of surviving. Hoskins (1987) recommends that nursery stock that arrives with a poor root system be transplanted to 8-inch pots or 1-gallon containers. Keep the container-grown plants in a wind-protected area out of direct, full summer sun. Before cold weather arrives, plant or store in a protected area. In either case, a heavy mulch is advised.

For the Upper Midwest, attempting to grow *true* kiwi does not seem very practical because of low temperatures and a short growing season. Some of the other "hardy kiwis" are possibilities for trial, but until more information is available, gardeners face a challenge and a great deal of experimentation.

Amelanchier—Juneberry

Except for a single species in Asia and another in Europe, *Amelanchier* is a rosaceous genus found only in North America. Here, more than 20 species are widely distributed in a variety of habitats. In the Upper Midwest, the following species are the most commonly cultivated. These species are hardy in all zones: *A. alnifolia*, Saskatoon, serviceberry, juneberry; *A. arborea*, downy serviceberry; *A. canadensis*, Shadblow serviceberry; *A. grandiflora*, apple serviceberry; *A. laevis*, Alleghany serviceberry; *A. stolonifera*, running serviceberry.

Fruit on all these species is edible, but *A. alnifolia* is most often selected for superior fruit quality. For details on the landscape value or gardening use of the other species see Snyder (1980).

Amelanchier fruit has a long history of use. American Indians cooked the berries with pulverized meat from buffalo and deer and then cooled the mixture and pressed it into cakes called pemmican. Jones (1946) also reported that the Lewis and Clark Expedition relied on the "berries" when food supplies dwindled.

From a botanical standpoint, the fruit of *Amelanchier* is not really a berry; it is a pome, like a pear or an apple. The fruit may be pea-sized on some of

'Pembina' is one of several Amelanchier *cultivars recommended for trial.*

the native plants or up to ⅝ inch in diameter on some of the named cultivars. Some white-fruited clones have been selected, but most of the superior cultivars have fruit borne in clusters of six to twelve, which mature to a purple, red, or almost black color. The fruit may be eaten fresh or used for wine, jelly, preserves, and pie.

Cultivars

About 20 cultivars of *Amelanchier* have been released, but most are Canadian introductions, and information on their performance in the Upper Midwest is scanty at best. Some are grown on their own roots; others are budded on rootstocks of European mountain ash, *Sorbus aucuparia*, and cotoneaster, *Cotoneaster acutifolia*.

Planting and Care

Juneberries have a reputation for being able to survive a wide range of climatic conditions. They are extremely cold tolerant and quite drought resistant. Except for waterlogged soils and heavy clay lacking organic matter, they will grow in most other soil types. They will also grow adequately in a wide pH range (6.0 to 7.8). The site selected for planting should be in full

Table 18. Some *Amelanchier* cultivars for trial*

Cultivar	Place and year of introduction	Comments
Forestburg	Canada, 1963	Shrub reaching 9–10 feet and producing few suckers. Fruit is large (⅝ inch) but of only fair quality.
Honeywood	Canada, 1973	Plant size unknown. Berry clusters large.
Moonlake	Canada, 1974	Plant size unknown. Berries large but the plant is not a consistent producer.
Northline	Canada, 1960	Free suckering shrub up to about 10 feet. Fruit is large. The highest yielding cultivar in trials conducted for 11 years at the Alberta Horticultural Research Station.
Pembina	Canada, 1956	Similar to 'Northline' but more spreading. The large berries produced in long clusters have been described as sweet and full flavored.
Regent	N. Dakota, year?	A shrub reaching a height of 5–6½ feet. Originally selected as a dual purpose plant. It may be satisfactory for landscaping but the fruits are low yielding and lack full flavor.
Smokey	Canada, 1956	6–10 feet, free-suckering spreading shrub. Fruit is large, sweet, and mild flavored.
Sturgeon	Canada, 1971	Shrub up to about 10 feet. Fruit is large with good flavor.

*Based largely on cultivar descriptions from Harris (1972); Hilton (1982); Laughlin et al. (1988); and Miller and Stushnoff (1971). The probable parentage for all these cultivars is *A. alnifolia*.

sun and away from low spots or areas likely to be affected by late-spring frosts.

Bareroot stock is recommended, and the 12- to 15-inch size is a good economical choice for home gardeners.

For a hedgerow, space the plants 5 to 6 feet apart, and in a few years they will grow together to form a continuous hedge. For spaced plantings, the minimum distance between each plant should be 8 feet. Set the plants slightly deeper than they grew in the nursery, and after planting prune off one-third of the top growth.

Little care, except for clean cultivation, is required until the plants reach bearing age after two to four years. At that time, pruning should be directed toward removing weak or damaged growth, eliminating lower branches, and thinning to keep the center open. In time, older branches should be removed because younger, vigorous branches will produce the best fruit. For ease of harvest, some of the taller cultivars should be pruned back to 6 feet high. Early spring is the best time for pruning.

As far as nutrients are concerned, juneberries do not seem to be a demanding crop, and in many areas little or no fertilization is required.

Pests

Birds are likely to be the most serious pest problem with juneberry culture. They are extremely fond of the fruit, and juneberries are frequently recommended for wildlife plantings to attract birds. Where a fruit harvest is desired, netting may be the most practical solution to the problem.

No comprehensive list of other pests of juneberry has been published for the Upper Midwest, but some common ones affecting other members of the Rosaceae can be expected. For additional details on pests and diseases affecting juneberries, see Laughlin et al. (1988) and Stang (1990). These publications are also useful for commercial production of this species.

Lonicera—Bush Honeysuckle

Lonicera coerulea edulis, a member of the family Caprifoliaceae, is one of the few members of the honeysuckle genus that produces edible fruit. Known in the Upper Midwest as bush honeysuckle or sweetberry honeysuckle, this attractive, low shrub reaches a height of 4 to 4½ feet and in June produces dark blue, oblong fruits, which are 6 to 12 millimeters (0.234 to 0.4728 inch) long. The fruit is quite tart but has a variety of uses and is prized for making preserves. 'George Bugnet' and 'Marie Bugnet' are popular cultivars. This variety is hardy throughout most of North Dakota, northern Minnesota, and northwestern Wisconsin. In some areas the species may be attacked by the honeysuckle aphid, a serious pest of many honeysuckle species throughout the Upper Midwest.

Ribes—Jostaberry

'Jostaberry' is the first cultivar selected from *Ribes nidigrolaria*, a hybrid species created from complex crosses involving black currant *R. nigrum* and the gooseberries *R. grossularia* and *R. divaricatum*. The name, pronounced "*yoh-sta-berry*," is derived from the German words *Johanisbeeren* (currants) and *Stachelbeeren* (needleberries or gooseberries).

'Jostaberry', first released in 1977, is the result of more than 30 years of breeding and selection by the late Rudolph Bauer of West Germany. Since this cultivar is a recent U.S. introduction and little is known about its performance and hardiness here, growers throughout the Upper Midwest are advised to plant it on a trial basis only.

North Star Gardens (1990) reports that the plants are quite adaptable to various soil types but perform best in a light soil with high organic content. A 5- to 6-foot spacing between plants in the row and a minimum of 10 feet between rows is recommended. Very little pruning is required during the first few years of growth, and after that pruning for shape and maximum sunlight penetration is all that is needed.

Some fruit may be produced the second year (assuming a start with one-year-old bareroot plants), but full production of 10–15 pounds per plant will require a maturity time of six to eight years. Fruit on 'Jostaberry' is produced on racemes similar to currants, and the mature berries are larger than black currants but smaller than large gooseberries. The berries are very high in vitamin C, and they may be eaten fresh or used for juice, freezing, or processing.

Sambucus — Elderberry

Elderberries belong to the genus *Sambucus*, a member of the family Caprifoliaceae. About 20 species in the genus are distributed in temperate and subtropical regions of the world.

In the Upper Midwest only three species — *S. racemosa* (European red elder), *S. pubens* (Scarlet elder), and *S. canadensis* (American elder) — are important horticulturally. These species have not been used extensively in landscaping but are sometimes used for naturalistic plantings and for attracting birds. *S. canadensis* is the only one of the species which produces desirable fruit for human consumption. Fruit in the other species is somewhat tasteless or has an objectionable taste quality.

Elderberries are hardy in all areas of the Upper Midwest and will grow in a wide range of soil types but perform poorly on light or sandy soils and on waterlogged soils. The ideal pH for elderberries is 5.5 to 6.5.

At planting time, incorporate well-rotted manure or compost into the soil. Supply additional nutrients in the early spring each year. For a nitrogen source, add ⅛ pound of ammonium nitrate for each year of the plant's age, with a maximum of 1 pound per plant. When phosphorus and potassium are required, use ½ pound of 20-percent superphosphate and ⅒ pound of muriate of potash. Avoid deep cultivation (more than 2 inches) because elderberries have very shallow, fibrous roots. Hand pulling of weeds and mulching are recommended.

Elderberries are quite shade tolerant and are often planted at the back of the shrub border or along the edge of a woods. One-year-old stock should be selected and planted in the early spring. Plants should be spaced 6 to 8 feet

Sambucus canadensis *elderberry in flower.*

apart in rows 8 to 10 feet apart. At maturity, the plants may reach a height of about 10 feet.

Sambucus canadensis has been cultivated since 1761 (Snyder, 1980), but attempts to select improved cultivars from superior wild plants did not begin until the end of the 19th century. Since that time, several cultivars have been released, but information on their performance in the Upper Midwest is very meager. The following cultivars seem worthy of trial:

Adams. Both Adams No. 1 and Adams No. 2 are vigorous plants with strong canes and very large fruit. Adams 2 is more productive than Adams 1.

Johns. This cultivar is not as productive as either of the Adams selections, but the fruit is larger and matures 10 to 14 days earlier.

Kent. The fruit is large and matures early and uniformly. This cultivar was selected from an open-pollinated seedling of Adams 2.

Nova. One of the most productive of all the cultivars listed here. 'Nova' plants are large and vigorous, and the fruit matures early.

York. The fruit is larger and the plants are probably more productive than any of the other cultivars listed here. The plants are larger than the Adams cultivars, and the fruit matures later.

Based largely on descriptions from Way (1981).

Elderberries are only partially self-fruitful; thus, for maximum fruit production, two different cultivars should be planted near each other for cross-pollination.

Prune elderberries in the early spring before growth begins. Pruning should be directed toward removing dead, weak, and older canes. Two-year-old canes are the most productive; canes older than three years produce very little fruit. At maturity, leave about nine canes consisting of an equal number of one-, two-, and three-year-old canes.

Elderberries have few pest problems other than viral diseases, which can be devastating. Diseases such as cankers, leaf spots, powdery mildew, root rots, and thread blight are rarely serious enough to warrant control measures. Stang (1990) reports that there are no insecticides or fungicides cleared for use on elderberries in the U.S. In contrast, the fruit of these plants is a favorite for several bird species, and in some cases netting may be necessary to protect the crop.

The flowers of elderberries are borne in large compound cymes and can be used for wine, vinegar, and flavorings. Hill (1981) reported that they can also be dipped in batter and fried.

The fruit should be harvested when it turns dark purple. For best results, harvest the entire cluster and then strip the individual berries. Fresh fruit is sour and unpalatable, but when cooked it is excellent for jam, jelly, juice, pies, and wine.

Shepherdia—Buffalo Berry

Shepherdia argentea, known as buffalo berry, silver buffalo berry, rabbit berry, and Nebraska currant, is a member of the family Elaeagnaceae. It is extremely hardy and drought resistant, and can be grown throughout the Upper Midwest. This large, thorny shrub reaches a height of 15 to 20 feet and is dioecious. For fruit production, both male and female plants are necessary. The small (4 to 6 millimeters long—0.1576 to 0.2364 inch) red fruit, which matures in August, is too sour for the palates of most people, but it was once used extensively by American Indians.

Vaccinium—Cranberries

Cranberries, *Vaccinium macrocarpon*, like blueberries, are members of the family Ericaceae. This native American species is rarely planted by home gardeners in the Upper Midwest, but it is the most important fruit crop grown in Wisconsin.

Worldwide, most of the commercial cranberry crop is produced in North America. Value of the 1988 harvest for the major producing states was

$86,164,000 in Massachusetts, $70,512,000 in Wisconsin, $16,687,000 in New Jersey, $6,915,000 in Oregon, and $6,062,000 in Washington (*Noncitrus Fruits and Nuts*, January 1990).

Stang and Dana (1984) report that Wisconsin cranberry cultivation began in 1850 in a native bog near Berlin in the south central region and gradually expanded to include nearly 1,000 acres by 1865. By 1900, an additional 1,200 acres were developed in the large, central-Wisconsin swamp area known as Cranmoor. During the 1940s, cultivation expanded, and new areas were added in west central Wisconsin and in the Northern Lake region. By 1983, 135 growers were utilizing 3,000 hectares (7,413 acres). By 1989, there were 9,200 acres of cranberries in Wisconsin (*Noncitrus Fruits and Nuts*, January 1990).

Commercially, cranberries are grown on boggy or marshy, acid soils where summers are moderately cool. Before planting, vegetation is removed, and the area is ditched and leveled. Dikes are constructed around the planting area because up to 300,000 gallons of water are required for each acre. Finally, a 2- to 4-inch layer of sand is spread over the peat surface. Unrooted, 6- to 8-inch cuttings are planted in the spring. To prevent winterkill, the area is flooded in late fall.

Few home gardeners have access to a swamp or bog, but, nevertheless, they can grow these plants in most areas of the Upper Midwest. Gardeners can create simulated bog conditions suitable for cranberry growth by using the following method. Begin by excavating all soil in the planting area to a depth of 18 to 24 inches. Next, line the bottom of the hole with polyethylene and fill with acid peat. At planting time, saturate the peat with water and space the plants 6 inches apart in each direction. During the summer, flood the area once each week, and if growth is slow, try light applications of ammonium sulfate at three-week intervals. Home gardeners can expect few, if any, pest problems.

With adequate snow cover, these plants will survive the winter nicely, but without it, expect extensive winterkill. For added protection, one successful grower simply covers the plants with an old tablecloth (do not use plastic). Other growers mulch with straw, marsh hay, or leaves.

The most effective pollinator of cranberries is the bumblebee, but honeybees and other insects also pollinate them. Only one cultivar is required since the plants are self-fruitful.

The choice and availability of cranberry cultivars are limited. 'Searles' (Searles Jumbo) is the most important cultivar grown in Wisconsin and is planted on 60 percent of the acreage. The 'McFarlin' cultivar ranks second (25 percent of the acreage) and 'Ben Davis' third (5 percent). 'Crowley', a relatively new cultivar, is gaining in popularity and is now being planted extensively (Stang and Dana, 1984).

Wild Cranberries

Two other close relatives of the cultivated cranberry occur in the Upper Midwest and are sometimes harvested for their fruit. Both species can be grown in areas with adequate snowcover, but details on their culture will not be presented since they are rarely planted.

Vaccinium oxycoccus. Known variously as northern cranberry, small cranberry, or marsh whortleberry, this native species produces small (⅓-inch diameter), red berries that are sometimes used as a substitute for the true cranberries.

Vaccinium vitis-idaea. The dark red fruit on this species is about the same size as in the preceding species, and according to Hendrickson (1981), it is the most delicious cranberry of all. Snyder (1980) reported that it makes a good ground cover on acid soils. Common names for this species are lingonberry, rock cranberry, cowberry, and red whortleberry.

Viburnum — American Highbush Cranberry

Like its close relative *Sambucus*, the genus *Viburnum* is a member of the Caprifoliaceae family. Several species in this genus can be utilized for their fruit, but only the American highbush cranberry, *V. trilobum*, will be discussed here. For details on the landscape-use of the other *Viburnum* species that can be grown in the Upper Midwest, see Snyder (1980).

American highbush cranberry in growth habit and size is similar to the elderberry, and it, too, can be grown throughout the Upper Midwest. This species is sometimes confused with the European highbush cranberry, *V. opulus*, which also produces red fruits, but these are highly acidic and are generally considered unpalatable. Fruit on *V. trilobum*, in contrast, can be used for jelly, preserves, or as a refreshing drink.

V. trilobum is not a demanding species, and there are no special cultural requirements. Ourecky (1972) reported that weed control is similar to that for currants, and that a light pruning may be necessary if the plants become too thick.

Most nurseries sell American highbush cranberry as the species since few cultivars have been developed. Examples of cultivars selected for superior fruit quality that seem worthy of trial include 'Andrews', 'Hahs', 'Manitou', 'Phillips', and 'Wentworth'.

SELECTED REFERENCES

Bauer, A. 1985. New Results of Breeding *Ribes nidigrolia:* Amphidiploid Species Hybrids between Blackcurrant and Gooseberry. *Acta Hort.* 183: 107–10.

Bauer, A. 1989. Development in *Ribes* Breeding with Regard to Mildew and Gall Mite Resistance. *Acta Hort.* 262: 141–44.

Bishop, B. H., and S. H. Nelson. 1980. Propagation and Transplanting of Saskatoon (*Amelanchier alnifolia* Nutt.) Softwood Cuttings. *Can. Jour. Plant Sciences* 60(3): 883–90.

Burkwood, A. 1947. The Genus *Viburnum. Jour. Royal Hort. Soc.* 72: 360–64.

Chandler, F. B., and I. E. Demoranville. 1959. *Cranberry Varieties of North America.* Massachusetts Agr. Exper. Stat. Bull. 513.

Craig, D. L. 1966. *Elderberry Culture in Eastern Canada.* Can. Dept. Agr. Pub. 1280.

Cruise, J. E. 1964. Studies of Natural Hybrids in *Amelanchier. Can. Jour. Bot.* 42: 651–53.

Dana, M. N. 1983. Cranberry Cultivar List. *Fruit Varieties Jour.* 37(4): 88–95.

Dana, M. N. 1990. Cranberry Management. In: *Small Fruit Crop Management.* G. J. Galletta and D. G. Himelrick (eds.). Englewood Cliffs, N.J.: Prentice-Hall.

Darrow, G. M. 1923. *Viburnum americanum* as a Garden Fruit. *Proc. Amer. Soc. Hort. Sci.* 21: 44–54.

Darrow, G. M. 1924. The American Cranberry Bush. *Jour. Hered.* 15: 243–53.

Darrow, G. M. 1975. Minor Temperate Fruits. In: *Advances in Fruit Breeding.* J. Janick and J. N. Moore (eds.). Lafayette, Ind.: Purdue University Press.

Eames-Sheavly, M., and M. P. Pritts. 1989. *The Home Fruit Planting.* Cornell University Inform. Bull. 156.

Ferguson, A. R. 1990. Kiwifruit Management. In: *Small Fruit Crop Management.* G. J. Galletta and D. G. Himelrick (eds.). Englewood Cliffs, N.J.: Prentice-Hall.

Harris, R. E. 1972. *The Saskatoon.* Can. Dept. Agr. Bull. 1246 (rev.).

Hendrickson, R. 1981. *The Berry Book.* Garden City, N.Y.: Doubleday.

Hill, L. 1977. *Fruits and Berries for the Home Garden.* Charlotte, Vt.: Garden Way Publishing.

Hilton, R. J. 1982. Registration of *Amelanchier* Cultivar Names. *Fruit Varieties Jour.* 36(4): 108–10.

Hoskins, C. A. 1987. *Hardy Kiwi Report.* Available from: Viking Kiwi Enterprises, 5678 Sunrise Crescent West, Surrey, British Columbia, V2S 7N9 Canada.

Johnson, D. M., C. A. Hanson, and P. H. Thompson. 1988. *Kiwifruit Handbook.* Available from: Bonsail Publications, 4339 Holly Lane, Bonsail, CA 92003.

Jones, G. N. 1946. American Species of *Amelanchier* Ill. *Biol. Memo.* 20: 1–126.

Klingbeil, G. C. and J. M. Rawson. 1975. *Wisconsin Cranberry Lore.* University of Wisconsin Coop. Ext. Ser. Pub. A2292.

Laughlin, K. M., R. C. Smith, and R. G. Askew. 1988. *Juneberry for Commercial and Home Use on the Northern Great Plains.* North Dakota State University Coop. Ext. Ser. Pub. H–938.

Madison, D. N. 1965. *Amelanchier:* Three Seasons of Beauty. *Annual Report Northern Nut Growers Assn.* 59: 133–35.

McDaniel, J. C. 1962. A Quick Survey of Serviceberries—Juneberries. *Nutshell* 9: 17–19.

Miller, W. S., and C. Stushnoff. 1971. A Description of *Amelanchier* Species in Regard to Cultivar Development. *Fruit Varieties Hort. Digest* 25: 3–10.

North Star Gardens. 1990. *Raspberry Nursery and Resource Catalog.* Available from: North Star Gardens, 19060 Manning Trail N., Marine on St. Croix, MN 55047.

Ourecky, D. K. 1972. *Minor Fruits in New York State.* Cornell University Inform. Bull. 11.

Pilarski, M. (ed.) 1984–89. *Actinidia Enthusiasts Newsletter.* Issues 1–5. Available from: Friends of the Trees Society, P.O. Box 1466, Chalan, WA 98816.

Ritter, C. M., and G. W. McKee. 1964. *The Elderberry.* Pennsylvania Agr. Exper. Stat. Bull. 709.

Scheer, A. H., and E. M. Juergenson. 1976. *Approved Practices in Fruit and Vine Production.* Danville, Ill.: The Interstate.

Snyder, L. C. 1980. *Trees and Shrubs for Northern Gardens.* Minneapolis: University of Minnesota Press.

Sole, P. R. 1985. *Kiwifruit Culture.* Available from: Ag. Access, P.O. Box 2008, Davis, CA 95617.

Stang, E. J. 1990. Elderberry, Highbush Cranberry, and Juneberry Management. In: *Small Fruit Crop Management.* G. J. Galletta and D. G. Himelrick (eds.). Englewood Cliffs, N.J.: Prentice-Hall.

Stang, E. J., and M. N. Dana. 1984. Wisconsin Cranberry Production. *HortScience* 19(4): 478, 607.

Stubbendieck, S. J., J. Stephan, L. Hatch, and K. J. Kjar. 1982. *North American Range Plants.* Lincoln: University of Nebraska Press.

Way, R. D. 1964. Elderberry Varieties and Cultural Practices. *Proc. New York Hort. Soc.* 110: 233-36.

Way, R. D. 1981. *Elderberry Culture in New York State.* Geneva, N.Y., Agr. Exper. Stat. Food Life Sci. Bull. 91.

Wiegand, K. M. 1912. The Genus *Amelanchier* in Eastern North America. *Rhodora* 14: 116-64.

Wright, P. H. 1969. The Saskatoon Bush for Fruit and Ornament. *Pomona* 2: 32-33.

Yerex, D., and W. Haines. 1983. *The Kiwifruit Story.* Available from: Agricultural Publishing Associates Limited, Box 594, Masterton, New Zealand.

Index

Don Gordon is professor of botany at Mankato State University. He received his Ph.D. in botany from Indiana University. Gordon has published a weekly newspaper column on horticulture and the environment since 1976 in the *Mankato Free Press*. For many years he owned and operated a commercial pick-your-own raspberry business.